Mazatlán
IS
Paradise

Charles A. Hall

Mazatlán IS Paradise
copyright ©**2003, 2004, 2005, 2006, 2007, 2012** Charles A. Hall
published by

Libros Valor

David W. Bodwell, Publisher

centro comercial Plaza Galerías, local no. 8
calzada Camarón Sábalo no. 610
fracc. El Dorado
C.P. 82110 Mazatlán, Sinaloa, México
Tel: (+52 *or* 011-52 *from the U.S and Canada*) (669) 916-7899
email: *mazbook@yahoo.com*

U.S. office:
6917 Montgomery Blvd. NE, Unit #E23
Albuquerque, NM 87109
Ph: (505) 349-0425

Typeset in Adobe Garamond Pro by 1106 Design

Cover Photo by Tom Tolman – used by permission

Interior photographs by Bodie Kellog – used by permission

Library of Congress Control Number: 2012949712

ISBN: 978-1-937799-33-5

Libros Valor
is an imprint of
Editorial Mazatlán

Sixth Edition
10 9 8 7 6 5 4 3 2 1

Printed in the United States of America

Table of Contents

Preface

My wife Katherine and I first arrived in Mazatlán in 1985, immediately fell in love with the city and purchased a timeshare at The Inn at Mazatlán. We returned to our timeshare for two weeks every year until 1998 when we bought a home in the El Dorado neighborhood near Rico's Coffee Shop.

My purpose in writing this book is to encourage others to enjoy the beauty and pleasure of Mazatlán. By providing a wide range of information, I hope to help not only first-time visitors, but also permanent residents, to enjoy this beautiful city. Most of my recommendations are based on first-hand experience. Exceptions are noted, and contributors are appropriately recognized. In any book involving recommendations, please realize that age and personal tastes of the author may be biased. My children and several grandchildren have visited Mazatlán over the years and they have provided input from the younger set. Many of the businesses and services in Mazatlán are exceptional, but it would be impossible to experience all of them. I apologize in advance for slighting any excellent businesses and services that I have failed to visit and mention.

I recognize that businesses come and go rapidly in any city the size of Mazatlán. Changes are a natural part of progress and time. This is the 2012 update of the book first published in 2003 and updated in 2004, 2005, 2006 and 2007. It has numerous additions and deletions.

All profit from book sales will be donated to my favorite charity, The Vineyard Church in Mazatlán, and to Bodie Kellogg's favorite charity, CONREHABIT.

Information about the Vineyard (La Viña) Church in Mazatlán:

The Vineyard Church is a mission with headquarters in Illinois. Regular church services in the Golden Zone include one in English and the other in Spanish, every Sunday. The vast majority of monies collected during the services go directly to church projects in the poorer sections of Mazatlán. The mission's vision came in 1995 with 12 new works in Mazatlán. Thirteen Vineyard churches—either complete or under construction—are now spread throughout Mazatlán. These all double as feeding centers for needy children, filling a total of up to 1,000 hungry tummies weekly. That is just one of their many functions. The newest building opened in 2011. The new goal is for 50 Vineyard Churches. They are currently working on raising funds to build a feeding center just on the outskirts of the dump for the dump workers.

These multi-purpose buildings also serve as community centers, dental and medical clinics. Twice a month, local women from *colonia* Valles del Ejido and *colonia* Pueblo Urias gather in the respective churches to take hair-cutting and sewing classes. Eventually, they will be able to start their own businesses from the skills they learn.

Another way the Vineyard serves the community is through its various clinics. The dental clinic in Valles del Ejido is open two days a week, providing dental care at just 20 pesos per visit. There is no charge for those who cannot pay. In Urias, just down the road from the city dump, the dentist sees patients. Children 12 and under are treated free. And finally, in *colonia* Renato Vega, volunteer doctors provide medical consultations once a week for people who otherwise would not be able to afford it.

Since many residents of the poor *colonias* eat only sporadically, The Vineyard provides them with a hot meal as often as possible. In one week, they might serve more than 3,000 meals.

Tres Palmas was a small, unofficial *colonia* of mostly dump scroungers that you could see on the right side of the highway right after you passed the electric plant coming from the airport. In 2001, La Viña began construction of a school and children's feeding center. Since most of the people who lived in this *colonia* depended on "dump scrounging" for a living, they were too poor to send their children to school. The Vineyard built and started a school (kindergarten through third grade) to fulfill this need. The children that attended this school were all sponsored by the Children's Scholarship program. Teachers were provided for this school by the Mexican government. The children's feeding program was held every Saturday at 10:30 A.M.; a kid's club and Bible study was held at the same time.

Unfortunately, during the spring of 2007 the Federal police arrived and informed the residents that they were unlawfully on land owned by a developer. Thankfully, Pastor Fred Collum arrived on the scene and worked with the police to sort matters out. The people were moved to a new *colonia* – a type of subdivision – called *Colonia* Loma Bonita and all were given a lot to build a house upon. The Vineyard church was also given some lots to build a community center. Each day the church sent a mobile kitchen to Loma Bonita to feed the displaced people; they also made a makeshift building for the kids to finish out the school year. The real good news is that the Vineyard is working on building a new community center there and the owner of the Tres Palmas land is allowing the church to keep the building/school there for the new community when it is developed.

The Center for Affordable Water and Sanitation Technology (CAWST) developed a biosand water filter that could eliminate more than 96% of waterborne disease worldwide by the year 2015. The filter is based on a simple technology that empowers people anywhere in the world to create affordable ($10–$30 per unit) and effective water filters out of locally available materials. La Viña was asked by Friends Who Care Charities Ltd. (FWC) to participate in a program to manufacture and distribute the filters in the Mazatlán area. Labor to fabricate the filters is provided primarily by local Mexican residents, and, as of spring 2008, La Viña had distributed more than 200 filters in the Mazatlán area, with production continuing.

The Vineyard church provides other services for visitors from north of the border. In addition to the free dump tour and Sunday morning English language services, there is a Wi-Fi hot spot, a computer and Vonage phones to make long distance telephone calls to the States or Canada, free of charge. The main church is located on Camarón Sábalo, about 200 meters north of Panama Restaurant in the Golden Zone. A satellite English language church was opened near the Pemex station in

La Marina in 2012. The office is located next door to the main church, with the entrance on the side.

I sincerely hope this book provides you with information that will make your Mazatlán experience enjoyable, and that you come to love this tropical paradise as much as I do. If you have any recommendations for input to future editions of the book, please pass the information to me via email, *cahallone@comcast.net*.

Information about CONREHABIT:

Martha Armenta is the founder and president of CONREHABIT, a Mexican non-profit, conservation organization that provides wildlife rescue services as well as community outreach programs in the rural areas of southern Sinaloa, Mexico. CONREHABIT has a hectare – 2½ acres – of land within a large piece of private property north of Mazatlán, with modest facilities to care for injured or orphaned wildlife. CONREHABIT has dealt with several hundred baby parrots at one time as well as raccoons, boas, coyotes and once a very angry bobcat. The latest mission for the community outreach arm of this organization is to utilize education and eco-tourism to preserve both the jaguars and the rural communities along the western flanks of the Sierra Madre. The village of Tacuitapa, with their resident *bramador* – jaguar caller – is CONREHABIT's first effort to benefit both the beleaguered jaguar populations of western Mexico as well as the lives of the subsistence farmers. The mission is to keep the villagers and hunters from killing more jaguars.

CONREHABIT is working to educate the villagers, both young and old, to the virtues of living with nature as opposed to seeing the natural world as something that needs to be dominated, feared or exploited. The concept of resource utilization to generate revenue, doesn't need to be defined as resource extraction or depletion, a symbiotic approach to living on the land can also generate revenue for some of the rural communities.

Martha's plan is to demonstrate that the jaguars and their unique habitat hold an economic opportunity when left unmolested and intact. Eco-tourism is a rapidly growing industry as many folks seek out distinctive and exceptional encounters with the natural world, which are abundant in the areas surrounding Tacuitapa.

If you wish to become a volunteer, go on a tour, donate to the cause or contact Martha, please go to the website: *http://www.conrehabit.org/*

Acknowledgements

THIS TYPE OF BOOK always requires many people to put it together. This book is no exception. My heartfelt thanks go to the following people:

Dee Hulen, my research assistant, critic, and informal editor, who claims to have gained several pounds checking the many restaurants in El Centro district of Mazatlán. Without her assistance, the book never would have been completed on schedule.

David Bodwell, who provided editing assistance and expertise in the complicated world of Mazatlán business and publishing.

Larry Robinson, technology assistant, who kept my computers going so that I could remain on task doing something that I knew something about.

Katherine Hall, my wife and inspiration, for everything creative that I have accomplished in my life.

This book is dedicated to the two communities of Mazatlán—the Mazatlecos and the expats—who have melded together to make one of the finest communities in the world. Special thanks go to the members of the Internet forums Whatsupmaz.org and MazInfo, a YahooGroup forum, who without knowing it provided valuable input to the book. Their communications not only gave me questions that begged to be answered, but in many cases, answers to the questions.

About the Cover

THE PICTURE ON THE COVER is meant to show the beauty of Mazatlán. The woman is Lissy Bernal, the 1995 Queen of Carnaval. Mazatlán is also known as the city of beautiful women because so many have won the Miss Mexico title. The gold, red and blue masks in the basket represent the annual Carnaval celebration—the third largest in our hemisphere. Lissy's jewelry shows the quality of work done by the artisans of Mazatlán. The necklace is a creation by Justina de Cima influenced by the historic petroglyphs located 45 minutes north of Mazatlán. The basket was provided by Casa Etnika shop, which has many top-quality arts and crafts of Mexico, and the make-up and hairdo was done by Laura Delia Habif of Fibah Beauty Salon. In the background is the remodeled Malecón with its miles of beautiful public beach.

climate in Mazatlán during the "tourist season". I enjoy the best of both worlds…year round! I must add that climate is a matter of acclimation. I also realize that many people like hot weather and if that is what you're looking for, Mazatlán in the summer is the place for you.

I heard a great story about an incident during the hurricane season, which is from July through October, although, due to the protection Mazatlán gets from the Baja California peninsula, hurricanes here are pretty unusual. It seems there was a big hurricane in the 1980s that caused a lot of damage and flooding. The flooding was so bad that some cattle were washed out to sea. The Alejandra Coppel family owned a sardine fleet, and like many locals, headed out fishing right away because the flooding washes food out into the ocean and the fish come in to eat.

The family threw out their nets at night and the nets became so heavy that the boat tipped to one side. They thought they really had a lot of fish and were mentally counting the pesos as the nets were raised. To their surprise, the nets contained live cows. The cows were probably tired of treading water, and glad to be netted. The fishermen couldn't throw the beef-on-the-hoof back, so they left them grazing on the decks, returned to port and emptied their cargo so they could return for some "serious fishing."

Location

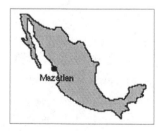

Found on the west coast of Mexico, due east of the tip of the Baja Peninsula, Mazatlán is easily accessible by air, land and sea. Among the resort cities of the "Mexican Riviera", Mazatlán is the closest to cities in the western and southwestern U.S. and Canada. Modern, high-speed, air-conditioned buses run from the border at Nogales to Mazatlán, 720 miles away. The trip can be made comfortably by vehicle in two days on a four-lane divided highway. There are also buses from

Tijuana, Phoenix, Tucson, Denver, Albuquerque, El Paso and many cities in southern Texas. For those coming to Mazatlán from points east, by auto or bus, the new highway over the mountains from Durango to Mazatlán is projected to be completed by the end of 2012, and it will cut the time of those trips by several hours.

Economy

I have visited Puerto Vallarta and Acapulco and found that Mazatlán certainly deserves its reputation for being the best resort buy on the "Mexican Riviera". It is far less expensive than Hawaii. If you like to travel first-class, there are luxury resorts. There are many other outstanding living quarters, but they all have one thing in common—the dollar stretches further in Mazatlán. The strength of the U.S. dollar compared to the Mexican peso helps even more. Several years ago, someone at the airport complained that his luggage did not arrive with his plane. I told him not to worry about it. Mazatlán is the only place I know where one can get along with just a swimsuit and toothbrush.

Shopping

If your luggage is lost and you feel you need more than a toothbrush and swimsuit, don't panic, you can shop till you drop in Mazatlán. I have visited Pier 1 in Olympia, Washington and markets in San Antonio, Texas where I found the prices to be two to three times higher than those in Mazatlán for Mexican jewelry, pottery, glassware, leather and other crafts. Further, I have met friends at the cruise dock in Mazatlán and taken them shopping and they all expressed amazement at the lower price of those items in Mazatlán compared to Los Cabos, Puerto Vallarta and Acapulco.

Easygoing way of life

While Mexico may not have invented *mañana,* the Mazatlecos (Mazatlán citizens) do their part to perpetuate it. But they are incredibly friendly and helpful to a fault.

A couple of years ago my friend Vicki, visiting from the States, came down with a stomach ailment and was confined to her room. My amigo, Paco, a shop owner and beach vendor, saw us at The Inn at Mazatlán. Not seeing her, he said, "Where is your friend?"

"She is sick with the 'revenge'," her husband replied.

"Get her dressed and I'll get my car and take her to my doctor," said Paco.

Thirty minutes later he arrived with his vehicle and whisked her off to his doctor. He stayed with her during the doctor's examination as an interpreter, and an hour later they were returning to The Inn at Mazatlán with a prescription. Twenty-four hours later she was back to her normal happy self.

Fishing

Mazatlán was famous for its great sport fishing long before it became a major tourist destination. There are a large number of charter boats that take aboard about 9,000 sailfish and marlin annually. There are charter bottom fishing boats as well as fishing from the beach. There are countless lakes nearby that produce excellent bass fishing.

The City

Mazatlán has more than 12 miles of wide sandy beaches that seem to go on forever. The picturesque Malecón (an oceanfront promenade) is a center for Mazatlecos and tourists alike for walking, exercising and people-watching.

Unique among other tourist cities along the coasts of Mexico, Mazatlán is a commercial city. Without question, it has the mega-resorts in the Golden Zone and north, but there are not the big housing areas occupied permanently by expatriates like those near Guadalajara. I live on a block in which I am only one of two foreign families. I have Canadian and U.S. friends who live in almost all areas of the city. Many of them have integrated into their Mexican communities with few problems.

The downtown area of Mazatlán is only a short bus ride from the tourist zone and completely different from the resort areas. It has a bustling central market where shopping daily for fresh food is a way of life carried over from the days prior to refrigeration.

The Old Town (downtown – El Centro or El Centro Histórico and the Olas Altas area) has been rejuvenated over the past two decades, mostly by expatriates and winter residents who have bought and restored formerly derelict homes and restored them to their former Mexican beauty. Reasonable rents, the old Mexican beauty of the old buildings and the charm of the area has attracted artists, dancers, musicians, chefs and other creative types more than ever before. The Plazuela Machado, six short blocks from the central market, has sidewalk cafés where one can sit quietly in the shade enjoying a local beer or soft drink while watching senior citizens on the park benches talk and children laugh and chase each other around the gazebo.

During the evening hours, tourists enjoy themselves with the loud music in the discos and sports bars in the Golden Zone or take an inexpensive taxi ride to El Centro Histórico and visit the renovated Ángela Peralta Theater for classical music and dance. Student bands and other musical groups often perform at the Plazuela Machado and other venues in the evening.

Good restaurants abound throughout the city and prices range from very cheap to very expensive (by Mazatlán standards). While the specialty is shrimp—Mazatlán is the shrimp capital of the world—seafood, beef and chicken are also in abundance. Unfortunately, Mazatlán has no vegetarian restaurants as of this printing, although most restaurants can serve a vegetarian meal if requested. The restaurants Panama Bakery, Pura Vida and Jungle Juice (see Chapter 7, "Where do you eat?") do have some vegetarian selections on the menu.

Modern shopping centers are abundant throughout the city. A Wal-Mart opened in 2002, and Home Depot opened in 2006. La Gran Plaza mall was remodeled in 2011 and is just four blocks from the tourist area. It features many excellent shops and boutiques, department stores and a multiplex movie theater. Sam's Club is a block away.

One of the "13 Wonders of Mexico": Mazatlán was voted one of the "13 Wonders of Mexico" in 2007. While I don't recall the other 12, I can tell you that there are 100 reasons for Mazatlán being selected as one of them.

Areas of the city

Golden Zone: This is the major tourist area and extends from the El Cid Marina south to Valentino's, the large white building that appears to be an Arabic castle, but in fact is a complex of discos and restaurants. The Golden Zone is where most of the tourists stay and play, although El Centro Histórico has become increasingly popular as the cultural center of the city.

Malecón: This is a beautiful boulevard with a beach-side promenade called Av. del Mar that runs from Valentino's south to the Fisherman's Monument where the street becomes Paseo Claussen, and continues on to become Av. Olas Altas. The promenade was widened and resurfaced in 2009.

El Centro Histórico and Olas Altas: This is the older section of the city where tourism began. In the last 10 years or so, it has experienced a rebirth, and museums, cafés, shops and art galleries abound.

Beaches

The beach – *playa* – seems to go on forever. There are, however, a few breaks along the way. I'll describe the beaches going from north to south:

Playa Delfín: The northern-most beach is relatively isolated except for the Pueblo Bonito Emerald Bay Hotel complex and a scattering of homes and condos. To get there, take the Sábalo Cerritos road from the new Marina to the Highway 15 bypass, then turn north just before you reach the railroad tracks. Very few people go there, so you'll have a lot of privacy. The downside is that once you pass Pueblo Bonito Emerald Bay, the road is dirt and can be dusty and rutted. No bus goes to Playa Delfín. The south end of this beach, in front of the Pueblo Bonito Emerald Bay, is sometimes called Playa Emerald Bay.

Playa Cerritos: Is between Playa Delfín and Cerritos Point. It is at the north end of several bus lines. During the week, tourists go there to explore, while on the weekend locals use it as a picnic area and children explore the tide pools. There are some souvenir shops and restaurants in a small strip mall.

Playa Brujas: Is the name of the beach that starts at the south end of Cerritos Point. Going south, the long sandy beach with no specific boundary, becomes:

Playa Escondida: This beach is used primarily by hotel renters and timeshare owners and extends nearly four miles. Multi-story condos are multiplying along this beach, which stretches almost all the way to the mouth of the inlet to Marina Mazatlán. Most of the beach is excellent for swimming. If you want to watch the more daring surfers, head up to the north end where it becomes Playa Brujas.

Hotel El Cid Marina beach: A lovely small stretch of beach, just before the jetty at mouth of the inlet to Marina Mazatlán. The only easy way to get to this beach is to take the water taxi from the El Cid Marina to the beach.

Playa Camarón Sábalo and Playa Gaviotas: For most tourists, this is where the action is. It extends from the Hotel Pueblo Bonito Mazatlán all the way south to Valentino's. The vast majority of the beaches are okay for swimming, but some stretches are a little better, as the offshore islands block any heavy surf in many areas. This is the area where my dog and I take our daily walks and I do most of my people-watching.

With all the beach vendors in this area, it is a virtual shopping mall. There are volleyball and soccer games, beach fishing, swimming, sun bathing, walkers and dancers and even an occasional traveling mariachi band. During college spring break, you may even catch a dance or "hard body" contest. This is where most of the "fun-in-the-sun" takes place.

Playa Norte: This beach parallels the Malecón and extends from Valentino's to just south of the Fisherman's Monument, three miles away. It is great for swimming, and most days you can sit on the Malecón wall and watch the surfers or on Sunday see the locals playing baseball, volleyball or soccer. Between 6 and 7 A.M. go just south of the Fisherman's Monument and watch the fishermen sell their daily catch—or buy some for yourself!

Playa Los Pinos: After a short rocky area at the south end of Playa Norte is this lovely, nearly hidden small beach, just before the long rocky area around Cerro de la Nevería – Ice Box Hill – to:

Playa Olas Altas: Popular in the 1940s, this is the original tourist beach in Mazatlán, located just south of Ice Box Hill. You can sit on the small beach and enjoy watching the surfers. Afterwards, cross the street and sit in one of the many sidewalk cafés and do some people-watching while sipping a cool one.

Stone Island: It is not really an island, but a peninsula, with miles of great beaches. It is a 5-minute boat ride from any of three docks: one near the east end of the street going east from the Fisherman's Monument, one adjacent to the La Puntilla Restaurant (probably the most popular) and another near the corner leading to the lighthouse.

The ferry is really an outboard motor boat – *lancha* – that carries 10–15 passengers for a cost of only 25 pesos – about $2.00 – round-trip. Walking, swimming, people-watching, quad-riding and horseback riding are among the many activities there. Cafés, *palapa* – palm thatched – restaurants such as Lety's, two small hotels and a small trailer park are strung along the first kilometer – about ⅔ mile – of this beach. If the cruise ships return to Mazatlán, I suggest you avoid Stone Island on days cruise ships are ashore as prices of rentals increase.

Video clips of Mazatlán

By far the best video to watch before coming to Mazatlán is this information packed one. WARNING! Once you watch this you WILL want to come to Mazatlán right then.

http://blip.tv/next-stop/next-stop-mazatlan-6333341

For superb promotional information go to these sites:

http://www.mazatlaninteractivo.com.mx. Just click on videos.

http://allaboutmazatlan.com/gallery/video-gallery/. Click on the video "Mazatlán the Pearl of the Pacific".

http://www.mazatlanmycity.com/

Click on Cultura videos.

State Department of Tourism/Tourist Services

Located midway between the Fisherman's Monument and the Golden Zone on Av. del Mar – the Malecón – it gives exceptional assistance to tourists. There are English-speaking receptionists ready to answer questions, give directions and advice and provide many colorful leaflets, maps, and tour information.

The Tourism Office also has professionals available to assist individuals and businesses considering investment opportunities. Prior to making large investments in construction or other businesses, I suggest that you contact this office that will help you develop your projects successfully. Tel: 981-8888 (if calling from the U.S. or Canada, use the prefix 011-52-669).

Safety

No discussion of tourism in Mazatlán would be complete without a discussion of safety. Since 2007 when President Calderon declared war on the drug cartels that smuggle drugs into Mexico and then into the U.S., various areas of Mexico have seen an upswing in violence. Has it affected Mazatlán? Yes, because the northern part of the state of Sinaloa is the home of one of the country's drug cartels. However, during that six year period there has been only one Canadian snowbird wounded by a stray bullet in a drive-by shooting (not at him) while crossing the street in an area far from the tourist area (and he has already said he's coming back for certain). Mazatlán tourists have not been affected by the increase in violence.

Unfortunately, it has had an adverse effect on the number of tourists in Mazatlán as international news sources have used a large brush to paint a dismal picture of violence throughout Mexico. I have happily continued as a snowbird every year and have not changed my habits at all.

Wonderful resort activities are available in Mazatlán and will be discussed in detail in another chapter of the book. Have I talked you into a trip to the most beautiful city south of the border? Then read on for tips for your trip!

Mazatlán, by H.F. Feucht

What is there about Mazatlán?
That makes one want to linger on?
That leaves nostalgic memories?
Is it the diamond dazzling azure sea
With stretching immensity
Endless like infinity?
Is it the island-studded majesty?
Relieving seas monotony
With crimson "end of day" display
When flaming sun sinks in the bay
With awe inspiring afterglow
And its prismatic rainbow show?
Is it the Playa's "in vacation mood"
Dispensing Spirits-exotic food?
And Vendedores everywhere
Plying tourista native ware
It's these.
But that which adds priceless charm
Are friendships made sincere and warm.
These all are why you linger on
And oft return to "Mazatlán."

Chapter 2

Let's go on that dream trip!

Y OU'VE JUST TOLD YOUR BOSS that it's time for your winter vacation, and you've called your travel agent or started looking online. Many first-time trips to Mazatlán are through a package travel deal involving both airline tickets and accommodations. Prices vary, depending on distance from Mazatlán, class of hotel and length of stay. Now your real planning begins. What are the things you **must** take?

Immigration

The Mexican government requires that all U.S. citizens present proof of citizenship and photo identification for entry into Mexico in the form of a passport, and you cannot re-enter the U.S. without one, which is a U.S. government requirement.

Mexican law requires that any non-Mexican under the age of 18 entering Mexico must carry written and notarized permission from his or her parents or guardians. If only one parent or guardian has legal custody, this has to be documented. The permission letter must include the name of the parent(s), the name of the child, the name of anyone traveling with the child and the notarized signature(s) of the absent parent(s), or a copy of any document(s)—court order or death certificate—explaining the reason there is only one parent or guardian. The child must carry the original letter—not a faxed or scanned copy—as well as proof of the parent/child relationship (usually a birth certificate) and an original custody decree, if applicable. These documents are absolutely necessary, as Mexican officials are notoriously inflexible in this regard.

All travelers, including children, will need a visitor's permit (FMM), which is an official form that will be given to you on the airplane while en route to Mexico. You complete and sign it prior to landing. If you're coming by land, there is a customs and immigration checkpoint 21km south of Nogales where you get these papers and the correct papers for your vehicle.

While processing through immigration at the airport in Mazatlán, the immigration officer will stamp it and return your part of the form. Keep it(them) in a safe place with your return airline ticket(s), as you will be asked for it when you leave the country.

No one will ever ask you for your permit, or even passport, while in Mazatlán EXCEPT if you change money at a bank (or unless you run afoul of the law, of course). I suggest that you make a copy of each and carry the copies with you—just in case. Put the permit(s) and passport original(s) in a safe place.

If you are not a U.S., Canadian or Mexican citizen, I suggest you contact the Mexican consulate or Embassy nearest you for identification and visa requirements.

The airlines will take the permit as part of check-in for your flight home. If you lose the visa it can be rewritten at the Migración – Immigration – office in the airport. The replacement permit usually costs around $40.

New brides, please note that the name on your airplane ticket must match your passport. I suggested to my granddaughter, who used our timeshare for a honeymoon, that she travel under her maiden name. She did so, but once in Mazatlán, she told everyone who would listen that they were newlyweds. They were amazed how many free drinks and special favors they received—from both guests and business proprietors.

Miscellaneous good advice

People always seem concerned about *bandidos* in Mexico. I'm sure rip-offs exist, but there is crime in all the cities the size of Mazatlán in the U.S. and Canada. It is my belief that you are safer here than in large cities in the States.

Someone asked me, "If you say the crime rate is so low, why do I see so many cops carrying automatic weapons in the tourist zone?"

"They carry the weapons and remain visible in the tourist zone to deter criminal activity," I responded. "The police, local, state and federal, carry automatic weapons all over Mexico...it's normal." It only makes sense that extra precautions would be taken by the government to protect tourists, since that is where businesses in Mazatlán get a significant percentage of their revenue.

Another common question is why so many of the houses have wrought-iron bars on the windows. I've been told that it is an architectural thing, brought to Mazatlán by the Spaniards. My house has ornamental iron bars in all the windows that not only add to the attractiveness of the house but also provide security. On the other hand, as I watch houses being built in the gated communities these days, I notice an absence of the iron bars.

Are there petty thieves in Mazatlán? Yes. Can your purse/wallet be stolen? Yes. But that can happen anywhere in the world. Our adult offspring expressed their concern about my wife and me driving to Mazatlán. They said it was too dangerous in Mexico. In fact, we feel safer in Mexico than we do while passing through Los Angeles and Phoenix!

This information is passed on not to alarm you of the possibility of petty theft in Mazatlán, but because forewarned is forearmed. Remove everything from your purse and wallet that you will not need before you go out. Make copies of both sides of your credit cards, driver's license, ID cards, etc. Now you know what was in your wallet before it was stolen or lost. You'll also have all the account numbers and telephone numbers to call and cancel. Don't place these copies in your wallet/purse, but take them with you on your trip and keep them in a safe place.

Ladies, do NOT set your purse on the floor beside your chair, either set it on the table, hang it on the back of the chair or keep it in your lap. Just good advice for any resort area anywhere in the world.

If your credit or debit cards are lost or stolen, call the phone numbers on your cards and cancel them. Also, call the three national credit-reporting organizations immediately to place a fraud alert on your name and Social Security Number:

Equifax 001-880-525-6285
Experian 001-880-397-3742
Trans Union 001-880-680-7289

Call the Social Security Administration fraud line, 001-880-269-0271 to let them know of your loss. By doing so, you may avoid someone using your identification to take out new credit. These numbers are the way to call from a landline phone in Mexico, they may not be toll free. The U.S. numbers would have the prefix 1-800 rather than 001-880.

I also call my credit card company and let them know the dates that I will be in Mexico, so that if my card is stolen and used for large purchases, the credit card company can stop the purchases. You may never have to use this information, but if you do, you'll have it. Warning: If you don't notify your credit (or debit) card bank or company, they may automatically block your card when it's used in Mexico.

File a police report right away with the local police. This will help you prove to credit providers that you were conscientious.

Clothing

Mazatlán is a warm weather area and very laid-back. You should load up on swimming suits, sandals, short sleeve shirts/blouses and shorts.

Bring along a pair of casual slacks and/or dress for evenings at that special place. Be sure to pack a good pair of walking shoes for there will be ample opportunity to stroll the city streets, taking in the sounds, sights and smells of this beautiful metropolis. I always recommend packing a light jacket or sweater for those cool evenings sitting in an open-air beachside restaurant while watching the breathtaking sunset.

Someone asked me if formal or semi-formal attire was needed in Mazatlán. My response was while there must be places that they would be needed, but I have never been to any of those places. Leave the suit, tux or fancy dresses at home! If the opportunity arises where you need to wear such attire, there are several formal clothing rental places in town. One is:

Arnold's: Arnold's is located at the corner of Canizalez and 5 de Mayo in El Centro. Very high quality men's suits and tuxes, including accessories for rent. All sizes are available from two-year old boy's to men's 55/56. They are open Mon.-Sat., 9 A.M. to 8 P.M. For weekend rental, the merchandise may be picked up on Thursday and returned on Monday. Tel: 982-8002.

Most hotels have laundry facilities and there are reputable laundries that give one-day service throughout the city and at least one coin-op laundry for those who really do want to do their own laundry. It's Galerías Speed Laundry, right across the street from the Hotel Costa de Oro behind the Modelorama "Super" next to the Banco Santander.

Plus, there are two favorite pastimes here: shopping for new clothes and hats…and wearing them. In fact, shopping is so good, I recommend one or both: bring along an extra suitcase filled with old clothes (if you can afford it with the new luggage charges), especially children's clothing. Your hotel or the La Viña Mission – The Vineyard – church on Camarón Sábalo in the Golden Zone will gladly take them for distribution to needy local families and orphanages. If you're a super shopper, there are numerous stores selling good leather luggage. Then you will have plenty of room for all those items you bought in Mazatlán.

If you are traveling from a cold climate, have a carry-on bag and place a pair of shorts and short-sleeve shirt/blouse in it so that when you arrive in Mazatlán, you can go to the restroom and change into them. It will make the motor trip to your resort much more comfortable. On your return trip, pack your heavy clothes to wear after the plane trip home in the carry-on, and make your change at your home airport. You'll be far more comfortable for that last minute shopping and long trip to the airport.

Other items

Sunscreen is a must. It is available in stores in Mazatlán, but I suggest you buy it in the States because it is not only cheaper, but also because the first place you will want to go is the beach, and you'll need the sunscreen then…EVEN IF IT'S CLOUDY.

The electric current is the same as in Canada and the United States. Mazatlán is so laid-back I'm not sure you'll even need your electric razor or blow dryer anyway. *Note:* Although becoming more common, there are still many two-prong electric outlets in Mazatlán. If you have anything that MUST be plugged in that is three-prong, you should bring an adapter with it, just in case.

Be sure to pack away an adequate supply of your prescription drugs because your prescription may not be available in Mexico. However, many prescription drugs are not only easier to get, but cost much less than in the U.S. Prescriptions by U.S. doctors are not always accepted in Mazatlán pharmacies, but many drugs that require written prescriptions in the

States are sold "across the counter" in the city. Antibiotics, psychoactive drugs (most anti-depressants) and the strong, opiate painkilling drugs definitely DO need prescriptions. Many small pharmacies – *farmacias* – are doctor-owned and can get you a prescription on-the-spot for a nominal doctor's visit sum. The larger, chain farmacias, like Farmacias Moderno, Farmacias Guadalajara and Farmacias Benavides are usually less expensive than the smaller *farmacias*, but you would have to get the prescription for those sorts of drugs on your own.

Since the NAMES of many drugs are different in Mexico than in the U.S. or Canada, be aware that only the large chain *farmacias* (particularly Farmacias Moderna) may have the latest cross-reference book or online reference ability, so it's wise to have your doctor or pharmacist give you the generic name if available.

If you have a prescription with the generic name of the drug, several *farmacias* specialize in government-certified generics only…at rock-bottom prices, the most common one is Farmacias Similares.

Just like traveling in the U.S. or Canada, keep a list of all the medications you are currently taking, notation of allergies or hypersensitivities and diet restrictions. Your health insurance card with the name and phone number of your family physician may be helpful for medical history if needed. Most U.S. health insurance covers medical needs in Mazatlán, however, prepayment by user is required, and with sufficient copies of bills, reimbursement will be made when you return home. Medicare is not good outside the U.S.

If you need eyeglasses or prescription sunglasses, bring either a prescription or a pair of glasses with you. Eye exams are available by professionals at excellent prices. Optometrists in the resort area sell designer type glasses for less than $100 Allow at least two days for delivery.

I always have a pair of good earplugs on the nightstand. Mazatlán is a busy city, and in some parts of town there can be traffic late at night or early in the morning. You non-party people don't want to be awakened in the middle of the night by the "fast-lane" people next door, and you partiers don't want to be awakened by the early risers or maids (especially if you're hung-over).

A good camera is a must. You want to capture those "Kodak moments" so that you can bore or make envious those friends and relatives who did not make the trip to paradise with you. You can find places providing four-hour digital photo printing in the tourist zone and most still give fast service for film developing and printing. Farmacias Benavides is located on Camarón Sábalo, just north of Gaviotas Cinemas. They have one-hour developing/ service for either film or digital, and there are Kodak photo stores both in El Centro and the Golden Zone that offer the same services.

Bring along a small backpack and/or a fanny pack. Wallets or purses are a nuisance, and you will want to take only what is needed while at the beach. While shopping, the fanny pack is safer for your cash or credit card. The backpack can be used for the bottles of water you should be carrying around to keep yourself hydrated. This book will fit nicely in your backpack as a quick reference and for directions.

While most merchants and store clerks in the tourist zone are bilingual, at least to some extent, there may be occasions to use Spanish. If you cannot speak Spanish, I suggest that you bring a pocket Spanish-English dictionary or electronic translator. Dictionaries are available at most bookstores, and Radio Shack has a large variety of pocket electronic translators. A list of helpful Spanish words and phrases are in Appendix 1. Metric-American conversion tables are in Appendix 2.

Money

Throughout the book I will try to convert pesos to U.S. dollars for simplification, however since U.S. coins are useless in Mexico, I use pesos where appropriate. U.S. dollar prices will have the $ (dollar sign) and peso prices won't (but they do in Mexican stores!) but will have the word "pesos" following the price. *NOTE:* Please remember, all the prices in U.S. dollars are APPROXIMATE. The exchange rate to pesos changes daily, but usually by only a small amount. As of this writing, it has been running between 12 pesos to the U.S. dollar and 13 pesos to the U.S. dollar.

Don't exchange U.S. currency at the airport booth as the rates are usually much lower than at the banks and exchange offices that are all over the tourist zones. There are ATM machines at the airport near the immigration office if you want to take the time to get some pesos before leaving for the beach. The best exchange rates are at ATMs. There are ATM machines in all the major grocery stores and banks scattered throughout the city that are safe to use. They charge a small withdrawal fee (20–40 pesos) for each transaction. Remember that the amounts on the screen are PESOS not dollars!

I have heard of several cases where ATM cards have been either eaten, or the user walks away and leaves the card in the machine. If your card is eaten, go in the bank immediately and inform an employee of the problem. If the bank is closed, be certain to be there at opening time (usually 9 A.M.) the next morning to see if you can retrieve it. This won't always be possible, as different banks have different regulations on this. Always put your ATM card on top of the cash you receive and put it away in your wallet before you exit the bank booth. If you rely completely on an ATM card, I suggest you bring a duplicate and keep it in a safe place. A number of major stores have swipe ATM machines. Use one of those and there is no danger of your card being eaten.

If for some reason your transaction goes through but you receive no cash don't bother going to the store or bank to get your money. Keep the transaction receipt, ATM number and location and call your ATM bank or credit union for redress. IT IS THE ONLY WAY TO GET YOUR MONEY BACK!

I don't know of any salesperson or shop in Mazatlán that does not accept U.S. currency, but note that the exchange rate, and that of your resort hotel, will usually be the lowest of all.

Leave your U.S. coins at home. Not only will you not have to go through the trouble of adding them to that little plastic box at the airport metal detector, but no one in Mazatlán accepts them.

Travelers' checks can be exchanged, but remember that most exchange institutions require picture ID and some banks will not cash them. I suggest that ATM cards provide the best rates and are far more convenient. After all, who wants to go all the way to Mazatlán for vacation and stand in a long line at the bank?

Many shops, restaurants and most resort hotels accept credit cards, but they don't always display on the window or cash register which cards are acceptable. If you have no alternative to the credit card, check with the cashier prior to placing your order. Generally, exchange rates are very good on credit cards, except that some charge for a foreign transaction. Some shops also charge you the same percentage they pay when someone uses a credit card – generally around 5% in Mexico. I've found that paying cash, in pesos, is less complicated and is money-saving.

Emergency money

Western Union sends money from the States to Mazatlán, but it can cost up to 10%. Wire transfers can be made, but that is complex and costly. My advice is to have a friend or relative make a deposit in your checking account so you can use your ATM card to access the money.

Pets

I bought a puppy in 2007 and she is already an international traveler. We kennel trained her right away and pay $100 each way and place the kennel under the seat in the plane. This cost varies with each different airline, and some don't allow it at all. Be certain to check with your airline directly for **their** requirements, not with your travel agent. Most airlines will transport pets in the luggage compartment, except, due to U.S. government regulations, in the summer months.

All you need to bring pets into the country is an up-to-date, veterinarian issued, health certificate less than five days old, available from any vet in the U.S. or Canada. To bring a pet into Mexico a rabies shot within the past year is a requirement, and a new requirement is certification of freedom from intestinal parasites. Your airline may have additional requirements

We have found many of the restaurants here are very tolerant of our little dog. You'll have to check with your hotel as to their pet policy. Maybe your beloved little friend deserves a vacation as well!

Don't bring guns and ammunition or explosives into Mazatlán unless you have proper documentation – check with your nearest Mexican Consulate or Embassy – the Mexican government discourages arming its citizens…and especially discourages foreigners from having ANY sort of handguns or other guns. Possession of illegal arms (practically any gun or ammunition—or just one cartridge!) can bring you some serious jail time—and I'm told any jail time in Mexico is serious.

Spring break for students

It happens every year in Fort Lauderdale and Palm Springs, Cancún or Padre Island, but Mazatlán is different. Although hundreds of young people will descend on the city between February 21 and Easter, older tourists don't need to worry, as that scene in Mazatlán is very, very mild compared to Daytona Beach, Florida or Padre Island, Texas. Don't get me wrong—they will be here, but don't cause disruptions or problems, and you might not even know that spring break is happening. I do want to point out to students reading this book that an excellent website for a spring break tour is:

http://www.paradiseparties.com.

Inexpensive travel to Mazatlán

Your first trip to Mazatlán may be through a travel agent that offers a package deal. That's great, but it does not have to be that way. There are a couple of good websites where you can get good airline tickets cheap, and I'll discuss hotels in Chapter 11. The websites are *http://www. cheaptickets.com*, *http://www.hotwire.com* and *http://www.bestfares.com*.

Daylight Savings Time

Mazatlán's STANDARD TIME is the same as Mountain Time in the States. Several years ago, the Mexican government went to daylight savings time, but the United States later shifted the start and end dates for Daylight Savings Time by three weeks from that used in the rest of the world. Here, clocks "spring forward" an hour on the first Sunday in April, and "fall back" on the first Sunday in October.

Landing in Mazatlán

You remembered to do all the things I suggested and you've finally landed in paradise. As you leave the plane, look for that restroom and hope not many people have read my book and taken my advice. Exit the restroom resplendent in your shorts and shirt and follow the crowd to immigration. Once the immigration officer stamps your passport and visitor's visa (issued and filled out on the plane), place the form he returns to you and your passport in a safe place because you will need them when you head home. Next, follow the crowd to the baggage claim. Don't worry about carrying your bags. There are lots of strong young men eager to help you schlep your stuff to the bus or taxi. Tip as you would in the U.S, about $1 per bag. Once you pick up your bags go to the station where they will be x-rayed. Then, you will be asked to push a large button. As you push, say a silent prayer for a green light because if you are unlucky and get a red light, all your bags will be opened and customs officials will inspect everything, including your "unmentionables". You are allowed to bring in $350 of goods duty-free.

Once you are allowed to leave the baggage area, you will enter a room with counters on two walls. Unless you are interested in spending some of your vacation time listening to a timeshare presentation, put your head down and continue walking through the small (by U.S. standards) airport terminal until you are outside on the sidewalk.

As you exit the terminal lobby numerous people will approach you offering you a free ride from the airport. No Virginia, there is no such thing as a free ride, not even in Mexico. These nice people are all timeshare salespeople, and you will be required to sit through a sales presentation to collect your free ride. Trust me.

Some tour package deals provide a ride to your hotel. If your transportation is provided, look for someone holding up a sign with your hotel's name on it. Before you exit the terminal lobby, you will find the ATMs if you need pesos.

Since ATMs are by far the best and most economical way to exchange foreign money for pesos, just after you pass the news stand in the main airport lobby look to your right and you will see four ATM machines: BaNorte, HSBC, Bancomer and Banco Del Bajio.

People always ask me the best deal for transportation from the airport. My response is always, if you are in a hurry, and don't mind spending the money, take a taxi. If you have plenty of time, prefer to spend less and want to see more of the city, take a shuttle van, although taxis charge the same for up to 4 persons, which sometimes makes them less expensive than a van.

Taxi

As you walk toward the exit of the airport, people will ask you if you want a taxi. There are three taxi companies in Mazatlán. The yellow (or white and yellow) airport taxis (and vans) operate **only** from the airport to anywhere else, but won't take you back to the airport. The fares are non-negotiable, and payment is made in advance to a cashier near the parked taxis. At printing, the cost regardless of the number of passengers (up to 4) and their baggage, but depending on the "zone" or distance from the airport, was $31–$55 (340 to 550 pesos—note that you save quite a lot when you pay in pesos, due to their very poor exchange rate, just another good reason for going to the ATM before exiting the terminal). They are not disagreeable to your sharing a cab, but the split in cost would be negotiated between you and the other tourist(s), not the driver.

The other taxis are red and white or green and white in color, both called "Ecotaxi", and take passengers all over Mazatlán, **except** from the airport to town. Their fares are negotiable (It has been announced that all taxis in Mazatlán will be metered taxis by the end of 2012—but the taxi drivers I have spoken with say it won't happen.) I will discuss them and other modes of transportation later in the book.

Van

The cost for travel on the van is about $10–$14 (100 to 150 pesos—see note above) per person. You could wind up on a circuitous route to your hotel. The other problem with this option is that many vans allow timeshare salespeople on the bus and they do their darnedest to offer you anything from free breakfast to tours to cash, just to hear a two-hour presentation.

I'll discuss timeshares later in the book, but since you will receive many more opportunities during your vacation, I suggest you resist the urge for all the "free" stuff and enjoy the ride to the city.

Car Rental

As you exit baggage claim there are rental car agents from Avis, Europcar, Budget, National, AGA, Alamo, Hertz and Dollar. I don't recommend car rentals in town, but if that's what you want, they are available for pick-up and drop-off at the airport. If this is your choice, be sure to take ALL of the insurance offered. Your U.S. or Canadian car insurance won't cover you in Mexico. And that credit card insurance you think you have might pay some of the costs, but only after long hassles with them.

At the hotel: When you check in, be sure and ask if safety deposit boxes are available. Usually they are free unless you lose a key. Place your return airline ticket(s), passport(s), tourist permits(s) and any other valuables in your safe deposit box. Once you've dropped your luggage in your room, head for the beach or the main drag (Camarón Sábalo in the Golden Zone) for some scouting around and fun.

Babysitters: Most hotels can help you get babysitting service. Current cost is $5 to $6 per hour. So as not to be disappointed, be sure to arrange for them 24 hours in advance.

Police: If you have a problem, don't be afraid to contact the tourist police, 986-8126. English-speaking officers are available and they are courteous and helpful.

U.S. Consular Agency: It is located in the Golden Zone, across the street from the Hotel Playa Mazatlán. The consular agent recommends that you register with them as soon as possible after you arrive, so that people in your hometown can get in touch with you if there is an emergency. The telephone number is 916-5889, and the business hours are from 9:00 A.M. to 1:00 P.M., Monday through Friday. Closed on both Mexican and U.S. legal holidays.

Canadian Consulate: It is located north of the Golden Zone near the new Marina. The telephone number is 913-7320, and they are open 9:30 A.M. to 12:30 P.M., Monday through Friday. Closed on some Mexican legal or bank holidays and all Canadian legal holidays.

Grocery stores: Mini-markets, called "Supers" are located all over the city. OXXO stores, like U.S. 7-11s, are also all over the city. Most resort hotels have stores that sell groceries and sundries too. If you need more than just a few soft drinks, beer and chips, I suggest going  to supermarkets such as Soriana, Mega, Ley (at Plaza del Mar or Plaza Ley) or Wal-Mart. *NOTE:* Wal-Mart Mexico does NOT carry most of the same brands/products that Wal-Mart in the U.S. carries. The prices are about the same or somewhat lower than in the United States—higher if imported from the U.S., usually lower to much lower if Mexican products—fruits and vegetables are a great bargain. If you are a member of Sam's Club in the States and are staying more than a week, I recommend you stop there, particularly for bulk purchases and wine/liquor.

Calling home: I've never been able to figure out why anyone would travel all the way to Mexico, then call home…but if you are so inclined, or have an urgent need, here is the information.

Dialing direct to the States or Canada is expensive, but can be done with any telephone in the hotels by prefixing the number with 001- instead of just 1-. For the best rates, bill the call to a calling card. An even better rate is to call collect—that way someone else is paying the ridiculous toll fee. Dial 090 and request an English-speaking operator. If calling to a local, i.e., Mazatlán, cellular phone, dial the prefix 044-669.

1-800 numbers are not toll free from Mexico to the U.S. or Canada, but you might have occasion to call one, especially if you lose a credit card or ATM card. The following are the numbers to dial:

1-800 dial 001-880
1-888 dial 001-881
1-877 dial 001-882
1-866 dial 001-883

Don't forget that free calls to the U.S. and Canada can be made at the Vineyard church in the Golden Zone, and if you brought your laptop, cheap or free calls can be made through Skype.com and other VOIP services anywhere you can get a wireless connection.

Some people want to leave a telephone number where they can be reached from home while they are on vacation. I don't understand that either, but here are the special instructions. Your friends and relatives will need to dial a bunch of numbers to get through to you. If dialing from the U.S. or Canada, first dial 011-52-669-, then the seven digit local number. But if they are trying to reach a cell phone you have purchased in Mazatlán or any other Mazatlán cell phone, they must dial 011-521-669- plus the seven digit number.

BE AWARE: Those two prefixes will be important to you if you want to call Mexico prior to your coming here. Throughout this book, Mazatlán landline numbers will be shown as ONLY the seven digit local number and cell phone numbers shown as the 044-669-XXX-XXXX numbers, where you have to replace the 044 with 011-521- if calling from the States or Canada.

Internet connections: Internet cafés are available throughout Mazatlán. There are a couple of cyber shops in the tourist zone as well as the downtown area, although this is rapidly changing as Wi-Fi becomes more common and cyber cafés less common. Wi-Fi connections are in most resorts and many restaurants/coffee shops, so bring your laptop if you need your Internet "fix".

Food delivery: Many restaurants have delivery service. Before ordering, I suggest you contact the front desk of your hotel for the policy for delivery. Some allow delivery to your room door, while others require you to pick it up in the lobby. Be sure to give the delivery person a tip.

Tipping: Everyone always has questions about tipping in Mazatlán. Keep in mind that most of the people who provide services only receive wages of $5–$6 a day. Your tips allow them to make a living wage.

TIPS SHOULD BE IN MEXICAN CURRENCY.

Although your generosity is appreciated, it is counter-productive to tip in foreign currency. Coins cannot be exchanged, and the worker either needs to save up the small one and five dollar bills he or she receives in tips until there is a substantial amount to justify taking time off from work to go to the bank and exchange the foreign currency for pesos or sell it at a deep discount…often as little as the equivalent of 50 cents on the dollar.

At restaurants, I tip 15–20% depending on the service. For buffets, I tip 7–10%. Some (very few) restaurants put the 15% tip on the bill so unless you want to really be generous, check your bill.

I always tip someone when I ask them to do a special service, such as moving lounge chairs and umbrellas. It is customary to give the gas station attendant a couple pesos for a fill-up. Maid service is as good as you get anywhere and I always tip two-four bucks a day and just leave the cash on the kitchen counter before check-out. Some hotels require a note signed by the guest that the amount of money and groceries were a gift to the maid—by name. The maids always appreciate the leftover food and drinks from the refrigerator and cupboards. The children and seniors at the supermarkets who bag groceries typically receive 2 or 3 pesos from customers, as they do not receive a salary. Give them ten pesos if they carry your groceries to your car or taxi.

That guy in the "make-shift" uniform standing in the parking lot at the mall or grocery store does not usually receive pay. Be sure and give him a couple pesos for watching your vehicle. In general, I always try to be an ambassador of the richest nation in the world and show my thanks for the service I receive.

During my first visit to Mazatlán, and before the 1994 changeover in currency, I inadvertently gave a waiter a $20 tip for a $10 meal. Since then, I always recommend carrying single dollar bills with you in case you get confused with the foreign currency, but much better is to hoard 10 peso coins and 20 and 50 peso bills for use only as tips.

Beggars: In the hotel zone, you will see mothers with little babies cradled in their laps, holding out a Styrofoam cup or selling trinkets, or they may have young children selling Chiclets.

These are poor indigenous Mexicans who come to Mazatlán to beg, particularly during the November to June tourist season. They have little or no other way to generate actual money except by begging, as most are from remote areas and are subsistence farmers (unless the crops fail, then they go hungry or starve).

They will ask you for a donation and you can put a coin in the cup or shake your head and move on. They will not follow you. There is an urban myth that the beggars live in good sections of town and even rent children to help them. I've never been able to confirm that it is anything but a myth. I usually pick out a different lady each day and give her a donation then shake my head to the others.

Extend your vacation: I know you will have so much fun that you will consider staying in paradise longer. You should confirm your airline reservations a day before scheduled departure. This can easily be done online, and you can print your boarding passes too. The following telephone numbers are provided for your convenience:

Mazatlán airport	982-2177
Aeromexico	914-1034
Alaska	981-4813
Continental/United	985-1881
Frontier	001-800-432-1359
U.S. Airways	001-800-428-4322
West Jet in Mexico	001-800-514-7288

Massage: If I haven't convinced you to extend your vacation, at least treat yourself to a body massage the day you leave for home. This is a must in Mazatlán. It will help you wind down from your vacation and inspire you to get yourself ready for the "old grind".

MYO Massage for Life is located on Camarón Sábalo, across the street from Hotel Costa de Oro in the Golden Zone. It is open seven days a week from 9 A.M. to 7 P.M. They have well-qualified massage therapists that can work out those "kinks".

Mayan Massage is located across from the Banamex bank on Camarón Sábalo in the Golden Zone. It features a 1-hour massage for about $12, manicures and pedicures. Tel: 916-5922.

Gyms: There are some people that want to maintain that "hard body" while on vacation, so there are several gyms in the Golden Zone and elsewhere in the city, where you can work out for a daily, weekly or monthly fee.

Body Factory: Above the Space Bowling alleys across from the Hotel El Cid Marina. Posted hours are Mon.-Fri. 6 A.M. to 10 P.M.,

Sat. 7 A.M. to 5 P.M. and Sun. 8 A.M. to 7 P.M. Their website is: *bodyfactorygym.com.*

GM Sport Center gym: One-half block east of Starbucks on the other side of the street. Tel: 913-3539

Departure home by air: Be sure and arrive at the airport two hours before departure. You will not only need your passport but the visitor's permit form that you completed when you entered the country. Your luggage must be inspected even though you may have checked in online so be sure and stop by the ticket counter. Following check in I suggest you go upstairs to the large waiting room. There are plenty of shops for last-minute shopping as well as a Carl's Junior and several other restaurants and cafés where you can load up to avoid the airlines food. Follow your airline's instructions as to boarding times and follow signs to your gate. You will find comfortable waiting rooms at each and of course, duty-free shops for any last-minute purchases. Don't be surprised if your carry-ons are inspected yet again at the departure gate. Have a safe flight and start counting your days till your return to "paradise."

Chapter 3

Getting there

Air: To get to Mazatlán from the USA, your choice of originating cities is limited.

Flights in and out of Mazatlán change rapidly. Below are the scheduled airlines that have had, may still have or expect to have flights available now or in the near future. Since we're not in the "future predicting business", for ticketing assistance, call the airlines direct (from the U.S. or Canada) at:

UNITED STATES

Alaska Airlines 1-800-426-0333   *alaskaair.com*
American Airlines 1-800-433-7300   *aa.com*
Cal Jet Air 1-866-226-4173   *caljetair.com*

NOTE: Cal Jet Air is very new and not scheduled to start flights to Mazatlán until December 2012. They MAY turn out to be a charter airline rather than a scheduled airline. We just don't have enough information yet.

Delta Air Lines. 1-800-221-1212   *delta.com*
Frontier Airlines 1-800-432-1359   *frontierairlines.com*

JetBlue Airways 1-800-538-2583   *jetblue.com*
Sun Country Airlines. .1-800-359-6786   *suncountry.com*

IMPORTANT NOTE: The Mexican government has given Sun Country, which is both a charter airline as well as a scheduled airline, a special privilege. They are the only charter airline to Mazatlán allowed to take on passengers in Mexico for a one way trip back to the U.S.—non-stop to Minneapolis, their home airport. In case of an emergency...a one-way, non-stop ticket out of Mexico to Minneapolis could save a life.

United Airlines. 1-800-241-6522   *united.com*
U.S. Airways 1-800-428-4322   *usairways.com*

CANADA

Air Canada. 1-888-247-2262   *aircanada.com*
Air Transat. 1-800-388-5836   *airtransat.com*
WestJet Airlines 1-888-937-8538   *westjet.com*

MEXICO

Aero Mexico. 1-800-237-6639   *aeromexico.com*
Viva Aerobus . . . . . .011-52-818-215-0150 *vivaaerobus.com*

NOTE: Viva Aerobus has very economical roundtrips from Mexico City, Monterrey(MX), and, with a plane change in Monterrey, roundtrip flights to Houston, San Antonio and Las Vegas.

Volaris 1-866-988-3527
*http://contenido.volaris.com.mx/SWA/Skins/VolarisSWA/en-U.S./
Frecuently_WebCIFAQ.html*

NOTE: Volaris has very economical roundtrips from Tijuana to Mazatlán. The Tijuana airport is quite easy to get to from the San Diego, CA airport or vice versa.

And here are the tour companies offering charter flights to Mazatlán:

From the United States
Apple Vacations *www.applevacations.com*
Funjet *www.funjet.com*
Travel Impressions *www.travelimpressions.com*
GOGO Worldwide Vacations *www.gogowwv.com*
Sun Country Vacations *www.suncountry.com*

From Canada
Air Canada Vacations *aircanadavacations.com*
Nolitours *nolitour.com* 1-866-556-3948
Signature Vacations *signaturevacations.com*
Sunquest Vacations *sunquestvacations.ca*
Sunwing Vacations *sunwing.ca*
Transat Holidays *transatholidays.com*
WestJet Vacations *westjetvacations.com*

Tons of thanks to Travel Judy for all this information. She's THE México travel specialist, who can make all your trips to Mazatlán seem easy, as she has her finger on each and every special deal… daily! You can reach her at: *traveljudy@hotmail.com.*

Bus: Buses in Mexico are not like those you've seen in the movies. They are not overloaded with passengers, baggage, and crates of chickens. No, they are modern, luxurious and comfortable. They have clean bathrooms, a sound system and current movies (often in English with

Spanish subtitles). They are definitely fast, as I always exceed the speed limit by five miles per hour and all the buses pass me.

Deluxe buses – **Ejecutivo** – to and from border cities include TAP and Elite. There are at least two departures a day from Tijuana to Culiacán. One-way fare is about $67 Driving time is between 20–26 hours. TAP is the bus line of choice for the discerning traveler. Phoenix to Culiacán one-way costs about $100 and takes about 16 hours. The cost from Laredo, TX is $90 Once you get to Culiacán, it's easy to catch a bus to Mazatlán as they run every hour on this two-hour route, but may not be the Deluxe buses, as those don't run as often. Tufesa goes from Mazatlán to Phoenix, and costs $300 round trip.

If you have an INAPAM card (Mexican official senior citizen ID) you can travel for half-fare most of the time…if tickets are purchased in Mexico. Since bus schedules change as often as airline schedules, I suggest you call and get the exact schedule. You can telephone TAP within Mexico at 01-800-001-1827 or in Mazatlán at 981-4659. Call Elite in Mazatlán at 981-3811. There are other bus companies both in the terminal and at other locations, but these two seem to be the major deluxe services to the border.

Here are some other bus lines to try:

Tufesa in Mexico 01-800-8883 (from the U.S., 1-520-294-3780 for their office in Tucson if you want to be assured of an English speaker).

Sea

La Paz Ferry: The ferry to La Paz, Baja California Sur, leaves at 4 P.M. and crossing time is about 18 hours, Monday, Wednesday and Friday (or La Paz to Mazatlán, Tue., Thur. and Sat.). One-way fare is $80 for salon (a seat only) per person, $60–75 additional for a two person cabin. Your car, van or SUV is $185 or $270, depending on the size of the vehicle. Fares and schedules change frequently (due to exchange rates and fuel cost adjustments, fares change most often, so these prices are approximate), and I suggest you call for information and reservations at 01-800-718-2796 from within Mexico. The telephone number for the Mazatlán office at the ferry terminal is 985-0470. The website is *www. bajaferries.com.*

Cruise Ships: Unfortunately, due to the economic downturn, Mazatlán was eliminated as a port of call in 2011, but I'm hoping they will return in the future.

Pleasure Boats: Or as my friend Ken jokingly calls them, "The boat people." There is ample moorage at four different marinas. Charge for moorage is by the length of boat and facilities available. I suggest that you contact each individually for accommodations and cost:

Marina Mazatlán has 196 slips and can be contacted by email at *marinamaz@prodigy.net.mx*, or by telephone at 916-7799 or 916-3614.

El Cid Marina has 90 slips and can be contacted by email at *marina@elcid.com.mx* or by telephone at 916-3468.

Isla Mazatlán has 110 slips and can be contacted via email at *islamaz@hotmail.com* or by telephone at 916-0833.

There is an anchor-out operation called Club Nautico, 981-5195.

Driving: I've found that driving in Mexico is as safe as driving in the United States. Before you decide to drive to Mazatlán, you should know the documentation requirements and costs. There are many two-lane highways in Mexico that do not charge tolls, but they are sometimes narrow and have numerous potholes and few shoulders. Toll roads are more like super highways in the U.S., but are costly—about $70 from Nogales to Mazatlán. Gasoline prices hover between $2.50 and $3.20 per U.S. gallon, depending on the dollar-peso exchange rate, and change by a small amount every month. Except for the border area, gasoline prices are the same at every station in Mexico. I've driven the toll road – *cuota* or *maxipista* – from Nogales, Arizona to Mazatlán and found it to be a beautiful, picturesque drive.

Documentation: You must have originals and copies of your vehicle title and registration. If your vehicle is currently being financed, a notarized letter of permission from the financing institution giving permission for the vehicle to be taken to Mexico must be provided. If you are leasing your vehicle, the same type letter must be presented. Be aware that most leasing companies will not issue the letter for more than a 30-day period. Before I left home I made copies of:

- My passport and my wife's passport.
- My driver's license.
- My car registration and title.
- Mexican insurance policy for the car.

Cars in Mexico are very expensive. It is completely illegal to take your car into the country, sell it for a healthy profit without paying duty, then scamper back north across the border. Be warned—follow Mexican law. Now that Mexico is computerized, you'll NEVER be allowed to bring another vehicle into the country.

Mexican and/or international drivers' licenses are not required for foreigners. You must have originals and copies of current U.S. or Canadian drivers' licenses of all drivers who will operate the vehicle in Mexico. Check to be sure that your license does not expire during your stay in Mexico.

A deposit of $200 to $400, depending on the year of the vehicle, is required for temporarily importing your vehicle. It can only be paid in dollars (cash) or by credit card, but there has been much confusion over using cash, so it would be much better to bring along a Visa, MasterCard, or American Express credit card in the same name as on the title/registration/ pink slip. The name on the credit card **must** be the same. The vehicle cannot be sold in Mexico, and the sticker on the windshield they provide **must** be surrendered when leaving the country. They will return your deposit as the vehicle exits the country, when you return the sticker and papers at the 21 km checkpoint. It usually takes a few days for the credit to your credit card to show up.

Vehicle insurance: Your U.S. insurance is not good in Mexico, so I highly recommend purchasing Mexican insurance, unless of course you like to live on the edge and are willing to gamble and don't mind spending some time in a Mexican jail. Like any insurance, you don't really know if it is good unless you have occasion to make a claim. There are several insurance agents in Nogales, Arizona that will be happy to sell you Mexican auto insurance. Remember that offices do not open until after 9:00 A.M., so plan accordingly. Most insurance company rates are based on the value of the vehicle and the sectors of Mexico that you will operate the vehicle.

I have used the following insurance companies:

Lewis and Lewis Insurance: They are located in Beverly Hills, CA and can be reached by calling 1-800-966-6830, or email at *cbrettnow@cs.com*. They also have a website at *www.mexicanautoinsurance.com*. They are agents for the Mexican insurance company Qualitas, CIA de Seguros, S.A. de C.V.

Juan Fco. Chong Robles: Juan is a Mazatlán agent for the Mexican auto insurance company Seguros Comercial America. Tel: 982-0260 or cell: 044-669-918-2504. From the U.S. or Canada: 1-619-488-3717 or email: *juanchong@telmexmail.com*. As a last resort, if all you have is your laptop with Skype, his ID is juanchongmaz

You can also get insurance from Seguros Comercial America through International Gateway Insurance Brokers, Inc. in Chula Vista, CA.

While I have never personally filed a claim, both insurance companies are highly recommended and have reasonable rates. I also recommend a legal assistance policy.

Customs: It is possible for you to bring in a reasonable amount of personal effects. For good or bad, the amount varies depending on the customs inspector you get. There is an official list of property allowed, but is not often followed. The inspectors usually look for desktop computers, items in boxes they originally came in, articles with price tags on them or merchandise that may be sold in Mexico. Laptop computers get by every time, as long as they are not in the original box and any price tags are removed.

If you are taking in new household items, remove them from the original boxes, try to make them look worn and run the linens through the washing machine and dryer. I made the mistake of not doing that and paid over $100 in duty. What was even worse, I spent over two hours convincing the customs inspector I should not have to pay $400

Pets: Mexico welcomes dog and cat visitors. All you need to be legal is for them to be veterinarian certified as free of parasites, have a current rabies vaccination and up-to-date shots and a health certificate from a veterinarian less than five days old. I've been told that in most cases, no paperwork is requested.

Pesos: At the 21 km immigration/customs stop, there is a money exchange available, but the exchange rate is not very good. There is a Pemex station about 90 kilometers (56 miles) south of the immigration stop. Next to it is a restaurant called "D'gymon". It is a great place for lunch. Between it and the gas station is a small ATM building. Remember, ATMs have the best rate of exchange. The pesos you get can be used for tolls and fuel.

I keep a pocketful of small change in pesos (coins) handy, because in most large cities and in some smaller towns, young boys lie in wait for you at stoplights. With rag in hand they leap on the hood of your car and wipe your windshield. If I need the windshield cleaned I pay them two pesos. If I don't want it cleaned I wave at them, yell *no más* – no more – and give them two pesos to get off my car. I know, I'm paying ransom, but I guess it keeps the kids busy (but not off the streets)—and besides I haven't been able to figure an alternative.

All Pemex gas stations have clean restrooms, but some have an attendant who expects a couple pesos payment. We always carry our own toilet paper and have had occasion to use it, as many public restrooms in Mexico won't have any. Some have coin-operated restrooms that cost five pesos.

Fuel: The only gas stations in the entire country are franchised by Pemex. Something I had never understood is that Mexico exports a great deal of oil, yet gasoline is very expensive throughout the country. Gas stations are plentiful on the roads leading from the U.S. to Mazatlán. Now I understand that Mexico, at the present, doesn't have the refinery capacity to produce enough gasoline for internal needs and therefore must re-import some of that exported crude oil as gasoline and diesel fuel. The high price, although still less expensive (usually) than in the U.S., both makes up the difference and generates additional funds to build new refineries.

There are three kinds of fuel sold: Magna Sin, which is rated 87 octane and is unleaded; Premium, which is a high-test unleaded gas rated at 89 octane and, of course, diesel fuel.

Prices will always be marked in pesos per liter on the pump. Be sure to get out of your vehicle and watch the attendant zero out the pump before he starts your order. The problem of overcharging tourists seems to persist. I recommend filling the tank each time because you never know where the next station is or if it happens to have the fuel you need.

If your Spanish is limited, simply tell the attendants "*Lleno, por favor* (YAY-noh pohr fah-bohr)," point at the pump you want the fuel from (Magna Sin is always the pump with the green dispenser) and give the thumbs-up sign. It works for me! Try to get as close to the final price as possible when you pay, as some of the tourist route station attendants have switching your big bill for something smaller, then asking for more money, down to a fine art.

Most gas stations on the route from Nogales to Mazatlán take U.S. currency (although this is becoming less common) and generally have the conversion rate posted on the pump. Tips are not required, but I usually give the gas attendant a tip of 5 pesos if they clean the windows, check the oil or tires for you, etc. Like stations in the U.S., almost all Pemex stations on the main highway also have small grocery stores that sell packaged snacks, coffee and soft drinks.

People always ask the price of gasoline. Here is a way to compute: Turn on your calculator and enter the price of gas per liter, currently 10.18 pesos, multiply the price by 3.79, divide the results by the current peso-dollar exchange rate, about 12.5 to 13.0 at this time, to get the price per U.S. gallon in U.S. dollars.

Green Angels: If you have a breakdown, look for an emergency phone along the highway, dial 078 and ask for help. If you call from one of these phones, a tow truck will take you to a mechanic and there is no tow charge. Also the Mexican government operates a fleet of green and white trucks called Green Angels. The trucks patrol the highways and provide professional assistance to people with vehicle problems. The trucks carry a first-aid kit, short-wave radio, gasoline and an assortment of common auto parts. Two uniformed employees operate each truck. Usually, at least one of them speaks English.

The operators perform minor repairs for the cost of parts and also provide tow service for up to 15 miles. If they are unable to solve the problem with your vehicle, they will tow it to a nearby mechanic. They will also give you a ride or arrange for other assistance. They expect a tip for their services, but will not ask. This is their website: *http://www. sectur.gob.mx/es/sectur/sect_9453_angeles_verdes.*

Driving tips: My experience has been that most drivers in Mexico are much more courteous than in areas that I have driven in the U.S. (as a former military officer, I drove all over the country), especially the large truck and bus drivers. Cross-country buses make frequent stops to pick up passengers, etc., so I think that is the reason they travel so fast. I was surprised my first time driving the posted speed limit south of Nogales and all the buses went zooming by me.

Don't drive at night. There have been stories about *bandidos* cruising the highways looking for rich tourists to rip-off (but no hard facts or reported incidents on the toll routes from the U.S. to Mazatlán). The main reason is that in some areas, cattle roam the roads day and night. Not to mention the potholes and speed bumps (both fairly rare on the divided highways) that are difficult to see during hours of reduced visibility.

Every town has a number of *topes* – speed bumps – for speed control. There is usually one on the outskirts of town and more within the city limits. They place warning signs, but sometimes they are placed very close to the speed bump, and you are rudely awakened from your daydream by the roof of your vehicle meeting your head. If it is raining, slow down. I mean really slow down, because the blow-off from the trucks and oil leakage from the vehicles make the roads very slick. It usually takes several hours of rain to wash the road.

The left turn signal is kind of tricky in Mexico. My rule of thumb is if the driver of a truck or bus turns on the left turn signal in the country, the driver is giving you a signal that the road ahead is clear and you may pass. In the city, a left turn signal means the driver is actually planning to turn left and you should not pass to the left.

Flashing your headlights to a car in front of you means you want to pass them. If you are traveling in the opposite direction and see a car flashing headlights, you don't have to slow down and start looking for the speed trap.

Left turns are different. At stoplights, it is only legal to make a left turn when the green "left" arrow is lit (unless there is a sign stating otherwise, but that's rare), whether there is a left-turn lane or not. No green arrow, no left-turn allowed. Turning right at a red light is not usually permitted—unless there is a sign saying that it is—except in Mazatlán.

Driving from Nogales to Mazatlán: Have I convinced you that driving through Mexico is an adventure worth trying? Then let's hit the road. Mazatlán is approximately 720 miles from Nogales, Arizona, depending on how many times you get lost going through towns or cities. It can be made in one day along Mexico's toll route 15D. You have to get up very early, drive fast and drive long. I've done it and don't recommend it—especially if it's your first time. I'm told the Mexican police have entered the 21st century and have radar guns now. I personally have never seen them used. I suspect that they have found that making signs that say "Speed laws enforced by radar" are cheaper than buying radar guns.

Starting in Nogales, Arizona just follow the signs to the border. The initial crossing was no problem for us. In fact, we drove past the border, but just past the first toll gate is a check point. I have been stopped there and they looked in the trunk of my car. On other occasions I have driven through without as much as a wave. The "real" border doesn't happen for another 21 kilometers. When you get to the immigration stop, plan on spending anything from an hour to four hours to get through the process, depending on how busy it is. Park your car in the large parking lot and take your papers with you. There are four stations, and in a manner of speaking, they are numbered.

Station 1 is immigration. If you do not have a *No Inmigrante* (formerly known as FM3) card, or *Inmigrante – rentista* (formerly known as FM2) card you will need to fill out a tourist permit and present your passport. The officer inside will stamp the permit and give you a copy to take with you.

Next, proceed to Station 2, which is a copying station. If you do not have all your documentation copied, stop and have it copied. You should also have your new tourist visa copied at $.25 per page.

Go to Station 3, present these copies and pay the fee and deposit for the "temporary import permit". The person behind the window will fill out the form and collect the $200–$400 deposit, which must be paid by U.S. cash or credit card. You will be given a holographic sticker and certificate. Place the sticker on the inside of the windshield, in the upper left hand corner in front of the driver. Place the certificate in a safe place.

You may let a Mexican drive your car as long as you or your spouse or family members are with him. If you are not, and a Mexican is caught driving your car, it will be impounded, and you will wish you never heard the word Mexico. Finally, you are only allowed to keep your car in Mexico for 180 days if here on a tourist permit (or whatever your tourist permit shows). On your trip home, you must stop at the customs kiosk and the immigration office and surrender the sticker and tourist permit and collect your vehicle deposit.

Get into your car and drive to Station 4. If you have something to declare, drive through the lane and to the customs inspector. I drive into the lane that says "Nothing To Declare", even if I have something questionable (but not really illegal). If a red light comes on, you will be escorted to a customs inspector who will look inside your car.

If you are lucky, and the customs inspectors are busy, you will get a green light. Don't stop and ask questions, accelerate and move on! Once on the road again, we decided to take the toll roads all the way down. Look for the signs that say CUOTA or MAXIPISTA, which means toll rather than LIBRE, which means free.

The cost of tolls for the entire trip from Nogales to Mazatlán is approximately $70. *Note:* Some toll stations do not accept U.S. dollars.

Be sure and keep the toll tickets that you receive because if your car is damaged while on the toll road, the government may reimburse you for damages.

We make the trip in two days and spend the night in Ciudad Obregón. We were stopped twice along the way by checkpoints. The first time they motioned me to an auto checkpoint and the guard looked at the sticker on my car and waved me on. At the border of Sinaloa, the man asked me if I had any plants or fruit, and when I replied in the negative he waved me on.

We stopped at a Best Western motel and had breakfast about 80 miles south of Ciudad Obregón. They have an exquisite buffet and also serve excellent American meals.

About half way between Navojoa and Los Mochis, the road is flatter, straighter and has less traffic. The speed limit was posted 110 km per hour. I set my cruise control on 70 mph and still had several cars pass me. From there to Mazatlán, the scenery literally whizzed by on both sides of the car.

If you are starting from Texas, chances are your trip will take you through Durango. The roads from Texas to Durango are straight and fast. The drive from Durango to Mazatlán will take you about seven hours because of the narrow and winding mountain road. The road is being re-worked and re-routed and the construction is scheduled for completion in late 2012 or early 2013.

Regardless of which way you travel to Mazatlán, sit back and enjoy the trip. In fact, you may consider trying all of them.

Chapter 4

Have more fun by recognizing local customs and history

REMEMBER THAT YOU ARE in a foreign country, and customs are different. The best way to enjoy your stay is to be courteous and respectful to everyone—regardless of his or her station in life. Mexico is an old-fashioned country where its citizens value traditional ideals of honesty, respect and devotion. Crime rates are low, and visitors are usually safer in Mazatlán than in their own cities.

Language

It will help a lot if you learn to use *por favor* – please – and *gracias* – thank you – even if you don't know another word of Spanish. If you can speak Spanish (even a little), remember that when addressing a stranger, it is best to use *Usted* and/or its corresponding verb form. By doing so you are showing respect.

No hablo español, is a comment to use when you do not speak Spanish. Ask the person if he or she can speak English: *¿Habla inglés?* If not, don't get excited. Most places in the tourist areas have someone who is bilingual and will translate. Just don't go into a business and expect everybody to speak English. Remember that you are in another country, and they have no requirement to speak your native tongue.

Don't make this common mistake: shouting in English does not translate to Spanish—no matter how loud. If using a taxi, carry a map and point to your location, or write the address and show the driver. I know very little Spanish, but have found ways to communicate with people who could not speak English. A little pocket dictionary or electronic translator could come in handy.

I decided to take the advice of friends and am taking Spanish lessons. It seems that my vocabulary is expanding daily. Books such as *Enjoy México in Spanish,* by David Bodwell, can be very helpful for those with no, or very little, Spanish.

Etiquette

Mexicans are POLITE! You should always use *Por favor* and *Gracias.* It's not possible to overuse these terms. *Buenos días, Buenas tardes* and *Buenas noches* – Good morning, Good afternoon and Good night – are the greetings that are almost as important. *Hola* – Hi! – should ONLY be used to greet those you are already acquainted with. It is considered much too "familiar" to use with strangers.

Mexicans value the family above all else. They spend a great deal of time with their family circle. Restaurants in Mexico, unlike some in the U.S., do not discourage children, and Mazatlecos take small children out to nice eating establishments. Don't be afraid to take your young children out to the best eating places in town.

Mexicans are the most hand-shaking, hugging, kissing people I know. If you are a woman, shake the hand of both another woman and man when meeting for the first time. With friends and acquaintances, women and men, a hug and a kiss on the cheek are appropriate. If you are a man, shake the hand of the man or woman you are greeting for the first time. If the woman is a friend or acquaintance, a hug and kiss on the cheek is customary. It may seem stilted at first, but practice makes perfect. I see Mexican friends every day, and every day they shake my hand and/or embrace me.

It is quite an honor to be invited to a Mexican family's home for dinner or a party. It is the custom to take a small gift such as flowers or wine to the host. Discussions should be limited to family, friends or the beautiful city of Mazatlán. Leave the business talk for another day. You will earn their trust and admiration if you take an interest in their values and culture.

Mexican people are very proud of their culture and heritage, so understanding the culture is extremely important. The concept of time is probably the single most conflicting difference between the U.S. and Mexico. Mexicans see far more value in interpersonal relations than a business deadline. It is quite reasonable for a Mexican businessman to put off completing your project to take care of a family matter.

If you want to know more about the Mexican culture, *Magic Made in Mexico*, by Joanna van der Gracht de Rosado, is the book for you, particularly the part (over one-half the book) titled "The Alphabet", which gives complete, correct cultural guidance to those living in or visiting Mexico.

Machismo

The "macho" culture of male superiority—particularly over women—that is still very prevalent in Mexico. If confronted by a male braggart, remain cool and in control. If he is yelling, stay calm, speak softly and get out of the area as soon as possible. *Machismo* requires even more cautious behavior for women. Mexican women's liberation is miles behind that of the north, but this is changing as more and more young women are breaking the bonds of *machisimo*, getting an education and becoming independent. Few women occupy positions of power in Mexico, (although in 2012 one ran for president!).

Wear bathing suits only at the beach. Foreign women should not go out in the evening unless with friends. Many Mexican men think a woman alone is looking for male companionship. If alone and a Mexican man is hitting on you—and you don't want to be picked up—ignore him. Even a "no" response may be taken as encouragement. If there is a Mexican man that you would like to meet, arrange an introduction through a friend or relative.

Business culture

Business culture in Mazatlán is almost the exact opposite of that of the U.S. or Canada. In Mexico, communicating is mostly indirect and subtle. Being redundant and diplomatic is an extension of courtesy. The conversations are more about relationships than information and facts. On the other hand, we are more familiar with the U.S. business style of directness and frankness. Mexicans see our business style as insensitive and rude.

It has been my experience that the more I get to know my Mazatleco business friends, the easier it is to do business. The reason is because I have finally understood their culture. Don't misunderstand, I am still a skilled negotiator, but now I have a lot more fun negotiating with the Mexican business people.

For complete information about the business culture in Mexico, read *Mexicans and Americans: Cracking the Cultural Code* by Ned Crouch. You'll not find anything else as helpful and knowledgeable.

History of Mazatlán:

Compared to other Mexican cities, Mazatlán is not very old. There is evidence that people lived here prior to the recording of history. Archaeologists uncovered beautiful pottery with elaborate black and red designs in the 1930s. The indigenous Totorames who created the pottery were hunters, fishermen and farmers, but primarily fishermen. They disappeared prior to the arrival of the Spanish *conquistadores*.

Nuño Beltrán de Guzmán, a Spanish *conquistador*, ravaged the state of Sinaloa. Mexican historians believe that a Náhuatl-speaking interpreter for Beltrán de Guzmán thought of the name Mazatlán – Place of the Deer.

The small village of San Juan Bautista de Mazatlán, first mentioned in 1602, is now called Villa Union and is about 20 minutes south of the present city and definitely inland. The Mazatlán harbor was used by French and English pirates to attack passing galleons, and reports say that Drake and Cavendish intercepted Spanish galleons filled with gold and silver from the mines of nearby towns Copala and Cosalá.

The colonial government countered by locating a *presidio* – small fort – in the village and a manned watchtower with a cannon on the hill, Cerro del Vigía, at the mouth of the harbor. The pirates disappeared by 1800 but left legends of chests of stolen jewelry, gold and silver stored in caves or buried in sandy beaches.

By 1820 trade restrictions had been lifted, and in 1821 independence from Spain was won. In the 1830s the municipal government was established and Mazatlán became an important seaport. The port grew as German immigrants moved to Mazatlán and helped improve international trade. Mazatlán appeared to have a prosperous future, however it didn't last long. The area was hit with yellow fever, plague and cholera epidemics that devastated the population.

Mazatlán's architecture is a portrait of the substantial German, Spanish, Filipino and French merchants who came here after Mexico's independence from Spain. Between 1835–1848, the Monroe Doctrine spread into Mexican territory by way of the Mexican-American War. Mexico lost nearly half her territory to the U.S., including the present states of California, Arizona, New Mexico, Nevada, Utah, Texas and parts of Oregon and Colorado. War was inevitable after Mexico abolished slavery in 1831.

The American immigrants in Tejas, a state of Mexico at the time, felt a need to keep their slaves, so an insurgency broke out that escalated to war in late 1835. Texas declared independence in 1836 and later became a state in the Union. Now, only the Alamo is remembered.

By 1846, tensions between the U.S. and Mexico over Texas and California in particular, got out of hand, and the fight was on, although now only the "The Halls of Montezuma" in the Marine hymn memorializes that war. In 1847, the U.S. Navy blockaded the port of Mazatlán and then occupied the city for several months.

Many U.S. soldiers fell in love with Mazatlán, but a naval officer, Lieutenant Henry Wise, was perhaps the most impressed. After spending six months in Mazatlán, Lt. Wise wrote, "I regard the half-year past as among the most contented in my existence and shall ever refer with many a yearning to those pleasant days in Mazatlán."

In 1864, the French bombarded the port and occupied the city in support of the Austrian prince Maximilian's drive to become Emperor of the entire country of Mexico.

Mazatlán served as the capital of the state of Sinaloa from 1859–1873, even though the British Navy occupied it for a short time in 1871.

Mazatlán enjoyed a period of prosperity from 1876–1910, during the reign of *el dictador* – the Dictator – Porfirio Díaz. The port and lighthouse were remodeled; the railroad arrived, making shipping inland less costly; and the cathedral was completed. Education, journalism and the arts flourished. The opera house, Teatro Rubio, now restored and called Teatro Ángela Peralta, was completed in 1874.

Mazatlán was not heavily damaged during the revolution of 1910–1917, but in 1914 it was the second city in the world to be bombed from an airplane (the first was Tripoli, in Libya). General Álvaro Obregón had a biplane bomb the ammunition depot atop Cerro de la Nevería – Ice

Box Hill – near the center of city. The pilot, Gustavo Salinas Carranza, missed the target with his crude bomb, filled with nails and other metal, and it landed in the city, killing two civilians and wounding several others. The 19-year old Salinas became an international celebrity for his pioneering military feat and went on to a distinguished career in military and civil aviation.

Many noteworthy Americans have visited Mazatlán and returned many times. Among notable scientists who visited Mazatlán were Josiah Gregg in 1849 and again in 1894 and David Starr Jordan, the first president of Stanford University and a founding member of the Sierra Club. The great ornithologist, Andrew Greyson, lived in Mazatlán for a decade, working on his *Birds of the Pacific Slope*. The famous American photographer Edward Muybridge took some classic photos in Mazatlán in 1875.

It was the American, Edward Weston, who visited Mazatlán with Tina Mendotti in 1923, who was so impressed with his trip abroad that he wrote, "We found life both gay and sad, but always life—vital, intense, black and white but never gray." Weston also took a historic photo, a classic called "The Great White Cloud in Mazatlán", which sold in 1994 for $156,500.

Another well-known celebrity-visitor to the "Pearl of the Pacific", was author Anaïs Nin, Henry Miller's lover. She loved Mexico and was a regular at the Belmar Hotel in Olas Altas. Actors John Barrymore, John Wayne, Gregory Peck, Yul Bryner and Tyrone Power were also among the frequent visitors to Mazatlán. Writers like Vicky Baum, Richard Willis, Emma Lindsay, E. Howard Hunt, Lee Parker and others came and chose Mazatlán as either the title or the setting for their novels.

During the 1920s Mazatlán prospered, but shortly thereafter was plunged into the Great Depression. Following World War II, port improvements, an international airport (located where the present Plaza de Toros – bullring – is) and a new highway connecting Mazatlán to the outside world, led to improved tourism during the 1960s and 70s.

The city expanded northward with high-rise hotels occupying the new tourist area called the "Golden Zone". The tourist industry provided thousands of new jobs, attracting skilled workers and professionals from other parts of Mexico.

Local industry remains the foundation of Mazatlán's existence. It is a leading manufacturing and seafood packing center in the state of Sinaloa. A huge commercial and sports fishing fleet brings in thousands of tons of shrimp, tuna and swordfish annually.

Tourism is a big part of the local industry, and, as many Americans and Canadians have bought and remodeled older homes, retaining their historic appearance, there has been a rebirth of the Olas Altas and El Centro Histórico areas. Old hotels along the beach in Olas Altas have been and are being renovated, and small charming B&Bs and boutique hotels have sprung up too. In the last 10 years, the beautiful architecture of the buildings, streets and plazas in this part of the city has begun to attract tourists, snowbirds and also many full-time retirees.

Chapter 5

What to do in Mazatlán

THERE ARE SO MANY EXCITING THINGS to do in Mazatlán; regardless of your length of stay, you'll feel like you missed something. Many people have asked me what fun things are available for children in Mazatlán. Fortunately my friend, Diane Hofner-Sapphire, has compiled a list. My contribution is that all items on the list are not limited to kids. Some things will be discussed in detail later in the book.

Kids love Mazatlán! The to-dos are organized alphabetically

Aquarium – **Acuario de Mazatlán** – *and bird show:* The Aquarium in Mazatlán is a lot of fun. The most exciting thing is that you can swim with the sharks and porpoises! In addition to the indoor marine exhibits there are entertaining bird shows on an outdoor covered stage. The Aquarium was built on two acres of land in 1980 and expanded in 2011–2012. The address is *calle* de los Deportes #111, one block east of the Malecón, just minutes from the Golden Zone or from El Centro. Look for signs on the Malecón. Hours are from 9:30 A.M. to 6:00 P.M. Tel: 981-7815. Tickets are very reasonable for adults and reduced rates for children. Aquarium staff do most of the rescue of marine mammals and birds here in town.

Beach day: Pick a beach, any beach, as they are all government-owned. You can get chair-side service and see lots of vendors at a hotel beach. You can dine on fresh, affordable seafood in a *palapa* – palm thatched hut – restaurant on Playa Norte and Stone Island. Make sand castles, pick up sea shells and sea glass, play soccer or football, volleyball or catch…you name it, you can't go wrong with kids and a beach.

Biking: Biking along the Malecón is gorgeous, easy and fun! From Valentino's south to the Pedro Infante Monument is about six miles one-way. It's a very level ride for most of the distance and safely out of the traffic. Borrow a bike from friends or your hotel if you can. Various shops and some cafés rent bicycles too; check out Kelly's Bike Rental that is located in *colonia* La Marina. Av. Carlos Canseco (used to be Av. de la Marina) #6020 L-6 is the address and the phone number is 914-1187.

Bird-watching, hiking and picnicking: The lush *Estero del Yugo* nature preserve on the north end of town makes for a day of hiking and bird-watching. Bring a picnic lunch, binoculars and your camera. Don't forget your *Peterson's Field Guide to Mexican Birds* book, as it's not available in Mazatlán.

Boogie board: Bring your own, rent one at the beach or buy one at one of the many shops along Av. del Mar or Av. Camarón Sábalo. It's a whole lot of fun!

Main City Park – **El Bosque:** Located about two blocks off the Malecón, adjacent to the aquarium, this park has a large pond with waterfowl, swing sets and climbing gyms, a small zoo, open spaces for team sports and a walking trail. There are many playground areas in small parks throughout the city, though I recommend you check their safety before letting your kids climb up and slide down.

Bowling: Space Bowling, on the north end of town near the Hotel Marina El Cid, has laser-light bowling at night, and makes for good refuge if you happen to be here during rainy season.

Boxing: Older teenagers and young adults may enjoy a night of boxing. You get up close and personal to the boxers. They are held on Friday nights about once every month, downtown in the *Gimnasio German Evers* (pronounced heem-NAH-seeoh HAYR-mahn AYB-ayrs). Your hotel concierge will know dates and times. Take a taxi or pulmonía, you'll never find it on your own.

Catamaran: You can have one of the *playeros* – beach attendants – take you and your family out for a cruise around the bay for a very small cost. Watch the sea lions, cruise past Bird and Deer Islands and see the city from the sea. Sailboats are also available, or you can go out on a party boat and  enjoy music, dinner or sunset. Again, your hotel's concierge is the best resource.

Climb to the lighthouse – **El Faro:** One of our very favorite family activities, we do this once a week. The climb only takes about 20 minutes (if you're in good shape! Even then, carry some bottled water with you.), and the view from the top is gorgeous!

Dolphin, whale and sea lion watching: Also one of our favorite activities! Definitely do this while in town.

Fishermen: Sitting near the *pangas* – small open motor boats – at the south end of Playa Norte in the morning, watching the fishermen bring in their boats, unload and clean and sell their fish, can make for a very enjoyable morning for a family.

Fly a kite: Buy one anywhere, and spend a few hours flying it on the beach. Enjoy some *ceviche* – fresh fish or shrimp and chopped vegetables marinated—actually cooked—in fresh lime juice – fresh fruit or *empanadas* – turnovers – from a strolling vendor, and maybe some live music from a passing band.

Horseback riding: There is nothing like a family horseback ride on the beach or through a forest of palm trees. Rent horses on the north end of town at Playa Emerald Bay or on Stone Island.

Inline skating: That six-mile Malecón is calling your name! You and the family can walk it or rent skates in Olas Altas at the Looney Bean coffee shop.

Island day: Spending a day at either Deer Island or Stone Island feels like going back in time to a simpler, more charming era. Pretend you're shipwrecked, or that you own your own private piece of paradise. On Stone Island there are plenty of restaurants with lots of adult beverages, and the beach is great for kids as the ocean is almost always calm. Stone Island tours often include horseback riding.

Deer Island is an environmentally protected nature preserve, and facilities are very limited.

Tours to either place can include banana boating, snorkeling or jet skiing;

Kayaking: Rent a couple of kayaks on the beach in front of one of the hotels and enjoy some terrific family time paddling in the bay.

Movies: Movie theaters in Mazatlán are much more affordable than they are north of the border. If you don't speak Spanish, be sure to see an English-language-Spanish-subtitled – *subtitulos* on the posters – movie, rather than one that's dubbed in Spanish. See the article later in this chapter for details. *NOTE:* Children's movies, e.g., Disney, Shrek, etc., are almost never subtitled in Spanish, but dubbed in Spanish, but they're still fun…the Spanish is pretty simple.

Paint ball: For some weird reason, paint ball is called "Gotcha" in Mazatlecan Spanish. The nearest location is Master Gotcha located behind the Casa Country restaurant in the Golden Zone. It is closed on Tuesdays. Check their Facebook page for specials.

Parasailing: It is amazingly fun and exciting! Book a trip on the beach in front of your hotel.

Commercial Port: Watch the workings of the port from the Mirador Restaurant or the Old Observatory. Drive, walk or bike through Olas Altas and up Paseo del Centenario (a continuation to the south end of Av. Olas Altas) to where it makes a Y (the second intersection), then take the left-hand branch to either of these places, and you will be rewarded with incredible views of the city of Mazatlán and the workings of its port. See the loading and unloading at the docks, the boats of the largest shrimping fleet in the Americas as well as the tuna fleet.

Sea turtles: Release baby sea turtles or see their mothers lay eggs. Sea turtles come in to the beach to lay their eggs starting in late August or September every year. It is an amazing process to watch, but please don't bother the nesting Moms! If you call the aquarium or Estrella del Mar, you and your kids may be able to participate in a release of baby sea turtles, something which the kids love.

Skate park: Bring your skateboard, rip stick, BMX bike, inline skates or just your eyes and good humor to watch. The Skate Park is next to the outdoor gym in Playa Norte near the Fisherman's Monument.

Snorkeling: Playa Los Pinos, near the Fisherman's Monument, has a sheltered beach, just south of the swim club and the outdoor gym, which has pretty interesting snorkeling: lots of colorful fish and sea glass. On Deer Island you can snorkel for octopus or scallops.

Surfing: Many kids would love to learn how to surf! In Mazatlán there are many options: Jah Surf School, Puras Olas or just do a web search. Surf In Mazatlán has a shop, rentals and gives lessons; it's upstairs next to the Gaviotas movie theater in the Golden Zone.

Swimming: This would seem to be a no-brainer. In the pool or in the ocean, Mazatlán is a swimmer's paradise. Something our family loves is to go down to Playa Norte in the early morning and watch the swim club swimmers do their ocean swims. Many are grandmas and grandpas and boy can they swim! In November each year the club does a *travesía* – crossing – during which swimmers swim out to Deer Island.

Tide pools: One of the best activities on the planet for families with young children. Bring a book of tide pool life (be sure to bring it down with you, as it won't be available in Mazatlán), put on some water shoes and take a walk when the tide is low along the beach south of Valentino's. Starfish, crabs, small fish, sea urchins (don't touch!)…Gotta love it!

Video arcade: The best video arcade that I know of is in the Gran Plaza shopping mall. There is also a small, "cooler" one for teenagers just north of Valentino's, on the second level.

Water park: If the kids want more slide action than the hotel pool can provide, take them up to MazAgua, on the north end of town on the way to Pueblo Bonito Emerald Bay. Full details under Water Fun later in this chapter.

Zip lines: Huana Coa Canopy Adventure tour: If you are into zipping above the tree tops you'll be crazy about this tour. It opened in December of 2007 with state-of-the art equipment and well-trained, bilingual guides. You are either picked up from your hotel or from their office on the Malecón and bused about 20 miles to the foothills of the Sierra Madres. There you are outfitted with zipping harness and helmet and given a safety lecture.

Veraneando Adventure Zipline Tour and River Ride Tour: About 35 miles southeast of Mazatlán, this is a relatively new operation, but it is getting good reviews.

In addition to the above year-round activities—excluding the water park, which is closed in January and February—there are also terrific seasonal events. These include:

Carnaval/Mardi Gras is a very family-oriented five days worth of activities, up until the wee hours of Ash Wednesday. Terrific parades on Sunday and Tuesday.

MotoWeek is a huge gathering of motorcycles from around the continent during the week after Easter. It includes concerts, an expo and a huge parade.

ExpoCar is November 16, 17 and 18 this year (2012), and features a car show and usually a drag-racing event. Exhibitions, concerts and lots of burning rubber.

Festival de la Frasca/Shrimping in the estuary in Aquaverde, Rosario, about 50 miles south of Mazatlán, is a once-in-a-lifetime experience for families, and occurs on a Saturday (the last or next to the last—when January has 5 Saturdays—Saturday in January), right after shrimping season opens, but even if you miss the Festival itself, the trip can be terrifically interesting and fun—really cheap buys on fresh shrimp and fresh crab too. You will need a car and someone to speak Spanish or have an interpreter or guide. A licensed guide would be the best for most folks, unless your Spanish is darn good.

Day of the Dead, November 2, altars and in the evening of November 1 the *callejoneada* parade, a fun parade that begins at the Plazuela Machado about 6 P.M. and goes through the streets of El Centro

Histórico to many of the home altars in the area—accompanied by one or more burro-drawn beer carts, live banda music and costumed dancers.

Holy Week/Semana Santa processions—various, although usually unpublicized, during that week before Easter. Another thing your hotel concierge will probably know.

AeroFest is usually held in November along the Malecón (Playa Norte area) and is a beautiful air show.

Revolution Day: The legal holiday is the 3rd Monday in November, but the traditional day is November 20. There will be various parades along the Malecón on either of these dates. The school children's parade, with all the Revolutionary costumes is one of the best, but as these are mostly unpublicized, it's difficult to give you a date for them. Your hotel concierge should be able to help you with this.

Independence Day, Sept. 16, especially "El Grito" the night before in the Plaza de la República – the main plaza in front of the Cathedral in El Centro.

Look for signs for special events such as Monster Truck shows, Lucha Libre (professional wrestling...with a VERY Mexican flavor. Also held at the Gimnasio German Evers), circuses (one going on somewhere in town at least once a month), carnivals/fairs (5–7 every year), etc....

Shopping

A favorite pastime for most tourists in Mazatlán is shopping. A little advice on negotiating a price is in order. Price haggling is not only a way of life in Mazatlán, but also a true art for many of its citizens. A few years ago my teenage granddaughter was with us and wanted to

buy a hat from a beach vendor. She tried a few on; found the one she wanted and asked the price. When she was told the cost, she reached in her pocket for the money. The vendor shook his head and waved the money away, and said, "No, Señorita, we must first bargain for the price."

I realize that most North Americans would rather just pay the asking price and move on to the next store. Sometimes I think American women especially hate to negotiate a price because it takes time away from serious shopping. My wife, even in the States, departs the area when I make the comment to a sales clerk, "How much will you really take for this item?" I'm one of those rare U.S. citizens who loves to haggle over prices. I even negotiate prices in Nordstrom's!

Sometimes I have been known to get carried away and lose track of reality. On a quick buying trip to Mazatlán, my good friend Alberto Ochoa, owner of Realtymex, provided his son, Roberto, as a driver, guide and interpreter. My wife, Roberto and I had found furniture for about $2,000 After some haggling with the sales person, I went to the store manager and continued negotiating. After the process exceeded an hour, I made my final offer, and when it was not accepted, I thanked the manager and told him that I would look elsewhere.

As my wife and I were leaving the store, she stopped to look at a mirror. A couple minutes later the clerk tapped me on the shoulder and said, "Okay, it's a deal." I shook hands and went to pay for the furniture. When I saw the bill, I noticed that there was a difference of $6 U.S., but they were not charging me for it. When I inquired why, she said that the young man, pointing to Roberto, had paid the difference. In my negotiating zeal, I had somehow gotten carried away and almost let a $2,000 deal disappear over $6 My wife and I got a great laugh and I thanked Roberto and paid him the $6.

Aside from my belief that everything is negotiable, let's talk about where one can generally negotiate. Most stores in the Golden Zone will haggle. Some stores that show price tags do not negotiate, but it's worth asking. Street and beach vendors will always negotiate. Keep in mind though that these are business people, and they are trying to make a living. Don't waste their time with trivial questions or small talk. Be friendly, respectful and courteous. Far too many times I have witnessed beach vendors being loudly berated by "ugly Americans". I have spent many happy hours haggling with vendors—and have made friends with most of them.

The "hows" of haggling are complex and difficult, but once learned can provide not only enjoyment but can also make your vacation dollar will go further. My teenage granddaughters were reluctant to negotiate prices, but after a week they were quite good at it.

I offer this only as a simple, personal way I have found successful. I'm sure there are other, more successful methods. For beach vendors, my goal is to pay 60–70% of the asking price. For storeowners I usually pay 80–90% of the asking price. The reason for the difference is the overhead for the storeowner.

I start the negotiation by inquiring about the price. I make a low-ball offer of 30%. After some laughter, the seller counter-offers and then I counter-offer, eventually arriving at an agreed price. I always initiate some joking, which allows the vendor to joke back, but I never downgrade the merchandise. Sometimes the price can be lowered by offering to buy more than one. I always smile and shake hands once the deal is made.

If a deal cannot be made I simply say, "No thanks, maybe tomorrow." Sometimes the vendor will return and counter offer, or maybe you can make a better deal with a different vendor.

Something to remember during negotiations: the advantage the vendor has is that he knows what he can sell the item for without losing money; the advantage you have is that you have the cash, and you don't really need the item. Don't feel guilty if you get a good deal, because the vendor is not giving away his merchandise. He'll make it up with a tourist that is not as good a negotiator.

Some stores in the Golden Zone and the Central Mercado in El Centro (downtown) offer good prices, but if the cruise ships return, I do not recommend shopping there on days when they are in port. The "cruisers" are generally in a hurry and do not negotiate. It will be difficult for you to negotiate with so many of them around! The shopkeepers love those customers with the little paper tags identifying the ship they arrived on. Mazatlán is sometimes the last stop before returning to Los Angeles. Since prices are generally higher in Puerto Vallarta, Los Cabos, Zihuataneo and Acapulco, whatever price Mazatlán merchants charge looks like a bargain by comparison.

Mazatlán's gift shops stock a huge amount of handicrafts from all over the country. There are many shops that sell similar items, so comparison-shopping is quite easy. Many of the shop owners buy their merchandise from the same suppliers, so the quality is the same. As previously mentioned, the advice I give you is based on personal experience. I'm sure others have acquired good quality merchandise from other merchants. But many of you will be in Mazatlán for a short period of time and want to know where to get a good deal. I suggest that for the first day or two you wander around with a notebook, noting items you're interested in and jotting down cost and store location. Then take your notes to the following shops:

Here is Paco: Paco has three stores located across from the Balboa Club on Av. Camarón Sábalo in the Golden Zone. The Balboa Club used to be a private resort, but is now open to the public. It is the stone-walled property that starts  at the north end of the Dairy Queen strip mall and goes up to the Balboa Tower (now "called" the Acquamarina, but closed) He has quality silver and the best value in gold jewelry. For gold jewelry, I suggest you stop by the shops in before noon or in the evening when Paco is there. I have purchased from him and had the pieces appraised in the States at 100% or more above price paid. He also has a huge selection of pottery and giftware.

Pic N' Save: This shop specializes in clothing and T-shirts, but has some giftware. They are located at Camarón Sábalo #15, which is right next door to Here Is Paco.

Sharkey's Den #1: It is on Camarón Sábalo, near Sr. Frog's retail store across from the Dairy Queen.

Sharkey's Den #2: It is located across from the Balboa Club on Camarón Sábalo in the Golden Zone.

Bloomingdale's: Is near Paco's on Camarón Sábalo across from the Balboa Club.

Kmart (not what you're thinking): Right next door to Bloomingdale's on Camarón Sábalo.

All of the above stores are owned and operated by the Miranda brothers and sister, who have been in business for more than 20 years.

As I mentioned above, most shop owners buy from the same distributors and their merchandise comes from Mazatlán, Tonalá, Guadalajara, Dolores Hidalgo, Teotiguacán, Taxco and Quiroga.

Their merchandise includes, but is not limited to T-shirts, blouses, hats, leather belts, sandals, hammocks, pottery, silver, gold, papier maché animals, bathroom sinks, ceramic patio and garden ornaments, patio lamp ornaments, chess sets, fountains, Talavera pottery, glassware, pewter, sunglasses, Mayan masks, ceramic vegetables, clay wall ornaments, crucifixes, colorful lamps, metal mirrors, lamps, wall hangers, pewter picture frames, ceramic planters and marble figures—but you get the idea. If you saw something in another store, and can explain it to them, they can have it for you within 24 hours. Tell them you found out about their shops by reading this book and they will give you a special discount.

Be cautious when buying silver jewelry. Sometimes when you think you are getting a fabulous deal on silver, you may be buying a silver-coated item. They are nice pieces of jewelry, but if you are interested in sterling silver, look for the numbers "925" and "Mex" or "Mexico" on the back of the item. Counterfeit silver has been found with those markings so take along a refrigerator magnet and place it next to the jewelry. If they connect, you know it is not genuine.

Casa Etnika: This shop is owned by Elena Van der Heiden and husband Miguel Ruíz and has a vast and unusual assortment of goods, including jewelry, furniture, baskets, gifts, clothing, children's handmade toys, original art and Sinaloa wildlife photography. While in the downtown area visit them at *calle* Sixto Osuna #50 in the heart of El Centro Histórico. Email them at: *casaetnika@gmail.com* or phone them at 136-0139.

Juárez Flea Market – tianguis: While there are many stores open every day in *Colonia* Juárez, the flea market held every Sunday is worth a trip. To get there from the Golden Zone hop any bus heading south that has the word "Juárez" on the main sign or painted on the front windshield. About 6–7 minutes after you pass Soriana on Insurgentes (the **second** Soriana if it was a Cocos-Juárez bus that you hopped on) you will see the main Juárez market on the right, but the best landmark is the church, since it is right next door to the flea market. Here is where the bus turns left, so be sure you get off. The Just tell the driver, "Juárez Mercado – HWAHR·ays mayr·KAH·doh" – and he should let you off at the market.

There is oodles of stuff for sale along the street, so stop and look or buy, but walk toward the church. When you get to the statue of the head of Miguel Hidalgo, Mexico's George Washington, you are at the entrance to the flea market.

You will find stall after stall of new and used merchandise at outstanding prices. If you like to bargain for prices you'll love the flea market. Go early in the morning, hours are 4 A.M. to 2 A.M., as things get picked over pretty fast. There are plenty of places to grab a bite to eat and even an aisle with barbers cutting hair for about $2 per haircut.

To get back to the Golden Zone I could tell you to retrace your steps (plus one block) and catch the Cocos-Juárez or Cerritos-Juárez bus, but I know that you will have too many packages to carry. Just hail a cab or *pulmonía* and the driver will get you and your new treasures wherever you want to go.

Fábricas de Francia: These are large, elegant department stores in the Gran Plaza mall and downtown near the Cathedral. It is Mazatlán's answer to Nordstrom's and Macy's. They sell everything from clothing to home appliances and furniture.

Designer's Bazaar: It is located in the Golden Zone at Playa Gaviotas #217, next to the Playa Bonita Hotel (formerly the Tropicana). It stands out among gift shops because of the quality, uniqueness and variety of its offerings. There are two floors of hand-crafted items, from inexpensive pottery and jewelry to original paintings and hand-made rugs. Attractive resort clothing is also available. The owners, Roberta and Luis travel the country to hand-select items from small, family-operated artisan businesses. The quality is wonderful; the prices are very reasonable. All prices are marked and there is no bargaining here. Currently closed, but supposedly due to re-open in December, 2012.

Tattoo parlors: I put this one in the shopping section because as I walk the beaches I notice more and more women are getting tattoos.

> *Tattoo Tekato* is at Camarón Sábalo #L-23, in the little strip mall above Subway Sandwich and Dr. Backman, the chiropractor. The telephone number is 044-669-117-6675, a cellular phone.

> *Inkk Tattoo* is also on Camarón Sábalo across from the Bancomer bank in the Golden Zone. The phone number is 044-669-158-0967, a cellular phone.

Water Fun:

Long beaches of beautiful sand and warm green water offer many hours of water fun. All the beaches in Mazatlán are federal property up to the high tide lines, and are public. Be cautious of undertows and swim only with someone else who can swim. Only a very few resorts offer year-round lifeguards. Also be on the lookout for jellyfish. They look like small pieces of clear or dark blue Jell-O. Avoid them, as their sting is quite painful. Watch for the white flags on the beach, as they are the warning that there are jellyfish in the water or washed up on the beach where you could step on them.

If one actually stings you, here are the BEST steps to take:

1. Wash the area with ocean water OR cold fresh water, BUT DO NOT RUB, as rubbing could force more of their poison into the skin.

2. IF there are pieces (tentacles) still stuck to you, sprinkle with ANY commercial, unspiced meat tenderizer (available in any large grocery store and just as necessary for a visit to the beach in jellyfish "season" as sunblock, although the jellyfish are rare between early December and mid April...the sun is **always** shining.)

3. After about 10 minutes, wash the area again. Repeat if there are still pieces stuck to you. Continue repeating until ALL parts of the jellyfish are dissolved away.

4. Once all the pieces of the jellyfish have been dissolved away, treat with any benzocaine ointment, available in any *farmacia*, which will stop the pain. Omni Plus lotion or Noxzema are said to stop the pain also, but a benzocaine ointment will do it quicker and for certain. There are lots of "folk remedies", but the above is guaranteed to work.

Boogie boards: They can usually be rented on the beach near most resorts and cost about $3–5 an hour, but price is negotiable, unless the beach is busy. Inexpensive styrofoam ones can be purchased at the large supermarkets and some shops.

Parasailing: If you like being dragged around in the air by a speeding boat, this trip is for you. You'll see all the colorful para-chutes along the beaches in the Golden Zone. Getting up in the

air is easy, and handsome young Mexican men will give you a crash course in not crashing when you land. The cost of the 10-minute ride is about $25–30, but price is usually negotiable—especially if you have more than one rider.

Banana boats: If riding an air-filled plastic log at high speeds in the ocean is your thing, banana boats are your answer. You'll find them on the beach near several Golden Zone hotels, including Costa de Oro and El Cid, as well as on Stone Island. The cost is $6–8 per person.

Kayaks: Are available at various locations on the beach in the tourist zones. Rental is $10 per hour for a single and $20 per hour for double.

Jet skis: Uneven water makes jet skiing more fun than on your lake at home. They are available at several hotels in the tourist zone and run about $40–$50 per half-hour and $60 if you want to ride double. Again, if there is more than one rider a better price is negotiable. Thirty minutes doesn't seem long; but believe me, after a half hour of bouncing around on the waves, you'll be ready to get on your land legs again.

Scuba diving and snorkeling: A nice scuba diving area is just off Deer Island. Diving gear can be rented at El Cid or the Ramada hotels. Snorkeling is available at El Cid for $24 for gear rental and a ride to and from Deer Island. The scuba diving fee is between $70 and $80 for equipment and transportation to Deer Island.

Snorkeling off Deer Island can be dangerous because the water on the surface is sometimes murky. In fact, one year I went during

April and the water was so cloudy I didn't see the coral reef and skinned my knee badly.

Hobie Cat: Four-person catamaran-style sailboats are available along the beach. You can rent them for about $20–30 per hour, or you can ask them to sail it for you, but then it only carries two passengers. If you elect to use the "sailor", a tip is appropriate.

MazAgua Water Park: This water park is four acres of everything from wading pools to a 100-foot long water slide. It has fun for everyone with the same price for all—about $12. Infants three and under can toddle in for nothing. It is located out near the end of the bus lines that run to Playa Cerritos. Get off at the traffic circle and walk about 100 yards east on the road toward Pueblo Bonito Emerald Bay Resort. They are open from 10:00 A.M. to 6:00 P.M. daily, March through December on the days in green on their website calendar – *calendario*. Their website is: *http://www.mazagua.com/calendario.html*. They are closed during January and February. Tel: 988-0041.

Fishing: The Sea of Cortez provides some of the greatest deep-sea fishing in the world. The best fishing is from March through December, but fish are still hungry in the winter months and can be coaxed onto your line. The trophy fish are the large billfish—sailfish and black, blue and striped marlin. Other fish that are fun to haul in are grouper, sea bass and *dorado* – mahi-mahi.

Some of the fleets in Mazatlán participate in a tag-and-release program. When you catch a fish, you tag it and the next guy that hooks into that fish knows you were there first.

Fishing trips leave from the El Cid Marina, the Isla Mazatlán Marina or from the downtown sports fishing dock near the lighthouse. The going rates for an eight-hour day of deep-sea fishing on a 28-foot cruiser are about $500 for up to six fishermen.

This does not usually include fishing license, food, beverage or the gratuity to the captain. I usually give $10–$15 depending on our boat's luck that day. Check with the fleet managers if you don't have enough to fill a boat. There are always others like you who are willing to team up and share expenses. Light tackle fishing trips are also available at most charters.

My personal favorite is the Aries Fleet, which goes out of the El Cid Marina. I prefer them because the skippers are very experienced, and their boats are fast, well-maintained and get you to the fishing quickly. Their website is:

www.cortezcharters.com/maza.htm
and their email is: *cortezcharters@sbcglobal.net.*

Another reliable fleet that goes out of the downtown sports fishing dock is Star Fleet, 982-2665.

Many tourists join the regulars and fish from the beach and breakwaters, while others try their luck at the various freshwater lakes in the area. Bass are the big catch in the foothill lakes of the Sierra Madre Occidental. Fishing licenses are required when fishing from a boat, but not when surf fishing.

Bass fishing: World-class bass fishing is available at Lake El Salto, which is about 50 miles from Mazatlán. It is not difficult to get there by car and they have boats for rent. La Papalota Villas Resort has package deals for any type of fishermen that include round-trip transportation from your hotel. The resort provides all-inclusive tour packages for from 1–10 nights on a sliding scale. The price includes lodging, all meals, fishing guide, boat, tackle and license. The price does not include alcoholic drinks, tips or airfare, but it does include ground transportation to and from the airport (or your hotel in Mazatlán). Friends this year have told me that the resort is excellent and the food is delicious. The fishing program is all catch-and-release. It is not uncommon to see someone get 10-pound bass each day. Their website is: *http://mazatlan.com.mx/ tours/bassfishingtour/lapapalota.htm* or you can email them at *bass@ easymazatlan.com*. Their toll free telephone number is 1-888-800-9619 from the U.S. or Canada.

Other activities

Golfing: If golfing is your game, Mazatlán has three of the best courses around.

El Cid Mega Resorts has a 27-hole golf course in the Golden Zone. The great Lee Trevino designed part of it.

Estrella del Mar Golf Course is near the airport on Stone Island. Robert Trent Jones designed this world-class, par 72 course; green fees are about $110 with cart. There are no caddies. The above courses offer membership or a six-month discount card.

The Marina golf course is the newest and is located in the New Marina area, near the new Convention Center.

A nine-hole public course, Club Campestre ($30) is located just off the road to the airport.

Tennis: The warm winter weather is ideal for playing tennis and courts are available all over Mazatlán. Some courts are lighted and the surfaces are clay, asphalt and concrete. Courts may be found at El Cid, Costa de Oro and the Gaviotas Tennis Club.

Horseback riding: If you like to horse around, there are horses aplenty. But first a caution—the officials on the beaches in the Golden Zone do not sanction horses. That is not to say horses are not available. Sometimes in late afternoon, young Mexican men bring horses to the beach to rent to tourists.

Ever hear of bilingual horses? I don't know how to say "giddy-up" in Spanish, but the horses understand our lingo. Ginger's Bilingual Horses have their office at the Playa Emerald Bay. Just hop on any Cerritos bus heading north to the end of the line. The well-kept horses costs $30 per hour. The rides are on both trails and the beach. They are open from 10 A.M. to 4 P.M. every day except Sunday. Call at 922-2026.

There is a horse rental place on Stone Island where you can go for long rides on the secluded beaches or through the fields of palm trees. You can arrange for horse rides on Stone Island at *www.kingdavid.com.mx* or call 914-1444.

Biking: Kelly's Bike Shop is located in *colonia* La Marina. Service includes bike rentals, sales and repair. They usually have a three- to four-hour guided tours in the hills also. You can contact them by telephone at 914-1187.

Moped or scooters: How about scooting around town? There are several places in the Golden Zone to rent scooters. A valid driver's license is usually needed.

Pacific Moto is located next to the OXXO store south of Panama

Restaurant on Camarón Sábalo in the Golden Zone. They have scooters for rent and have ATV's or "quads" for rent. In addition they usually have 2½ hour guided tours. Helmets and goggles (and drinks in the tours) are provided. Tel: 191-8634 or cell: 044-669-120-0103 for information and reservations.

Quads are the latest fad in Mazatlán, and by far the best place to rent and ride them is on Stone Island. There are miles of sandy beaches that are free of traffic, so you can go "all out". There are stretches of the beach that are Federally protected turtle nesting ground, so be sure to ask the attendants just where you can ride and where you can't.

Gambling: While I do not gamble, Vegas arrived in Mazatlán in 2006 in the form of a popular casino called Caliente. It is referred to as "bingo", but that is as loose a definition as is possible. The Vegas-style slot machines have small bingo cards on the screen in addition to the blazing 7s, doubles and triples. They are all electronic and the only thinking required is the amount of the wager. You buy a ticket and program the machine with a number and a secret pin code. As you tire of one machine you can go to another and program that machine and your credit is automatically transferred. The staff is very helpful in answering any of your questions.

You can also bet on dogs, horses and sports if machines bore you. Caliente is located on the Malecón, one block north of the Aquamarina Hotel. Currently they open at 5 P.M. and close at about 2 A.M. In addition, they have an ATM machine next to the money/ticket booth that is a swipe machine, so now you have a place to go after-hours for cash without the danger of the machine "eating" your card. Of course it will also take some self-control to make it to the exit with at least part of the cash you got from the machine.

In the Golden Zone proper, just about a two blocks south of the Panama Restaurant and across the street, is a new casino, Monte Carlo. They offer about the same things as Caliente, but their hours are quite different, 7 A.M. to 3 A.M. There is another, Midas, but it's too far off the tourist track to bother with.

Jogging: The most popular jogging area is along the Malecón early in the morning. There is less traffic at that time and just as importantly, it is the coolest part of the day. Beach jogging is also good, but I would check the tide tables (available each month in the Pacific Pearl magazine) and run when the tide is lowest. The beach is flatter and harder at that time.

Hiking: Walking is a favorite pastime in Mazatlán, whether it is along the beach, the Malecón, looking at houses in the El Cid or El Dorado neighborhoods or window shopping. Be warned that Mexico is not a litigious society like the U.S. If you step in a hole in front of a shop, don't bother calling your lawyer.

Here is a guide to some of the best walking in Mazatlán:

El Faro – the lighthouse: For a beautiful view of the city, don your hiking shoes, put a big bottle of water in your pack and take a taxi to the base of Crestón Hill – Cerro del Crestón. It takes between 30–45 minutes to hike to the famous El Faro on top—depending on your age and physical conditioning. The last third of the way is all stairs.

The spectacular view from 500 feet above sea level is well worth it. Afterward, check out the fishing fleets in the harbor. You may be lucky and see a big billfish hanging with a proud angler having his picture taken.

A walk in the downtown area: Take the green Sábalo Centro bus from the tourist zone heading toward downtown and get off at the central market. Take in the sights and smells of the Central

Mercado – *Mercado José María Pino Suárez* – where Mazatlecos follow the time-honored tradition of shopping daily. You can find everything in the market from souvenirs to meat and vegetables. If shopping for souvenirs, be sure to negotiate prices with the vendors. There are restrooms on the second floor for a small fee.

Exit on the opposite side from where you entered the one-block square market. The street is called Benito Juárez. As you exit,

turn left (heading south), and walk past Panama Bakery/Restaurant and Fabricas de Francia. Cross the street and enter the famous *Catedral Basilica de la Purísima Concepción*, which is the centerpiece of Mazatlán. Built on a filled lagoon, the Cathedral was started by the Bishop Pedro y Pardave in 1856. Completion was delayed due to many circumstances until 1899. In 1937, it was elevated to the status of a Basilica. Its beauty and grandeur are breathtaking. The Cathedral is open from 6 A.M.–1 P.M. and 4–8 P.M. daily. It is still an operating church, so be respectful of masses or ceremonies that may be taking place. Instructions for behavior are posted at the entrances.

When you exit the front of the Cathedral, cross the street to the Plaza de la República, where there is a beautiful wrought-iron

bandstand. If you have time, enjoy an ice cream cone or a shoeshine and relax on a park bench for some people-watching.

On the west side of the plaza is the *Palacio Municipal* – city hall – where the mayor, at or a bit before midnight on the eve of Independence Day on September 16, has words of patriotism for the celebrating crowd, which always end with the famous Cry of Dolores – Grito de Dolores – *¡Viva Mexico! ¡VIVA MEXICO! **¡VIVA MEXICO!*** that went up in the church at Dolores (now Dolores Hidalgo) in what is now the state of Guanajuato at midnight, September 15, 1810, beginning the War of Independence with Spain. The city hall is also where property taxes are paid.

Continue south down busy Benito Juárez for 3 blocks, turn right at *calle* Constitución, and go one (long) block west to the Plazuela Machado. It is a beautiful plaza with a gazebo in the center and wrought iron benches scattered around the periphery. Restaurants offering a variety of different cuisines surround the plaza. Stop at one of the cafés where you can rest, enjoy your lunch and people-watch.

Once at the plaza and still facing west, turn left. On your left will be the famous Ángela Peralta Theater. Go in for a look at its splendor. They ask for a 15 peso donation to enter. The old traditional El Túnel Restaurant faces the entrance to the theater, along with Memorial Café, a coffee/pastry shop that has yummy desserts and espresso drinks.

On the opposite end of the plaza, at the southwest corner, walk west down *calle* Sixto Osuna a few blocks toward the ocean.

A block before the ocean, at #76 on your right, you will come to the Museo de Arqueología. The museum contains exhibits of the history and culture of Sinaloa. On display are petroglyphs, figurines of animals and humans and the ancient polychrome pottery of Sinaloa. Entrance fee is about $3. The museum is open Tuesday-Friday, 9 A.M.–6 P.M. and 11 A.M.–2 P.M. Saturday and Sunday.

The Mazatlán Membership Library is a few doors further toward the water, on your right. Stop and do a little browsing and even leave a small donation. More information about the library can be found later in this chapter.

Across the street, stop and visit the Mazatlán Museum of Art – *Casa de la Cultura*. There is a permanent exhibit as well as rotating exhibits of local, regional and international artists. Entry is free. Sometimes, in the evenings, there are concerts or poetry readings in the spacious courtyard.

Walk west one more half-block and you will find Olas Altas, the original tourist area of Mazatlán. Stop at one of the sidewalk cafes and have a soft drink or beer, enjoy the soft sea breeze, and soak up the flavor of old Mazatlán. Since the main tourist resort area is miles away, I suggest you hail a *pulmonía* for the refreshing ride along the Malecón to the Golden Zone, or to the new Marina area resorts and all the beach resorts north to Cerritos. Or you can wait at any corner along Av. Olas Altas for the northbound green Sábalo Centro bus back to your resort.

If you still have time and strength after your downtown tour, you can head north for a stroll along the Malecón—but I suggest you save this trip for another day.

A walk along the Malecón: For those staying in the main tourist resort areas, your stroll on the Malecón will start with a bus ride on the southbound green Sábalo Centro bus. Tell the driver to let you off at Fisherman's Monument. This monument has experienced a great deal of notoriety over the years, due to the full-frontal nudity of the figures.

Keep walking south past the fisherman unloading the day's catch from their boats at the south end of Playa Norte, till you get to Los Pinos beach. On one side is the Ciencias del Mar, a marine biology school, and on the other is the Casa del Marino, originally a fort built to repel the French invaders in 1868.

The Continuity of Life Monument, a fountain erected in 1993, is next. It is a naked man and woman poised on a snail shell, which stands for continuity in the Aztec culture. The fountain also features 13 leaping dolphins that represent intelligence.

You will next arrive at the Glorieta Sánchez Tabuada, a big oceanfront plaza with cliff divers who soar into the sea from a high platform. If you are lucky, divers will be performing. Across the street is Ice Box Hill – *Cerro de la Nevería*. Supposedly, in the late 19th century, ice was shipped from San Francisco, stored in a cave and used to keep the city's fish fresh. During the Mexican Revolution, dynamite and munitions were stored there. On the red wrought iron gate is a sign marked Cueva del Diablo, which means Devil's Cave. Satan, disguised as a handsome foreign tourist, is said to have once lured an unsuspecting *Mazatleca* – Mazatlán woman – to that cave during Carnaval. Climb up to the entry gate and you can still smell the lingering sulfur left behind when he dragged her off.

Cross the street again and you'll encounter the *Mujer Mazatleca* – Mazatlán Woman – monument. The state of Sinaloa is famous throughout Mexico for its beautiful women because so many locals have won the "Miss Mexico" title.

A short distance south is the *Monumento del Venadito* – Deer Monument – a tribute to the name of our city. Mazatlán is "The Place of the Deer" in Náhuatl, so the statue is "our" symbol.

Now you're in Olas Altas and can stroll over to one of the Olas Altas cafés for a cool drink, and wait to catch a bus ride back, via the Central Mercado, to your hotel in or north of the Golden Zone.

For those staying in the El Centro Histórico or Olas Altas areas, just do this walk in reverse, catching the bus or a *pulmonía* back to your hotel from the Fisherman's Monument.

A walk in the El Dorado and El Cid residential districts: If you enjoy looking at beautiful homes, walk along Camarón Sábalo in the Golden Zone until you get to *calle* Gabriel Ruíz, across the street from The Inn at Mazatlán at the stoplight. Walk along the boulevard or take the side streets. Mexican professionals own most of the homes in this neighborhood, El Dorado.

Many Americans and Canadians live in the gated community of El Cid. Walk on north on Camarón Sábalo to the stoplight

opposite the big Señor Frog's restaurant and club. Turn east, walk through the gates and continue past a white building that is the members' clubhouse and athletic center of El Cid. Continue east along the road and view the beautiful homes and well-kept lawns that butt up against the golf course. We've spent hours walking in this neighborhood. Be warned that

87

there are no service stations there, so the only bathroom facilities are on the golf course—and you have to look hard to find them.

The bullfights: Please note that regularly scheduled, traditional *corridas* – bullfights – were suspended in January 2004 and it is not known if or when they will resume.

There are irregularly scheduled bullfights sponsored by a group called *Los Forcados de Mazatlán*. Since each traditional *corrida* – bullfight card – has six individual bullfights, and the *forcados*, who represent a Portuguese bullfighting tradition are the sponsors, the corridas here in Mazatlán tend to be a spellbinding mixture of different styles.

One is the traditional Spanish/Mexican style *corrida* where the *matador* works the bull and eventually fights him to the death stroke, entirely on foot.

Then there is the traditional Portuguese style, where a group of eight *forcados* wrestle the bull to the ground to tire him, then the *torero* – bullfighter – called the *rejoneador* (rather than *matador*), takes charge from horseback and fights the bull to the death while still on horseback.

Then there is a new mixed style that's quite flashy, where the *forcados* do their thing, then turn the bull over to the *rejoneador* on his horse. The *rejoneador* fights the bull from horseback, until, in his judgement, the bull can be fought on foot. Then he dismounts and fights the bull to the death, entirely on foot, just as a traditional *matador* does.

Although irregularly scheduled, the bullfight season in Mazatlán is in the fall, very late September to probably no later than December 12 when the traditional Mexican Christmas season begins. However, more often than not, there is always at least one bullfight card scheduled during Carnaval, but since all of this depends on the funds available to *Los Forcados de Mazatlán*, which even they are unable to predict, there is no predictable schedule available until a couple or three weeks before each *corrida* takes place. No, not even the one during Carnaval.

It's a shame, since whatever the style of bullfighting, the bullfight is a marvelous spectacle, with its lovely costumes and pageantry and the fantastically artistic and athletic *matadors* and the *rejoneadors* with their fantastically trained horses.

Carnaval: If you're into huge crowds, loud music, festivities, fireworks, parades and spectacular pageants, then come and see the third largest pre-Easter celebration, behind Rio de Janeiro and New Orleans. Mexicans and foreigners descend on Mazatlán in droves for the weeklong activities. Wise people rent hotel space a year in advance—especially in Olas Altas and along the parade route on the Malecón. Carnaval is a moveable feast, the week before Ash Wednesday. Every year people ask when the celebration will take place. The late Jackie Peterson, a long-time expat resident of Mazatlán and patron of the arts, was kind enough to provide a schedule for the next several years:

Year	Start	End
2013	February 8	February 12
2014	February 28	March 4
2015	February 13	February 17
2016	February 5	February 9
2017	February 24	February 28
2018	February 9	February 13
2019	March 1	March 5
2020	February 21	February 25

On the Thursday before Ash Wednesday, there is usually some sort of show in the Ángela Peralta Theater on when prizes for painting and literature are given out. But this is variable. The Friday of

Carnaval is always the night of the *Juegos Florales* – Flower Games – pageant. Saturday is the Queen's Coronation pageant and Monday is a pageant for the crowning of the juvenile king and queen of Carnaval. All three pageants are held in the baseball stadium and include performances by nationally known (in Mexico) entertainers. Who, what and exactly when and where is to be found on this website once everything is finalized for the upcoming year:

www.culturamazatlan.com
or check with your hotel consierge.

On Saturday night, around 10:30 P.M. there's a stunning fireworks display in Olas Altas called the *Combate Naval*. Using fireworks, it is a depiction of the French navy assault on the harbor of Mazatlán. You can watch it from one of the buildings in Olas Altas, or take a "booze cruise" with Yate Fiesta.

The Yate Fiesta charges less than $60 per person (less than $50 per person if tickets are pre-purchased before Jan. 31, 2013), and you receive a three hour cruise, a great seat for the fireworks, live music, dancing, open bar and return transportation to your hotel/home.

Contact Rigo at 982-3130 or email *info@yatefiesta.com*. It can also be booked through the concierge at your hotel or a local travel agent. The cruise is well worth the money, and I believe it has the best view of the fireworks.

In 2008 there was an 8 P.M. fireworks display along the Malecón on Monday night. It has become a tradition and continued every year since then.

On Sunday evening and Tuesday afternoon of Carnaval, there are parades along Av. del Mar featuring more than three dozen floats. The parade on Sunday starts at the Fisherman's Monument and goes north to Valentino's. The Tuesday parade is shorter and goes from a few blocks north of the Fisherman's Monument south through Olas Altas. It is always a good idea to check the local newspaper or the schedule online at *www.culturamazatlan.com.*

If you want a decent place to watch the parade on the street, get there early and bring a chair. There are plenty of vendors and restaurants around so that you can buy refreshments as you wait. Remember that Av. del Mar is a boulevard, and the floats go along the west lane (nearest the water). Don't expect the parade to start on time—or even just a little bit late. You don't expect anything else in Mazatlán to be on time, so why would you expect the parade to start promptly?

During several parades, I rented a street-side room at Hotel Don Pelayo/Best Western for a minimum three-night stay. We used the room only one night, invited a dozen other people and had a dinner party while waiting for the parade. Then we watched the procession in comfort from our balcony. After the conclusion of the spectacle, we partied for an hour and by then the crowds had dispersed and we walked back to our homes in the Golden Zone.

Food booths, beer booths and bands for the street dancing are in abundance at Olas Altas all during of Carnaval.

Since Carnaval is a traditional, pre-Lent, Catholic festival, more Mexicans (coming from all over Mexico) celebrate Carnaval in Mazatlán than foreign tourists, and I believe that is too bad.

I think it is the fault of the expats living in Olas Altas and El Centro Histórico—many of whom leave town during Carnaval, as access to their homes may be affected, and those bands are LOUD until about 4 A.M.—warning tourists, even though **they** don't participate, that it is just a drunken brawl with huge crowds and noise. Carnaval is a fiesta, not a drunken brawl. It is masses of people having a good time. In the States we have no problem fighting the crowds at the State Fairs, Fourth of July fireworks demonstrations and the many state and national inaugural balls. It's the same in Mazatlán.

I only provide the following warnings. Don't try to drive downtown to Olas Altas for the fireworks demonstration or the street dancing. Take the bus. If you don't leave for the bus stop immediately following the fireworks display you may miss the last bus. If you don't want to take the bus back to your hotel, or you're too late, walk north about two miles to the Fisherman's Monument or inland a few blocks where many taxis and *pulmonías* are available.

Even though some expats head out of town or plan at-home activities during Carnaval week, my plans are to stay in town and enjoy the festivities.

Baseball: From October through December, baseball – *beisbol* – Mexican-style, is the thing to see. The local team, Los Venados,

play at the baseball stadium. As you ride down the Malecón at night, just look for the bright lights of the stadium—away from the ocean of course! For the price of a very cheap seat you get to drink cheap, ice-cold Pacifico beer, people-watch families and kids having a great time and cheering on the local team. There were times when we were the only gringos seated in the area, but people were fun and friendly, and everyone had a great time.

Games with their archrivals from Culiacán always guarantee a big turnout. In many ways it is the same as in the States, but there are so many delightful variations! Especially the cheerleaders! I have been a season ticket holder for several years.

The Venados are in a winter league officially classed as a AAA minor league level by the major leagues in the U.S. They always have a few Americans and other foreigners on the team.

The Venados were in the January playoffs for 12 years straight but missed it in 2012. They always seem to field a competitive team. During 2008 the Venados won the Mexican championship and represented Mexico in the Caribbean World Series in January 2009.

Ulama: This game is unique in that it is over 3,600 years old. Some exhibition games are offered for tourists throughout Mexico and Central America, but the Mazatlán area is the heartland of the renewed interest in the game and the state of Sinaloa is now the only place regular games (not just tourist events) are played. The game was originally part of the indigenous religions and was played for centuries, until it gradually faded away.

In the game, I saw there were three players (can be more) on a field that was 65 meters in length and four meters wide. The idea is to advance a solid, nine pound rubber ball, larger than a softball, but smaller than a soccer ball, past your opponent's goal line. Three styles of ulama games are played: one using only hips, one using only arms and one using only sticks to advance the ball. I'm told that the purest form of the game is to use hips only, and that's how it is played in the Mazatlán area. Ulama is much like a soccer game, but scoring is more like tennis. While the scoring is not this simple, in order to win a game, one team must score three straight times.

Los Llanitos is a very small town about 40 minutes north of Mazatlán is a center of the Ulama revival. This is where the purest form of the game is played during the season, October through April. Games may be scheduled one or two weeks ahead for visiting groups, with transportation and a light lunch provided by CONREHABIT. For details and prices call Martha Armenta at 986-2471 or by email at *spanish@prodigy.net.mx.*

Sightseeing

Cliff divers: The cliff in Mazatlán is not as high as the one in Acapulco, but the water is definitely shallower and requires better timing and skill. The cliff divers dive from a platform in the Glorieta Sánchez Tabuada just north of Olas Altas. A tip of about $1 per person is appropriate. When I visited last, I was introduced to three generations of cliff divers, who all gave me a demonstration that day. Dives take place between 11:00 A.M. and 1:00 P.M. during the high tide, but there are other times they dive also. If there is a nighttime dive with torches, be sure you don't miss it. Your hotel concierge may have more information.

Pacifico Brewery Tour: This brewery was built in 1900, but has been modernized several times since. They have tours Monday through Friday from 9 A.M. to 4 P.M. The English-language tour is on Thursdays. They are currently closed for tours until November, so be sure to call for a reservation before you go.

The tour takes just over an hour and ends in the brewery museum lounge where we looked at the artifacts while sipping free beer! You will see where all the malt is made, how the bottles are cleaned, and how the brew is bottled. The brewery bottles 3,100,000 bottles of Pacifico daily. I think they need every one of them during Carnaval.

While the tour is free, it must be scheduled on Wednesdays. The latest information is that they require 15 reservations to have the tour in English. Call 982-7900, Ext. 1642 for reservations. There is a dress code of no sandals or shorts.

Whale-watching and dolphin-watching: ONCA Explorations have daily guided tours on excellent boats. The best time for whale-watching is December through March, and cost is $85 for adults and $65 for children 6–10. From April though November the four-hour dolphin quest snorkeling combo trip costs $75 for all ages. There is a requirement for a minimum of four passengers. The trip includes lunch and water/soft drinks. There is also a four hour tour called "Ethnic Experience" costing $75 for adults and $45 for children 6–10. The office is located at Rio de la Plaza #409 in Av. Las Gaviotas (next to apartment Siesta) and the telephone number is cellular: 044-669-116-0301, or 913-4050. Check out the manager, Oscar Guzon's website at *www.oncaexplorations.com*, or email him at *oxinfo@gmail.com* for answers to questions.

Fiesta Shows at Resorts

El Cid Resorts: Their fiesta is a Carnaval theme and is on Wednesday nights. There is plenty of food and drinks, combined with the show making it well worth the $35.

The Inn at Mazatlán has a Mexican Fiesta every Wednesday night with dinner.

Late-Night Activities

Bora Bora: It is located in the Valentino's complex on Camarón Sábalo in the Golden Zone. This is a nightspot that also may still feature beach volleyball.

Joe's Oyster Bar: On the beach behind the Ramada hotel in the Golden Zone, Joe's is another party place for the 18–40ish crowd.

Valentino's: Mazatlán's favorite disco. It is the castle in the Fiesta Land complex. No tennis shoes or shorts allowed. There is a cover charge and drinks run $3–$5 each. Thursday and Sunday women drink free from 9–11 P.M. There is a classic strobe-lit dance floor, but it has several hideaways including a karaoke bar and romantic music nook.

Gus & Gus is a perennial favorite with visitors. Besides their long-time location across from the Hotel Costa de Oro, they also have a new location in the new Marina. Consistently good reports from visitors to both locations.

LGBT bars/clubs

Vitriola's: Heriberto Frias #1608 (between Ángel Flores and 21 de Marzo, one block north of the Plazuela Machado in El Centro Histórico. Vitriola's attracts a generally well-dressed, upscale clientele (customers seldom show up in shorts), both male and female. Featuring both food (it's a popular place for pizza) and music videos, it's open from 8 P.M. Thursday through Sunday.

Pepe Toro: in the Golden Zone on *calle* de las Garzas #16, one and one half blocks west of Camarón Sábalo (where the Panama Restaurant and the Oxxo Store are on the corners). Pepe Toro attracts a younger and more diverse crowd, male, female and transgender. Open Thursday through Sunday (and the rest of the week during Semana Santa, Carnaval and major Mexican vacation periods), doors open about 8 P.M., but normally there are few customers before 11 or 12 at night. Dancing, videos, drag shows at 2 A.M. Friday and Saturday nights (or Saturday and Sunday morning), outdoor patio and a dark room (at your own risk).

Bar La Alemana: is at Zaragosa #14, just east of the 5 way intersection with Av. Juan Carrasco and Aquiles Serdán several blocks north of the Central Mercado. La Alemana is listed as a gay bar by the largest Mexican gay website, sergay.com.mx, but draws a diverse (male) clientele.

Ángela Peralta Theater: Presents just about everything from traditional deer dances to contemporary ballet, flamenco and modern dance to John Lennon's music to a Mozart trio. There are films, lectures, plays and readings as well. Sitting in the old restored theater is alone worth the admission price of any show, which is very inexpensive when compared with prices up north. There are two great stories that are of interest about the theater.

Ángela Peralta, named "The Mexican Nightingale," was one of the world's most famous opera divas. She was supposed to perform at Mazatlán's relatively new opera house in 1883. Huge crowds met her on her arrival, and she was so overcome by them that she performed from the balcony of her hotel. Before she could do her theater performance, she fell ill and died of yellow fever at the age of 38. The theater was named after her in 1943.

For a period around World War I, the theater fell on hard times. It was used for Carnaval balls and boxing matches and later a movie theater. In 1964, due to deterioration, it was closed to performances. Just as plans were in the works for restoration, in 1973 "Hurricane Olivia" blew the plans away and the building to ruins. By 1986, civic- and arts-minded locals got together and began the restoration project that has restored the theater to its original state.

Movies: There are several modern movie complexes in Mazatlán. The good news is that they usually have American movies in English with Spanish subtitles. The other good news is that a ticket costs around $4.00 (may vary, depending on the day and/or movie) and popcorn, candy and snacks are equally inexpensive.

Cinepolis is in the La Gran Plaza mall;

Cinemas Gaviotas is an older theater a little north of Valentino's in the Golden Zone; and

There are two Cinemexes, one next door to the Soriana superstore on Av. Rafael Buelna close to the Golden Zone and the other one next door to the Soriana superstore on Av. Insurgentes.

For you non-shopping guys, it gives you an opportunity to catch a flick while your spouse is shopping. For you shoppers, your spouse can save some money at the movies while you spend said savings in the stores.

Sightseeing tours

There are numerous organized tours of the city of Mazatlán and the surrounding areas. Some are best enjoyed with a tour driver in a van, while others must be taken in a boat or other vehicle through a tour company. Most of these destinations can be visited by public transportation if you are adventurous and budget-conscious.

King David Tours: This is one of the more popular tour groups in Mazatlán. It is best known for its van service to and from the airport at about $ 8 per person when pre-booked and prepaid over the Internet. They offer jungle tours, city tours, kayaking, golfing and more. Visit their website at *http://www.kingdavid.com.mx/* or telephone them toll-free at 1-866-438-7097 from the U.S. or Canada, 914-1444 in Mazatlán or email them at *info@kingdavid.com.mx*.

Vista Tours: Is located on Camarón Sábalo, in the Golden Zone, across from the Gaviotas movie theater and a bit south. Their telephone number is 986-8610, and you can visit their website at *www .vistatours.com.mx*. They have tours to Rosário ($60.00), Copala ($55.00 with lunch and $45 without lunch),  El Quelite ($50.00), La Noria ($40). They also offer a four-hour city tour for $25.

Huana Coa Canopy Adventure tour: If you are into zipping above the tree tops you'll be crazy about this tour. It opened in December of 2007 with state-of-the art equipment and well-trained, bilingual guides. You are either picked up from your hotel or from their office on the Malecón and bused about 20 miles to the foothills of the Sierra Madres. There you are outfitted with zipping harness and helmet and given a safety lecture.

Military ATVs that traverse the difficult terrain take you to the top of a hill. After a demonstration by the guides you are hooked up to a zip line and start your ride. There are nine lines that range from about 100 yards to 300 yards long, high above the treetop canopy where you can look down and see the hills and agave fields. After the "flying" you return to the start, turn in your equipment and board your bus that will take you to the popular Los Osuna tequila factory—about five minutes away. Following a guided tour and demonstration of the making of tequila you will be offered a free shot of tequila.

The office of Huana Coa is located in the Don Pelayo hotel on the Malecón. Visit their website at *http://www.facebook.com/home.php?#!/ profile.php?id=100001608972677.* Call 990-1100 for reservations. The cost for the five hour tour is $75 per person (but subject to change). Water and an apple are provided at the end of your zipline tour.

To go on the zipline tour, one must be at least nine years of age, able to understand directions and comply with rules and able to walk uphill for 15 minutes. The tour is not recommended for people with heart conditions, epilepsy, asthma, back, neck, or shoulder problems, or those that are pregnant. They also offer horseback riding and quad riding at additional costs.

Veraneando Adventure Zipline Tour and River Ride Tour: About 35 miles southeast of Mazatlán, this is a relatively new operation, but it is getting good reviews. Details may be had by calling 044-669-123-0785 or at their website: *http://veraneandoziplining .webs.com/pricesandservices.htm.*

Yate Fiesta: A big double-decker yacht, has a two and one half hour cruise with 2 drinks, that has an additional two and one half hour Stone Island tour that includes lunch and open bar. The boat leaves the dock near the lighthouse at 11:00 A.M. daily. There is a very entertaining guide on board. Price is about $30, with reduced prices for kids between the ages of 5–8 and free for those under 5. Tel: 982-3130 or *http://www.yatefiesta.com/paseos.html*

The following are towns around Mazatlán worth visiting:

Teacapan and Rosario: The shrimpers' village of Teacapan is about two hours south of Mazatlán (approximately 90 miles) on an isolated peninsula thick with coconut palm trees bordered by a mangrove swamp. The lagoons are a bird watcher's paradise. There are more than 90 bird species that have been identified there.

Rosario is a former silver and gold mining town that was founded by the Spaniards in 1655. I've been told that there are more than 40 miles of underground tunnels below Rosario, which is more than the above-ground streets. I have made no effort to go underground and check the figures though. Everyone who goes to Rosario visits the baroque cathedral. The entire church, with its ornate gold-leaf-covered altar, valued at $1 million dollars, had to be moved brick by brick to prevent it from caving in on the town's labyrinth of tunnels. There is a museum, the house of Lola Beltran, Mexico's famous singer; but it is only open sporadically.

Tours are available departing at 7 A.M. and lasting eight hours. They can be booked through your hotel concierge or through tour companies. The per-person cost is approximately $50 and includes lunch and cold drinks.

Concordia and Copala: If you want to see another side of Mexico, don't miss this visit. Tour companies usually depart at 9:15 A.M. and return at 3:45 P.M. The tour costs about $50 and includes lunch and cold drinks.

About 40 minutes southeast of Mazatlán is the town of Concordia, which was founded by the Spanish in 1571. It is best known for its solid wood, colonial-design furniture and pre-Colombian-style pottery. Delicious mangoes are grown here, and when in season, many stands sell them along the streets.

Copala is another old mining town that lies in the Sierra Madres, about 10 miles east of Concordia. It was founded in 1565 and produced tons of silver in the late 19th century. Now it is a small, picturesque tourist town, with cobblestone streets and white houses on rolling hills. Among the 600 inhabitants are some retired Americans and Canadians. Soon after your arrival, children will surround you wanting to sell you woodcarvings made in Copala. Please don't pay them in U.S. or Canadian coins, as they are not legal tender in Mexico.

La Noria: This small village, about 30 minutes northeast of Mazatlán is worth visiting. La Noria translates to "the waterwheel", either for the shape of the town or because sometime in the distant past there was a waterwheel driven mill there. Several leather factories are located here. You can stop and watch saddles, sandals, belts and other leather goods being made right in the shops. Other sights are the church of San Antonio and a very old jail that is still in use.

El Quelite: About 40 miles northeast of Mazatlán is a town named El Quelite. Besides having a beautiful main street, El Quelite is the home of a large cockfighting ranch. Row upon row of specially bred roosters can be seen individually tied to small white shelters. They will eventually be sold for sport-fighting. By request, the roosters will be pitted against one another to find out which ones are the best fighters.

I have checked with several Mazatlecos to find cockfighting arenas in the area, but to no avail. Apparently cockfighting is not illegal, but betting on the fights is against the law. My guess is that fighting occurs, but only advertised by word-of-mouth.

The town also has a great bakery near the cockfighting ranch and several cheese-making operations. The trip is worth it just to taste the great pineapple turnovers – *empanadas de piña*. Follow the signs to the ranch—then ask the caretaker at the ranch for directions to the bakery and cheese-making places.

Don't leave town without trying a meal at Dr. Marcos Gabriel Osuna Tirado's restaurant, Mesón de los Laureanos, a quaint little restaurant that is part of a hotel complex. They have what the owner calls "traditional rural Sinaloan food and ambiance". We had a barbecued beef Mexican dish that was superb. For information call 965-4465 or 965-4143.

Local cruises: The coastal city of Mazatlán is a great place for cruising in smaller boats. They can be booked through your hotel or through a local travel agency.

Yate Fiesta: A big double-decker yacht cruises for about two and a half hours around the bay. You will see the three islands, the shrimp fleet, Pacifico brewery tower, pirate caves and much more. The boat leaves the dock near the lighthouse at 11:00 A.M. daily. There is a very entertaining guide on board. Price is about $20, with reduced prices for kids between the ages of 5–8 and free for those under 5. The price includes pickup and return to your hotel. They also have a two and a half hour sunset tour with open bar for about $25 with reduced prices for kids between the ages of 5–8 and free for those under 5. It leaves the dock at 4 P.M. daily in the winter and 8 P.M. daily in the summer. Tel: 982-3130

Estero del Yugo: Hidden just north of the water park MazAgua on Av. Sábalo Cerritos are saltwater and freshwater lagoons and a tropical dry forest. It provides habitat for more than 200 species of aquatic and terrestrial birds and numerous mammals such as the bobcat and deer.

Tours may be arraigned by calling Martha Armenta 986-2471 for details. CONREHABIT sponsors these tours, so you're supporting a good cause. *NOTE:* For birdwatchers, bring your identification book with you—the best is supposed to be *Peterson's Field Guide to Mexican Birds*—as none are available in Mazatlán.

La Viña Dump Tour: Free tours, sponsored by the Vineyard Fellowship, are conducted Tuesday and Thursday of each week from November through May. The tours are billed as "an opportunity to visit the Mazatlán that tourists never see", and last about four hours. Participants help prepare simple meals with bottled water and serve them to the people who live near and support themselves by scrounging in the city's garbage dump.

Volunteer tour guides explain how to become active partners in some or all of these relief efforts through financial contributions, volunteering time and expertise or by sharing the message of the Vineyard when they return to their homes and through their prayers.

Tourists hear the Fellowship's mission statement and learn the principles that underlie the Vineyard's work with the poor. This work includes scholarships for children, the "Help a Child Smile" project that provides new shoes and gifts for more than 1,200 children each year and many other outreach activities.

Social and Charitable Groups

It is not hard to find social activities/meetings in Mazatlán. Most groups have permanent members, but welcome tourist visitors. They all seem to have one thing in common: To improve the lives of the people and animals here and learn more about Mazatlán.

Friends of Mexico: This is a group of foreigners that have a charter, and meet for the purpose of helping foreigners live better in Mazatlán.

Presently they meet at various restaurants once a month for regular meetings. They usually have a meal and guest speakers. Annual membership fees are about $16, but it entitles you to discounts at several restaurants and businesses throughout the city.

Money raised through dues, collections and fund-raising activities is spent for the education of needy children of Mazatlán. Help in various forms is provided to local school students. For more information about how you can become involved visit their website at *www.friendsofmexicoac.org.*

Amigos de Los Animales: It's the Mazatlán humane society. Their primary purpose is to assist the dogs and cats in Mazatlán. Most of what they do is care for the street animals and hold animals at their animal shelter for adoption.

They meet once a month at different days, times and locations. You can find out more by going to their website at *www.amigosdelosanimalesmazatlán.com* or by calling 986-4235. They have an animal shelter, pet supplies shop and a thrift shop in the *colonia* Francisco Villa—just off Av. de la Marina. The address is Bicentenario Juárez #3. Anyone is welcome to visit the thrift shop (all donations accepted) or volunteer at the thrift shop and/or kennel.

CONREHABIT—**Con**servation and **Re**habilitation of the **Habit**at—is a non-profit organization dedicated to increasing the awareness of the effects of economic development on the fragile Mexican tropical dry forest ecosystem. CONREHABIT promotes conservation efforts in northwestern Mexico, actively seeks to educate the public in the importance of conservation, works with governmental agencies to minimize the detrimental effects of development on the local ecosystem and maintains facilities for the study of and rehabilitation of wildlife.

It was created to honor the memory of Kittie Jepsen and Aldo Barragán, two people who during their lives gave their time to help others. Donations can be made through PayPal by going to the website at *www.conrehabit.org.* For additional information call 044-669-912-0890.

La Familia: Was started about 13 years ago by some Mexican women and a few foreigners. Their purpose is to assist a poor *colonia* called Genaro Estrada that is about halfway to the airport. Many of the shacks have dirt floors, no electricity and no running water. The group has been building a community center, about 45 x 60 feet. The kitchen feeds about 50 children a day. They also provide English, sewing and cooking classes. Their ultimate goal is to raise the standard of living for the community to the point that it will become self-sufficient.

They try to have a fundraising dinner every February, with the children providing the entertainment. La Familia is a charity recognized by both Mexico and the U.S. Internal Revenue Service and they accept cash donations. To have a tour of the community center or make a donation call 913-0037.

AA meetings: The La Mission English-speaking AA meets in the Golden Zone, across from Dolce Mami restaurant, kitty-corner from Burger King, inside the gate on Camarón Sábalo. Meetings are every night at 6:30 P.M. They also have a beach meeting and separate women's and men's meetings. Additional meetings in Spanish are held daily throughout the city.

Men's group—Beer and Beans – *Hermanadad de Frijoles y Cervezas*: meets at Bar La Alemana on Zaragoza at 11:00 or a little later the 2nd through the 4th or 5th Wednesdays of the month. The first Wednesday they meet at Loco Lupes on the Malecón for *Camarones y Cerveza*. This group is in hiatus for the summer. Generally the first meeting is the last Wednesday of October.

Rumor has it that this men's group has been meeting every Wednesday since the 40s. They have no program or agenda and membership is not a requirement. Just drop in, grab a seat and introduce yourself to your neighbors. They just sit around and eat, drink and swap stories and tell jokes. I'm told that if someone comes up with a sad story they will pass the hat—"at the drop of a hat".

Bridge: Duplicate bridge groups meet Monday through Friday at the Hotel Playa Mazatlán. They don't always meet at the same time, so call the hotel for that information. Don't have a partner? Not to worry, as they will partner you up with someone.

Church Services in English

The Vineyard—LaViña—Christian Fellowship of Mazatlán: Services every Sunday at their building on Camarón Sábalo, a block north of the Panama restaurant, on the same side of the street in the Golden Zone. Services in English are at 9 A.M. and Spanish services at 11 A.M. For more information call Fred Collum at 933-1880 or the office at 916-5114. Get to know the members better by attending a brunch at one of the local restaurants following the English service. They opened a new church in the new Marina near Rico's Coffee Shop. English language service each Sunday is at 11:00 A.M.

> *Templo de la Sagrada Familia:* It is located at *calle* Rio de la Playa #2 *fracc.* Gaviotas. They have mass in English at 8:50 A.M.

> *Jehovah's Witness English Congregation:* Services at noon on Sundays at Av. de la Marina #899, a few blocks south of Home Depot. Tel: 983-0843.

> *New Apostolic Church*: Services are Sunday at 10:30 A.M. in *colonia* Francisco Villa. For inquiries and directions Tel: 983-9716.

> *San Judas Tadeo:* English mass is 8:45 A.M. at Mojarra #55 *fracc.* Sábalo Country. English masses are seasonal. Tel: 916-6246.

Congregational Church (Blue church): English services are at 9 A.M. every Sunday year-round. They are located at the corner of 5 de Mayo and Melchor Ocampo in El Centro. Tel: 985-1607.

Reading Material

Mazatlán Membership Library: You can't spend all your time on the beach, touring the area and partying. The Mazatlán Membership Library is a non-profit circulating library specializing in mostly English, but with some Spanish books. Donations, dues and volunteer workers support it financially. They will be happy to accept your donations of books or cash. The library is stocked with 6,000+ books that are not easily found in Mazatlán. Operating hours change seasonally, but basically it is open weekdays 9 A.M. to 5 P.M. and Saturdays 10 A.M. to 2 P.M. For current hours call 982-3036.

Visit the library at Sixto Osuna #115 E, almost next door to the Archaeology Museum.

Mazatlán Book & Coffee Company: They specialize in exchanging paperback books for a nominal fee, but also have some new books, particularly ones about Mexico. You can find them on Camarón Sábalo, behind the Banco Santander that is across the street from the Hotel Costa de Oro, in suite #8. Call them at 916-7899. They have some of the best coffee, ground and beans, in town.

Something new! A real Farmer's Market opens Saturday, Nov. 17, 2012, 8 A.M. to noon, Zaragoza Park. That's south of Fisherman's monument and just off the Malecón a couple of blocks on *calle* Guillermo

Nelson or *calle* 5 de Mayo. The season generally runs to the last Saturday of April. More information at:

https://www.facebook.com/pages/Mercado-Org%C3%A1nico-de-Mazatl%C3%A1n-Mazatlan-Farmers-Market/338298116183371?ref=ts

As you can see, there is something to do for everyone, regardless of age. You, like most of us, will find that there will be so much to do and so little time.

Chapter 6

A basic calendar of events for the year

WHEN MAKING YOUR VACATION PLANS, it will be helpful to know what is going on that you don't want to miss. Exact dates for many events change every year however, so you must always check.

January

Baseball play-offs

1st – New Year's Day (National Holiday)

6th – Three Kings' Day. This is a traditional Mexican holiday. If you're invited to a party, look inside your piece of cake for the plastic baby Jesús toy. If you get it, you win the opportunity to throw a party on February 2.

February

2nd – party from Three Kings' Day, and *Dia de la Candelaria* – Candlemas – when, if you have construction workers at your house, you ARE expected to offer them a full sit-down hot *comida* and drinks – heavy lunch – around 2 P.M.

First Monday – Constitution Day (National Holiday)

14th – Day of Friendship—St. Valentine's Day

Five days before Ash Wednesday – *Carnaval* – Mardi Gras – is officially celebrated for five days. It is billed as the third largest Carnaval celebration in the world. Since the date is determined by the date for Easter, that varies every year.

Annual Pro Mexico house tour

Annual La Familia fundraiser dinner

La Viña Golf tournament

24th – Flag Day (not a national holiday)

March

Third Monday – Birthday of President Benito Juárez celebrated (National Holiday)

Annual Wine and Cheese fundraiser by Friends of Mexico

Tom Garcia golf tournament at El Cid

Don el Guia El Cid fishing tournament

April

Semana Santa – Holy week – The week preceding Easter Sunday.

Maundy (Holy) Thursday and Good Friday – The Thursday and Friday before Easter (ALL government offices and possibly banks will be closed, even though they are not National Holidays)

Semana de la Moto – Motorcycle week – Easter week – The week following Easter Sunday.

Annual Sailing Regatta

Tennis tournament at Las Gaviotas Racquet club

30th – Children's Day

Annual Triathlon

International Sailing Regatta

May

1st – Labor Day (National Holiday)

5th – *Cinco de Mayo* – always written 5 de Mayo in Spanish (not a national holiday)

10th – Mother's Day (the third most important traditional holiday in Mexico.) Most businesses—except tourist businesses, restaurants and bars—and offices will be closed in the afternoon.

Expo *Canacintra*: Held annually in the parking lot next to Sam's Club

June

Third Sunday – Father's Day

Annual Billfish tournament hosted by Club Nautica

Santa Rita bicycle races

August

International tennis tournament

International fishing tournament

September

1st – *El Informe* – The President's "State of the Union" address to the legislature (May be a bank holiday in some cities)

16th – Mexican Independence Day (National Holiday) It is celebrated as the first day of the revolution against Spain. The celebrations actually start about 6 P.M. on the 15th with *El Grito* shortly before midnight at the *Palacio Municipal* on Plaza de la República. Then there is a nice parade during the day and festivities in the Plaza de la República downtown in the evening.

October

12th – *Día de la Raza* (Columbus Day-not a national holiday)

Mazatlán Venados baseball season starts

Mountain bicycle race

The Sinaloa Cultural Festival begins during the latter half of October, with imported talent of all sorts. It could be anything from opera to symphony to jazz appearing in the Ángela Peralta Theater (by admission ticket) plus a few free events in either the Plazuela Machado or at the Mazatlán Art Museum. If you haven't experienced a concert in the Ángela Peralta, you're in for a treat. Check at the box office or look for posters outlining the various performances by date.

November

1st – *Día de los Angelitos* – All Saints Day

2nd – *Día de los Muertos* – Day of the Dead – All Souls Day – Mexicans go to gravesites of relatives, clean them and have a family picnic. The 1st is for dead children, the second is for all the family. (It is a bank holiday and many businesses will be closed, but it is not a National Holiday, just the second most important traditional holiday)

Baseball season continues

Jesús Arnoldo Millán Golf tournament at El Cid

Third Monday – *Día de la Revolución* celebrated (National Holiday)

Christmas shopping trip to Guadalajara and Tonalá sponsored by Friends of Mexico

Bisbee's Billfish Classic El Cid fishing tournament

Ángela Peralta Theater fall season begins

Martial Arts International Festival

Supercross Championship

Annual Pacific Marathon – A two day event, Saturday and Sunday. Either the last weekend in November (when November has 5 Sundays) or the first weekend in December. Traffic blocked in the Golden Zone early in the morning Saturday, and till noon or one o'clock on Sunday.

December

1st – Presidential Inauguration (National Holiday in 2012 and every sixth year after)

8th – *Festival de la Inmaculada Concepción*

12th – Day of the Virgin of Guadalupe (the most important of all the traditional holidays in Mexico. Most businesses and offices will be closed and it **may** also be a bank holiday.)

16th to 24th – *Posadas* – Traditional Christmas Parties, however the 24th is usually restricted to family and special guests, as the traditional "Christmas Dinner" is served around 10:30 P.M., and gifts are opened right after midnight (and those special guests must have a gift for them also!). It is also unique, as it is the ONLY party in Mexico where gifts are opened in front of everyone. Usually, in order not to seem presumptuous or embarrass those whose gifts are less than the gifts of others, gifts are only opened in private…AFTER the party is over and guests have gone home.

24th – not a holiday, but most business, even restaurants and bars, except in the tourist areas, close by about 7 P.M. in order to celebrate their Christmas dinner late that night.

25th Christmas Day (National Holiday)

Annual amateur golf tournament at El Cid

Ángela Peralta Theater winter season

31st – Regular baseball season ends

31st – New Year's Eve Parties all over town! Businesses are usually closed by 7 P.M., as nearly every family has a private party at home with a big dinner late that night, then the traditional glass of wine or cider with 12 grapes immersed for toasting the New Year at midnight. Then hugs, best wishes and kisses for EVERYONE!

Chapter 7

Where do we eat?

Eating is one of the most fabulous activities in Mazatlán—hence a separate chapter. Unlike in U.S. restaurants, in Mazatlán there's no pressure to eat quickly and be herded out the door. Meals in Mexico are considered a social and leisurely activity. It is unlikely that you will have your check delivered to your table until you ask for it. All restaurants use purified water and ice. It is not necessary to order bottled water, but if you insist on paying for water, go ahead and ask. Because eating out is such a tremendous activity in Mazatlán I do not recommend "all-inclusive" hotel packages.

Mexican Food

There are many restaurants in Mazatlán that specialize in Mexican food (but NOT the "Tex-Mex" or its relatives, Ariz-Mex or Cali-Mex, that usually is called "Mexican" in the U.S. or not even New Mexico style which is quite different also) It is not necessary to speak Spanish, but it could be helpful. Mexican restaurant menus may confuse you because some of the same "breakfast" dishes may reappear elsewhere in the menu. A Mexican meal is not complete without tortillas. They are flat, round, pancake-like flatbread, usually made of ground, nixtamalized corn without shortening or sometime (with some dishes) wheat flour with lard or vegetable shortening. Tortillas are eaten with nearly every non-dessert dish. I especially enjoy watching my Mexican friends rolling meat in a tortilla one-handed; much like my stepfather rolled cigarettes with one hand.

Soup: The most common soup in Mazatlán is called *sopa de tortilla*, which is artfully seasoned with chicken broth, and garnished with tortilla wedges, cheese and sliced avocado (maybe). My wife, Katherine, considers it a delicious meal in itself.

Salsas: There seem to be as many different salsas as there are restaurants in Mazatlán: Red, green, brown, salty, thin, thick, sweet, chunky and blended salsa. The most common are red and green salsas.

Fresh red salsa, salsa Mexicana or simply salsa *fresca*, ordinarily contains chopped serrano or jalapeño chile, chopped fresh tomato and onions, mixed with cilantro, lime juice and salt. It ranges from not "hot" at all to very, very "hot". This is the salsa often brought to your table with the complimentary basket of tortilla chips, but that could be about any red, green or brown salsa depending on the restaurant.

The green salsa, made with a base of *tomatillos* (small, tart, green tomato-like vegetables), is usually served with meat, poultry and seafood.

NOTE: All salsas are made with varying amounts and types of chile pepper, so...do as the Mexicans do when confronted with an unknown salsa, just put a drop on the back of your hand and taste it BEFORE ladling over your food. If it is just too *picante* – Spanish for "hot" – and since nearly all restaurants will serve several different salsas with your meal, you can change to one that you can tolerate (or really like) without embarrassment.

Guacamole: When served as a condiment in many restaurants, guacamole is mashed avocado, liquefied (in a blender) with salt, onions, chile and sometimes other ingredients. As a salsa, this liquefied guacamole is very, very mild.

When guacamole is served as a "vegetable" with your meal, or as a side dish with tortilla chips, it is never blended in a blender. The avocado is merely mashed or finely diced and mixed with finely diced green chile pepper (serrano or jalapeño), chopped fresh tomato, onion, lime juice and salt.

Desserts: The most common Mexican dessert in Mazatlán is a delicious egg custard called *flan* which nearly always has a topping of caramelized sugar syrup. Pastries in Mexican restaurants are not as rich or as sweet (no matter how they "look") as in the U.S., but equally tasty, but oh the cakes, some are very wonderful, particularly the *pastel de tres leches* or three-milks cake. Pie – *pay* – is quite common, but regardless of type, quite different than those up north. Always worth the try.

Other Mexican dishes: When you go to the restaurants that tourists usually frequent, reading menus is not a problem because they are either in English or are bilingual. If you really want to get a "taste of Mexico", try some of the smaller, more traditional restaurants. I've found some great meals by wandering into places or going because someone recommended a particular establishment. I have listed some of the more familiar Mexican dishes in Appendix 3.

My favorite spots to eat: Approximate costs are in U.S. dollars per person for dinner. Like the U.S. and Canada, prices for lunch and breakfast are usually less. Keep in mind that shrimp is usually the most expensive item on the menu. Mexican food (minus shrimp) and fish are the least expensive.

Expensive = $25 or more
Moderate = Less than $12 up to $25
Inexpensive = Under $12
Even less expensive = Under $7

Expensive

Señor Pepper: Is now located in the new Marina near the main entrance to the marina itself. This casual name is deceptive, as the fixtures are of gleaming wood and brass. The classy atmosphere is punctuated with well-dressed waiters. Steaks are the specialty but they also prepare scrumptious lobster, fish, pork and chicken. Go here for that special evening.

La Cordeliere at Pueblo Bonito Emerald Bay: Is in the newest Pueblo Bonito complex northeast of the end of the bus line at Cerrillos and past MazAgua water park. Emerald Bay is elegant, in a beautiful white, Spanish-plantation style décor with both indoor and outdoor seating. The menu is wide-ranging and includes Mexican dishes, poultry, beef, seafood and pasta. The tortilla soup is delicious and coconut shrimp are not only served in large portions, but tasty, with a delightfully flavorful sauce. Desserts are mostly pastry, and delectable. All the dishes were very attractively presented.

Reservations are required at least 24 hours in advance. If your name is not on the "pass" list at the gate, you will not be allowed to enter. For reservations call 989-0525.

Angelo's: Italian food is the specialty at Angelo's. Elegance best describes the surroundings with rich, cushy chairs, chandeliers and candlelit tables. An outstanding singer entertains almost nightly. The hot oven rolls that are baked in butter are a nice surprise. The pasta dishes are all tasty and in large portions. The restaurant is connected to the hotel Pueblo Bonito Mazatlán on Camarón Sábalo.

La Paloma at Estrella del Mar: Right at the golf clubhouse, this beautiful restaurant is worth the long drive from town and the Golden Zone. Call them at 982-3300, ext. 3005 for reservations. They have both indoor and outdoor seating. The menu includes delicious steaks, seafood, chicken and numerous Mexican dishes. They have live entertainment on Friday during the tourist season.

Moderate

The Papagayo: Most of the restaurants in Mazatlán have something unique to attract visitors. It may have a view of the sunset, a place for people watching, ambience, beautiful decor, great service, delicious food, wonderful music or reasonable prices. The Papagayo is the only place in Mazatlán I know that has them all.

Located on the beach side of The Inn at Mazatlán, on Camarón Sábalo, both indoor and outdoor seating is available. Most of the staff has worked there for decades, so the service is consistently good. Happy hour is from 12–2 P.M. and 4–6 P.M. daily, and a marimba band plays each evening.

The chef's personality has surfaced with food to tickle the palates of guests of all ages. They serve special dinners on Halloween, Thanksgiving, Christmas, New Year's Eve and Valentine's Day. We always celebrate Christmas there with a delicious turkey dinner. They also make a wonderful French toast for breakfast—or even for lunch. Don't miss this marvelous eating experience.

Topolo restaurant: This restaurant is loaded with atmosphere. It has two separate rooms and a garden patio. The walls are painted red and the black ironwork adds to the colorful décor. They always play nice soft music. They specialize in delicious Mexican dishes and seafood and are located on *calle* Constitución, one block east of the Plazuela Machado. The chef creates the most eye-appealing dishes in all of Mazatlán. I believe it is the best overall dining experience in the downtown area.

Sheik: If you are on the Malecón, you can't miss the Valentino's complex that looks like a white castle on the edge of the water. Sheik is a major part of this complex. Appropriately, its customers are treated like royalty. If you choose the terrace that sits out over the water you can sometimes watch surfers trying to "catch the big one". After sunset, the lights on the busy Malecón to the south are a dazzling sight.

The furnishings inside match up with any expensive restaurant in the world. There is a waterfall and fishpond with hundreds of goldfish. A piano is located near the entrance and live music is sometimes available.

If you like a romantic atmosphere, delicious food, and enjoy being pampered, Sheik is a must! I prefer the chateaubriand, French onion soup with banana flambé for dessert. Reservations are suggested, especially in the high season. Tel: 989-1600.

La Palapa restaurant: This is a huge restaurant inside a gigantic *palapa*, located inside the Tórres Mazatlán Resort about a mile north of the new Marina on Av. Sábalo Cerritos. About 80% of the building has windows that can be closed when the weather cools or opened for ventilation. The white tablecloths with red roses provide a colorful and classy atmosphere to the place that has both indoor and outdoor seating. The menu is an excellent mixture of Mexican and American dishes and breakfast, lunch and dinner are served daily. There is a dinner special every evening.

They also have diet dishes. But the hallmark of this special restaurant is the service. The staff is well-trained because they have been there for several years. Ask for Victor for even better service. The head chef and restaurant manager is Lani Wooll, and she can also set up a small party for you and your guests. Call her at 669-989-8600, ext. 5050 or email her at *laniwooll@gmail.com*.

La Palapa Del Mar is located on Camarón Sábalo next to La Casa Country restaurant. There is plenty of parking in the rear. The building is a huge *palapa* and the interior reminds you of the tropics. It's not just a restaurant but a place that vibrates. There are TVs on all the walls so it is also a sports bar. In the evenings there are all kinds of live music for your listening and dancing pleasure.

They specialize in seafood but also have delicious chicken, beef and pork dishes. The service is excellent. For reservations call 914-1900.

Sanborns restaurant: This well-known Mexican bookstore, general store and restaurant chain is in the La Gran Plaza mall. The place is packed with locals and the food is primarily Mexican, well-presented and tasty. There is a daily Mexican breakfast buffet and the service is excellent. The best way to describe Sanborns is that it is a more up-scale Panama's.

Pueblo Bonito restaurant: Inside the Pueblo Bonito Mazatlán resort is a restaurant that has both indoor and outdoor dining. They have a large menu and specialize in Mexican dishes. I highly recommend the Sunday brunch. They have plenty of fruit and juices, pastries and a large selection of both American and Mexican dishes on the buffet table.

Señor Frogs: If you're young—or even young at heart—go to the ground floor of El Cid Resort on Camarón Sábalo and follow the crowd. If you don't see the crowd, follow the sounds of the music. The crazy waiters still bring excellent food and provide their own show. My daughters have told me that the place gets wild after dinner, when there is usually standing room only. Be warned that the Jell-O "shooters" are deadly!

El Shrimp Bucket: It is the first and original restaurant of the Anderson group. The other is Señor Frogs. It is located in Olas Altas opposite the Venadito statue on the Malecón on the ground floor of the Hotel Siesta. It used to be known as the place where celebrities who visited Mazatlán went. It still has excellent food and good service. There is seating in the dining room, outside and an inside patio. They specialize in seafood, and my favorite is the bucket of shrimp, which consists of wonderful, big breaded shrimp and French fries served in an old-fashioned clay "bucket". Reservations are not needed except during Holy Week.

Gus & Gus (south): This is the original Gus & Gus that has been a popular eatery and night spot for years. The menu is varied and they not only have a large area for outside dining, but an enclosed, air conditioned room that they call the "non-smoking area". They are open at 9 A.M. for breakfast and are one of the last places to close nightly in the Golden Zone. The following are on the menu: shrimp, fish, steaks, barbecue chicken and ribs and all the usual Mexican dishes. It is on Av. Camarón Sábalo, across from Hotel Costa De Oro. Great food and a fun place to go.

Gus & Gus (north): Was opened in 2010 in the new Marina behind Portofino Justo condominiums. It is in a very modern, picturesque setting with both indoor and outdoor seating. You can admire the docked yachts while dining. The food and prices are about the same as the other Gus & Gus but the music and clientele appear somewhat more mellow.

Tony's on the Beach: It is perched at the end of a mini-mall on Camarón Sábalo, next to the Carravelle hotel, and adjacent to the Chile's Pepper Restaurant. I have known Tony since 1985 and I always go there for his Shrimp Special. My wife loves his fish. It is a family-owned restaurant that provides that something extra. It has, by far, the best red salsa in Mazatlán. The view of the sunset is breathtaking.

La Casa Country: This popular place is located on Av. Camarón Sábalo in the Golden Zone. They specialize in beef, but have a wide-ranging menu that includes Mexican dishes, seafood, barbecue ribs, chicken and pork chops. I prefer the petite filet mignon with breaded shrimp. It is served with a baked potato and mixed vegetables. They serve a warmed and spicy refried bean dip with the tortilla chips that is the best I have ever tasted.

The dining room has a lot of wood including the rails and huge beams in the ceiling. There is no question that it is a country western motif, and the waiters all wear *vaquero* – cowboy – hats. It is a fun place with country western and Mexican "canned" music. Every night at 7:30 P.M. there is a short show and dancing to country western music. It can get noisy in the evening, so don't expect to hold many conversations.

Los Arcos: Located just north of the El Cid Resort complex on Av. Camarón Sábalo. My choice for the best shrimp deals in town. For a change of pace, try the Hawaiian shrimp. Nice canned music, good service and excellent food. Many locals eat at Los Arcos.

Ernie Tomato's: Ernie Tomato's is located where Señor Peppers used to be on the northern edge of the Golden Zone, more or less across the street from the hotel Pueblo Bonito Mazatlán, but before you get to Space Bowling.

If you like salads, this is the place for you. I tried fried green tomatoes there for the first time, and now I order them with every meal. The place is usually crowded with a lively group of customers. I have never been there when I didn't enjoy the music—and I'm a self-proclaimed "fuddy duddy".

Terraza Playa: Is the large patio restaurant that is inside the Hotel Playa Mazatlán. The oldest hotel in the Golden Zone, many of the waiters have  been there for many years. Service is consistently good and the food even better. Try the surf and turf, which is jumbo shrimp and juicy filet mignon brought to your table flaming on a sword. Sunday brunch is a favorite for many of the locals.

Pedro y Lola: This popular restaurant is located in El Centro Histórico, right across from the northeast corner of the beautiful Plazuela Machado. They specialize in Mexican dishes, but I have had delicious steaks there, and my wife loves the chicken. Both indoor and outdoor seating is available with live musical entertainment every night. Enjoy a delicious meal at tables set up outside on the wide sidewalk while watching the activities on the plaza. I recommend that you call 981-0111 for dinner reservations on Friday or Saturday evenings during the tourist season.

Casa Loma: I went to Casa Loma the first time several years ago. I didn't know where it was located, but when the taxi driver started going into a residential area I must admit I got a little nervous. Off the beaten track, Casa Loma has beautiful Italian/Spanish style courtyard seating as well as a room with fabulous elegant Spanish/French décor inside. Each time I'm there I notice Ramón, the manager, going to every table to ask if everything is okay. They have an excellent assortment of food, period. I like the pasta. My wife and I have enjoyed an excellent meal of sharing a house salad and each ordering tortilla soup. You will experience a classy dining experience. Although it is on Av. Gaviotas, about six blocks east of Av. Camarón Sábalo in the Golden Zone, I suggest that you take a taxi or *pulmonía*.

Villa Italia: It is adjacent to the El Cid housing complex and right on Camarón Sábalo, across from Senor Frog's. If you like pizza, you'll love their pizza that is baked in a wood-burning oven. Every time I go in there I promise myself I will try something new, but

I invariably order the pizza with pepperoni and shrimp. The best I have ever tasted!

Vittore: This long-established Italian restaurant is located on Av. Playa Gaviotas, across the street from the Ramada hotel. It has Mediterranean decor with both indoor and outdoor seating and soft mood music. They have a large menu of Italian dishes and some excellent fish dishes. Their house salad is exceptional. But if you go you must try their wood-oven baked pizza.

La Puntilla: When you tire of the places in the Golden Zone and El Centro, try this place down by the Navy base, next to the main Stone Island ferry dock. It is all outside seating with a beautiful view of the harbor entrance. They specialize in seafood and have an excellent breakfast buffet daily.

I am a shrimp lover and found something called a shrimp hamburger. It has no beef, but large shrimp rolled together with bacon, served on a bun with pickles, lettuce and tomatoes—outstanding! Occasionally a mariachi band passes through to add some nice sounds. Tel: 982-8877. They close at 8 P.M. so get there early.

Al Agua: Owned by the same people that own La Puntilla, the menu is basically the same offerings of primarily shrimp, but a nice offering of fish, octopus and oysters. Al Agua is adjacent to and south of the El Cid towers—with an entrance on Camarón Sábalo and another right on the beach. There is plenty of free parking. It has a large straw and bamboo roof, with mostly indoor, but some outdoor seating. A great place to sit and watch the beautiful Mazatlán sunset.

Costa de Oro restaurant: Well-placed, on the beach side of the Hotel Costa de Oro in the Golden Zone, just south of The Inn at Mazatlán. It is one of the few places in the Golden Zone where you can eat and enjoy people-watching without being bothered by beach vendors. The outside eating area is about 10 yards above the beach. I order the shrimp omelet for either breakfast or lunch. They also have great Mexican dishes and the best *chilaquiles* in town.

Diego's Beach House: Is half a block off Camarón Sábalo in the Golden Zone, between the Oceana Palace hotel and La Costa Marinera Restaurant. It is owned and operated by acclaimed chef and TV personality Diego Becerra. There are three seating areas: right on the beach, a dining area and near the bar. It has a tropical ambience and is a great place for picture-taking. They advertise that it was not created to be a sophisticated dining experience, but a fun place to be. The menu is what everyone else has, but the preparation and service stands out. This is another place that specializes in barbecued ribs. Call them at 986-1816 for information and reservations.

La Costa Marinera: This fun place is a must! If you are celebrating a birthday, wedding or anniversary, tell the waiter and he will see that you are serenaded with a beautiful Mexican song. A wonderful mariachi band plays every night. Don't miss their favorite singing waiter—Ernesto—but be careful, as he may put the mic in your face to help him with a song. They specialize in seafood, but also have excellent Mexican dishes, beef and chicken. Try the seafood platter for two, served in a very large heated bowl. Located a block off Camarón Sábalo, just north of Oceano Palace hotel, they have covered seating right on the beach as well as indoor seating. Tel: 914-1928.

Pancho's restaurant (south): Arguably one of the most popular restaurants in Mazatlán. I have never been to Pancho's when it was not crowded. It has a large menu. Literally, the bilingual menu covers about half a four-person table! They have a wide range of selections with all the usual Mexican dishes, chicken, beef, seafood and even the pork chops are excellent. Located at the beach end of the shopping center across the street from Sea Shell City in the heart of the Golden Zone, the two-story restaurant has a Mexican atmosphere, with seating right on the beach.

Pancho's restaurant (north): This restaurant is another Pancho's, opened in 2011 on Camarón Sábalo across from Pueblo Bonito Mazatlán. The menu is about the same and it has both outdoor and indoor seating, upstairs and downstairs. The decor is very Mexican. The service is every bit as good as the original Pancho's restaurant.

Los Zarapes: If you can't have fun at this restaurant you don't have a pulse. Located in the Golden Zone, across the street from the Oceano Palace hotel, they have live music and dancing nightly. If you don't like that, ask Luis, one of the owners, to provide a little magic show. He performs like a professional. The food is superb and the salsa, prepared at the table, is delicious. It is hard to decide which is the best—Mexican, seafood, chicken or beef. It is all good, and well-prepared and presented.

The Water's Edge: This spectacular little restaurant is in the hotel Casa Lucila in Olas Altos, across the street from the Pedro Infante monument. This is the most luxurious eating establishment in Olas Altas, but the prices don't reflect that. While there is a large indoor dining room, the view is spectacular from the front patio, especially for sunset and at night.

The Water's Edge is open from 7 A.M. to 10 P.M., while serving breakfast from 7–12, and lunch and dinner from 12–10 P.M. While the lunch/dinner menu is somewhat limited, there is enough variety to serve the most discerning diner. I thoroughly enjoyed the Bean and Rice Bowl while my wife raved about the Penne Regate.

The wine list is large and extensive. Go to their website at *thewaters edgemaz.com* for more information.

Inexpensive

Panama Bakery/Restaurant: Meet your friends for lunch on Camarón Sábalo, in the Golden Zone, at Panama! Don't try to go there between from 9:00 A.M. to noon on Sunday as the place is usually packed. They have excellent American breakfasts and delicious Mexican lunch entrees. To help you choose, they make sample dishes and set them by the front door and also put pictures of the dishes on the walls. I'm not a cupcake eater, but my friends rave about the pastries—and they will also bake a cake to order. They serve excellent French toast. My friend Sherry claims the "divorced" eggs are to die for. There are many Panama restaurants around Mazatlán; in the downtown area, there is one about two blocks south of the Central Mercado on Benito Juárez, going south.

El Canucks de León: This is the former Canucks restaurant across from the Malecón in Olas Altas, a block up the hill north of the Shrimp Bucket. Like many restaurants in El Centro Histórico, it is frequented by many nationals but is still popular with expats. It has a varied menu with delicious Mexican food, seafood and beef. They are usually open for dinner and have live music almost every night.

La Bahia: This seafood restaurant, established in 1950, is at Mariano Escobedo #203, about a block from Olas Altas in the courtyard of an old colonial home. Beautifully prepared seafood, including shrimp, oysters, mahi-mahi, snapper, squid and octopus, is cooked to your taste. Try the grilled mahi-mahi or their famous *ceviche.*

Most menu items cost $8 to $13 and include vegetables, rice and salad. Tel: 981-5645.

Molika Bakery: Don't be fooled by the name. It is not only a place that makes wonderful baked goods, but a restaurant as well. The stylish bistro is at Belisario Dominguez #1503, about a block from the Plazuela Machado. They specialize in sandwiches made from their delicious homemade breads, but the menu also offers pastas, quiche, fish, prawns, beef, pork, soup, salads and more. You can order breads or pastries, and I recommend that you call them at 981-1577 or email them at *molikabakery@gmail.com* a day in advance.

The Saloon: This sports bar was taken over by a couple of Canadian women a few years ago and has fast become a very popular watering hole and hang-out for sports nuts and music-lovers. They have eight HDTV sets, music three nights a week, wonderful food and superb service. Customers can bring their laptop and use the free WiFi or phone to call anywhere in the world free of charge. They are open from 11 A.M. to 11 P.M. daily.

Twisted Mama's restaurant and bar: This restaurant is one of the best-kept secrets in Mazatlán. While the menu is limited, the most expensive items are fish and chips and shrimp and chips at about $10–$11 U.S.. They have specials at a slightly greater cost every night except Friday. The beer-battered fish and chips are the best I've tasted in Mazatlán, as is the coleslaw. They have a wonderful dessert called jalapeño apple crisp that is tangy and delicious. They serve breakfast, lunch and dinner. This restaurant, with both indoor and outdoor seating, is owned by a Canadian and is a bit hard to find. It is on Laguna Street in the middle of the Golden Zone. The best directions are to walk west from the Panama Restaurant, past Jungle Juice and take a right at Laguna—Twisted Mama's is across the street. Her cell phone number is 044-669-912-9201. There is live musical entertainment almost every night.

Hola De Bola, Saigon Sandwiches: Yep, a Vietnamese restaurant in the Golden Zone. It is located two doors north of the Señor Frogs outlet store, across the street from the Dairy Queen on Camarón Sábalo. They feature a large assortment of sandwiches with buns that are delicious. They also offer several types of fruit drinks. But the inexpensive Vietnamese dishes are superb. I had pineapple fried rice, which was pork and shrimp fried rice in a hollowed out half-pineapple. It is special! There is indoor and outside, upstairs and downstairs seating. They are open from 10 A.M. to 10 P.M. and have WiFi too. Check out their website at *www.holadebola.com.*

Jungle Juice: It is on the corner just west of Panama Restaurant in the heart of the Golden Zone. I have been going there since 1985. They have everyday specials of *carne asada* and fried whole or filet of fish that include salad, beans and rice, tortillas and a pitcher of *agua fresca* (flavored water of *tamarindo, horchata* or *jamaica*) for $5. Also, seven fine breaded shrimp with the above additions for $6 Several vegetarian dishes are included in their menu. They have an all-inclusive breakfast from 8–10 A.M. for $3.40 Try the hot cakes. It is a fun place to go with a great atmosphere.

El Bambu: It is between the La Gran Plaza mall and Sam's Club, about two blocks from Valentino's. Menu averages $8–14 and specializes in charbroiled steaks. It has both indoor and outdoor seating and a large staff that will cater to all your needs. Many locals frequent this establishment.

Carlos-Lucia's restaurant: This is another restaurant bar and grill, but features Cuban food as well as the usual Mexican cuisine. The owner offers inexpensive beer and margaritas to die for. They have indoor and outdoor seating and parking in the rear—which is important for a restaurant located on Camarón Sábalo, across from The Palms resort (previously the Holiday Inn) in the Golden Zone.

Beach Burger: A casual place on the Plazuela Machado, is best known for its delicious, huge (½ pound) burgers. The basic is a cheeseburger. There also are burgers with mushrooms, bacon or teriyaki sauce. All are served with choice of fries, coleslaw or potato salad and cost less than $7. The BBQ ribs are very good, and there are steaks, shrimp, snacks like fish fingers, chicken fingers, sandwiches and desserts. A bottle of beer is less than $1.50. Sit at one of the umbrella-shaded tables and watch life in the Plazuela.

El Aljibe de San Pedro restaurant: It is a newly re-opened restaurant in El Centro Histórico. It is located at *calle* Constitución #710, about one and a half blocks east of the Plazuala Machado—a half block east of the Topolo Restaurant. They serve Mexican food, spaghetti, steaks, fish, chicken and soups and salads. They have a generous wine selection as well. Service was excellent and food presentation is good.

What is unique is that the restaurant is that it is in a 150-year-old, 500,000 liter cement and brick water tank! The decor is what I call "old junk" and my wife calls "antique". Seriously, it is very tastefully decorated with antique items on the walls as well as some beautiful paintings. There are even old musical instruments on the ceiling.

Il Mosto: is located across from the southwest corner of the Plazuela Machado in El Centro Histórico. There is indoor and outdoor seating under umbrellas, like every place on the Plazuela, but you will want to sit outside and enjoy whatever is going on in the Plazuela while you dine. The owner, Apostolis, is a Greek/Italian immigrant and the menu reflects his heritage. The food (Mediterranean, not Mexican) and service are great. The atmosphere is a little more European than Mexican and the service a tiny bit more formal than most places around the Plazuela. There is music at night, mostly violins, and is kind of romantic. You will be served the house-made olive bread and olive spread when you arrive.

The appetizers are so good you can make a meal from them, especially if you have a group of 4–5 people. Try the fried calamari, eggplant or the mushrooms! Main courses include fish, beef, chicken, shellfish and lots of pasta dishes. Friends rave about the lasagna, which I have not tried. If they have it, be sure to try the mango flambé for dessert. It is wonderful!

The Place (**El Paraje**): This quaint little sidewalk café is a very inexpensive and popular place for tourists. They serve wonderful American-type meals for breakfast and lunch and specialize in Mexican food for dinner. They are located on Camarón Sábalo just north of the Oceano Palace hotel in the Golden Zone. They have a large area in the rear, with dance floor, bar, and pool table and a small indoor eating area.

Zab Thai restaurant: With a name like that you would expect Thai and Chinese food, right? Well it's true and both are excellent. For you folks that say you can't get good Chinese food in Mazatlán, you have to check this place out. It is located on Camarón Sábalo at the back of the little strip mall at the Pemex station near McDonald's. It is relatively small with little atmosphere, but it is clean and the food is wonderful. Some people avoid Thai food because it is spicy ("hot"!), but they aim to please and will temper the spice to order. They have all large portions and are delicious. The prices are reasonable as our meal cost about $9 per person. They have carry-out and delivery service too. Tel: 986-6343.

La Cueva del Leon: This is one of a row of favorite restaurants in Olas Altas. It does not have much décor of note, but good service and excellent food make up for it. It has a large indoor seating area and a nice, newly expanded, outdoor eating area. They specialize in Mexican dishes but have very unique ways of preparing shrimp, fish, chicken and beef. They also have a large variety of cocktails and of course beer and wine.

El Faro restaurant: Much like Cueva Del Leon, this quaint café in Olas Altas specializes in Mexican food and is very popular with expats in El Centro. They prepare many varieties of shrimp, fish, and beef dishes. You can even catch a traveling local guitarist singing and playing familiar Mexican songs. Stop by at lunch time for a great hamburger and fries. I've found the service here to be exceptional.

Copa de Leche: An old favorite facing the ocean at Olas Altas #1220. Indoor and outdoor seating, with friendly service and consistently good food. A variety of scrumptious entrees range from $4.50 to $13. Try the filet mignon and ask for baked potato and vegetable. There is karaoke and other live music in the evenings. They are open for breakfast, lunch and dinner, and can be contacted at 982-5753.

Super Cocina D'Paulina: This marvelous little café is located on Sixto Osuna, about two blocks from the Malecón in Olas Altas. There are a few tables out front on the sidewalk, but most of the seating is inside the rustic old building. They have traditional Mexican breakfasts as well as eggs, hot cakes and French toast. In the evenings you can order outstanding BBQ ribs, steak and chicken. They also have "super" shrimp dishes for $12–13. A large variety of smoothies are also available. The service is outstanding. On Fridays between 1–5 P.M. they have a special of soup, main dish (house-selected, but a variety available), soft drink and dessert for less than $5.

Pizza Moreno: The bad fortune of El Centro was the good fortune of the Golden Zone when Pizza Moreno moved to Camarón Sábalo #3001 in Sábalo County, just north of the Fiesta Inn and cattycorner from the OXXO. There is a small dining room and outside counters. Although their menu is limited, with salads, lasagna and spaghetti, their specialty is pizza. They still deliver anywhere in the city and you can order by phone at 985-5863 or cellular 044-669-993-5373.

Roy's restaurant: They are located in the strip mall at Cerritos and have lots of both indoor and outdoor seating. They serve lunch and dinner and have terrific coconut shrimp and other seafood. Roy's has a special steak night on Thursdays and ribs special on Sunday night. There is usually live music. Cell: 044-669-150-8779.

The Last Drop: This is another of those sports bar and restaurants that are becoming popular in Mazatlán. Located in Cerritos near Roy's at the end of the bus line. They feature delicious hamburgers and BBQ ribs. In addition to several TVs for sports they have live music many nights during the week. And if you're up for billiards, this is the place for you. Tel: 988-1111 for reservations.

Even less expensive—with atmosphere

El Chilito restaurant: This little restaurant in the heart of the Golden Zone also has a bar. The small, family-owned eatery boasts strictly Mexican food, yet has hot cakes and eggs for breakfast and sandwiches and soups for lunch. The most expensive item on the menu, Imperial Shrimp, is less than $10. Most items are less than

$8. My wife had enchiladas and raved about them. It is located on Camarón Sábalo, across the street from Royal Villas Resort. Open from 7:30 A.M. to 9:00 P.M.

Mary's: It is next to Rico's Coffee Shop across from The Inn at Mazatlán in the Golden Zone. Excellent sandwiches, such as patty melt, cheeseburger, Hawaiian burger, fried chicken breast, my favorite, the Philly cheese steak, and others, for about $6.25. They have onion rings and French fries, plus great salads as well, chicken, turkey and ham. All seating is outdoors and everything is available to-go. They also have a terrific breakfast menu. Call 913-0900 for reservations or home delivery.

Juanita's: A small sidewalk cafe across the street from the Oceano Palace hotel on Camarón Sábalo. She specializes in home-style Mexican food. My favorite is the special Mexican plate at about $5. She has American dishes of fish, shrimp, beef and chicken. The lunch menu includes a wide assortment of sandwiches. It has to be good because many beach vendors and taxi drivers eat there. You can have the same *comida corrida* (Mexican-style "blue plate special" type meals) they eat, but you must ask because it is not on the menu.

Las Brochetas: An outdoor café on Av. Rafael Buelna, east of Valentino's. After careful consideration, we chose the rib eye steaks served with baked potato and small salad. Absolutely delicious! The baked potato is a meal in itself. Las Brochetas is open Tuesday through Sunday, roughly noon till midnight. It is another of Mazatlán's well-kept secrets.

El Guamuchilito: This seafood restaurant, located on Insurgentes at the first stoplight east of the Malecón, is very popular with local residents. It offers a varied menu of fresh and well-prepared seafood, including *ceviches, zarandeado* (grilled whole fish), tacos and empanadas, shrimp paté, filets and seafood cocktails. Prices range from $4 to $10 per entrée. It is a warehouse-like space with a concrete floor, white plastic Coca-Cola chairs and tables, steel bars for walls and sliding doors, but everything is clean and well maintained. There are several other locations around town. Contact them by calling 986-6691.

Cocina de Ana: It is located in the Golden Zone behind the Banamex bank. While they specialize in Mexican food, they also have daily specials. Believe it or not, they have some of the best Chinese food in town. The food is sold by weight, so the average lunch is about $3.50–$4.

Lety's Restaurant: In my opinion a trip to Stone Island is not complete unless you stop at Lety's and try anything on the menu. It is a family restaurant that specializes in seafood and good service to customers. It is literally right on the beach, so it's a wonderful place for people-watching as well. You can sit in the beach chairs and be pampered by the waiters all day.

Really inexpensive, with character:

Several people have asked me for these types of places, so I asked my friends Dee Hulen and Lloyd Bodrack, who live in the downtown area, to do some research, and they came up with some real dandies.

Taqueria Martín: One of the best and most popular *taquerias* – taco restaurants – in town. It is large, very clean and well-maintained. A generously-filled taco with grilled onions on the side and choice of toppings is $.60, a quesadilla $1.20, and orders of *carne asada* – grilled beef – are $3–4. Fresh tortillas are continuously made on the premises. They are located on Av. Gutiérrez Najera, across from the

Juan Carrasco Mercado, about two blocks east of the Fisherman's Monument.

La Fondita: Is a tiny place located on Mariano Escobedo just off *calle* Aquilles Serdan, around the corner from Edgar's Bar, 4 blocks south of the Central Mercado. They serve breakfast and *comida corrida* from 9 A.M. to 4 P.M. daily except Sunday. The restaurant is usually crowded around 2 P.M. The daily *comida corrida* costs less than $3 and you have a choice of entrees (from about 15), plus soup, beans, rice and tortillas. Soft drinks are extra. I thought my *chile relleno* was very good, and so were the beef ribs in a rich, but mild, chile sauce. No one there spoke English, but the menu choices are printed on a chalk board.

Central Mercado: You will no doubt have an occasion to visit the Central Mercado, if only to look at the pigs' heads, the beautiful produce and all the other things for sale. No address is necessary as it is at the heart of El Centro. What many don't notice is that the second floor is surrounded by small, clean restaurants serving good, inexpensive food. The daily *comida corrida* is just over $2.50 and includes the main dish, rice, beans and sometimes beverage and dessert. The menus are about the same at all the places, and they look identical so take your pick. Nothing fancy here, just a lot of food for your *peso.* You can sit inside or on the little balcony overlooking the busy street.

Ceviche Cuate: It is located at Guillermo Nelson and Melchor Ocampo, one block west of the Central Mercado in El Centro. It is a very small place where you get a big dish of several types of *ceviche* for less than $2.50. Drinks are extra. *Jamaica* is about $.45 and a Coke about $.75

Specialty Restaurants

Puravida: If you like healthy, natural food and delicious smoothies, this is the place for you. They specialize in fresh fruit drinks that are not watered down. This is a favorite of locals and tourists who happen to stumble across it. The name means "pure life" in Spanish, and the food is purely delicious. They have vegetarian meals also. They are just up the street from the Hotel Playa Mazatlán, on *calle* Bugamvilias. They have special prices for children under 12 for lunch and breakfast. Overall, their prices are very reasonable.

Allegro Café: If you are a lover of gourmet coffee you have to try this place. The address is Camarón Sábalo #336, across the street from the Bancomer bank in the Golden Zone. There is both indoor and outdoor seating. I'm not a big fan of expensive, flavored coffee, but my wife, who is, says this place is "something special". As a people-watcher, I noticed there is a lot of foot traffic that passes by. They also have wonderful breakfasts and sandwiches, pastries, cakes, cookies and herbal teas. Tel: 913-0080.

Rico's Café: This is not just another coffee shop. Located on Camarón Sábalo, across the street from The Inn at Mazatlán, Rico's has Mexican coffee as good as Starbuck's but at not quite the cost. They have outside seating for people-watching while sipping a brew, and WiFi is available. They have a large breakfast menu that is available all day. Fresh homemade pastry is featured every day. Another unique feature is live music in the evening, Thursday through Saturday. This place is always busy. Tel: 913-1444. There is also another Rico's at the new Marina near the Pemex station.

Looney Bean: There is one in Cerritos at the end of the road and another in Olas Altas. The one in Cerritos is at the end of the bus line in the little strip mall. Owned by a California couple, Tom and Heidi Lonsdale, they specialize in all kinds of coffee and espresso drinks. They also have an assortment of delicious fresh fruit smoothies, bagels, oatmeal, healthy homemade muffins and some interesting hot breakfasts. Both places have beautiful rock wall décor, and are a must-see.

Starbuck's: Yes, Mazatlán has a place for the "Starbuck snobs". It is located on Av. Lomas de Mazatlán just off of Camarón Sábalo and right behind the HSBC bank on the corner, sharing the parking lot with Burger King in the Golden Zone. They have all the Seattle types of coffee as well as delicious pastry with both indoor and outdoor seating.

Pasteleria Gladys: This is a bakery that sells delicious bakery products including cakes, muffins, scones, croissants, cookies, quiche, empanadas and others. Telephone them at 044-669-116-4640 to see what is available and where it is to be delivered. Every Sunday morning from 8 A.M. to 12 P.M. they set up tables just inside La Viña Church and sell their pastries with the profits going to the church. All other profits of the bakery go to Douglas Rogers' Abandoned Children program, which is now administered by the La Viña Church.

A very special treat is to stop at a coconut stand and have the vendor open a coconut with a machete. Drink the milk through a straw, and then have the coconut cut into pieces. The delicious fruit inside tastes even better by adding salt, lime and salsa to your satisfaction. Yum!

Like in the States and Canada, there are restaurants to fit everyone's taste. One of my favorite pastimes in Mazatlán is checking out new restaurants. I'm not disappointed very often.

Chapter 8

Getting around Mazatlán

MAZATLÁN IS A BIG CITY, but getting around is easier than in most large metropolitan cities throughout the world. First, I'll tell you what I would not do in Mazatlán. With apologies to car rental agencies, I would not rent a car. "Why not?" you're thinking. Because there are so many better ways to get around Mazatlán, and you do not have to learn the Mexican traffic laws. But if you insist, here is a listing of car rental agencies in the city, and all are located on Camarón Sábalo:

Advantage	984-1700
AGA	914-4405
Alamo	913-1010
Avis	954-8146
Budget	913-2000
Dollar	984-1700
Europcar	989-0525
Hertz	913-6060
National	913-6000

My basic belief is the same whether I am in Seattle, San Francisco or Mazatlán. If I am in a hurry, I take a taxi, and if I'm not, I take a bus. Besides this, parking can be a nightmare in Mazatlán.

Buses

My choice in travel throughout Mazatlán, unless I am in a hurry, is the bus. The price is right—about $.45 on the older buses and $.80 on the newer, larger, air-conditioned buses called Sábalo Centro and Cocos Juárez.

Try to have as close to the exact change as possible—and certainly don't try to change a 100 peso note on the bus. Remember, the driver is jockeying a huge vehicle through traffic while trying to make change. The driver gets to keep 20% of the fares with the owner receiving the other 80%. When you pay the fare, the driver will give you a small piece of paper. Keep that ticket in your hand until you get off the bus because the owners' union inspectors sometimes board busses and spot-check. It lets them know that the driver is not trying to cheat them. There is not a transfer system in Mazatlán, so if you have to take two buses, you pay full fare for each.

Another convenience is that while some bus stops are designated, if you just stand on the curb and wave at a bus, it will usually stop, unless it is full or the driver decides it is too dangerous to stop. On some routes there are set bus stops and the driver will not stop except at those stops. Just look up and down the street for a bus stop or where people appear to be standing waiting.

The Sábalo Centro bus is the most popular for tourists and expats and runs from the extreme north at Cerritos south through the downtown area. If you want to go anywhere within the Golden Zone, just jump on any bus. Unless you like to ride on buses, or would like to go to various places in the city to look around, when in doubt, ask the driver if he is going where you want to go.

Here is a listing of the routes and places the buses go from the Golden Zone, heading south (in some cases you may have to walk two to three blocks):

Sábalo Centro

Cerritos point

Around the new Marina

Through the Golden Zone to the Malecón

Aquarium – one block east of the bus route

Fisherman's Monument

Central Mercado

Cathedral – one block west of the bus route.

Plazuela Machado – two blocks west of the bus route, as is the…

Ángela Peralta Theater

Stone Island *lancha* dock – **may** be a couple of blocks east of the
bus route (which sometimes varies slightly near the end).

The end of the line is near the cruise ship, La Paz ferry and Stone Island *lancha* docks. Then you can catch the return bus (but you have to pay another fare), and in minutes it will go through Olas Altas, then back through El Centro, past the Central Mercado and on to the Malecón, then north to Cerritos point.

Cerritos Juárez

Cerritos point

Around the new Marina

Through the Golden Zone to Valentino's

Left on Rafael Buelna past the Mega supermarket

Right past Sam's Club

La Gran Plaza shopping mall

estadio Teodoro Mariscal (baseball stadium) – about 2 blocks
south of where the bus turns left onto Insurgentes.

Soriana supermarket on Insurgentes

TelMex office

On to *colonia* Juárez

The end of the line is right behind/beside the Café El Marino plant.

Cocos Juárez
Right in front of the Pueblo Bonito Mazatlán resort
Through the Golden Zone to Valentino's
Left on Rafael Buelna past the...
Mega supermarket
Polimedica building and Sharp Hospital
Office Depot
Soriana supermarket on Rafael Buelna across from...
Home Depot
Ley #2 supermarket (Plaza del Mar)
Wal-Mart
Left at Insurgentes, then past...
Soriana supermarket on Insurgentes
TelMex office and on to ...
colonia Juárez

The end of the line is right behind/beside the Café El Marino plant.

Sábalo Cocos
Right in front of the Pueblo Bonito Mazatlán resort
Through the Golden Zone to Valentino's
Left on Rafael Buelna past the...
Mega supermarket
Polimedica building and Sharp Hospital
Office Depot
Soriana supermarket on Rafael Buelna across from...
Home Depot
Ley #2 supermarket (Plaza del Mar)
Wal-Mart

Central de Autobuses(or Camionera) – the main intercity bus depot.

Ley #1 supermarket (Plaza Ley)

Central Mercado

Cathedral – one block west of the bus route

Plazuela Machado – two blocks west of the bus route, as is the...

Ángela Peralta Theater

Stone Island *lancha* dock – **may** be a couple of blocks east of the bus route (which sometimes varies slightly near the end).

The end of the line is near the cruise ship, La Paz ferry and Stone Island *lancha* docks.

Urias Sábalo

Hotel El Cid Marina

Golden Zone to Valentino's

Mega supermarket

Polimedica building and Sharp Hospital

Office Depot

Soriana supermarket across from...

Home Depot

Since the end of the line is far, far away from anything of interest, out on the highway to the airport, visitors should get off at Home Depot.

Playa Sur and El Toreo

Cerritos point

south to the new Marina, then left to the...

Soriana supermarket across from...

Home Depot

Office Depot

Polimedica building and Sharp Hospital
Mega supermarket
Sam's Club
La Gran Plaza
estadio Teodoro Mariscal (baseball stadium)
Aquarium
Ley #1 supermarket (Plaza Ley)
Central Mercado
Stone Island *lancha* dock to the end of the line at the...
Lighthouse

Taxis: The air-conditioned green and white and red and white taxis will take you anywhere in Mazatlán for $2 up to $15 depending on distance and whether it is day or night. They are sedans, small station wagons, and yes, there are even covered pick-up trucks that I have

seen filled with partying tourists as well as families, although those are called *aurigas*. Always negotiate the fare before accepting the ride.

Stop at the front desk of your hotel and ask what is a fair taxi price from the hotel to where you want to go. Some resorts have the taxi fares posted on the wall near the reception desk. As I mentioned earlier, don't tip the driver unless you ask him to make a stop along the way or he provides some other service, such as carrying your bags to the hotel. Remember that the price of taxis increases when bus service ends, and during Carnaval and Holy Week. Ever hear of "the law of supply and demand"?

Pulmonías: These customized, open-air VWs can be seen scurrying around town all hours of the night and day. Unique to Mazatlán, these little vehicles not found else-where in Mexico, as they are a regis-tered trademark for the owners' union in Mazatlán. They are supposed to hold three to four passengers, but most drivers will attempt to accommodate more if you ask. Be sure to negotiate the price prior to entering.

The cute little vehicles with low-powered engines and high-powered amplifiers usually cost a little more than the taxis and provide the thrill of the wind in your hair and absolutely no protection in an accident, BUT, since they rarely exceed 25 mph, the rare accident is usually just a "fender bender". The drivers always seem to weave in and out of traffic like madmen, but I have never actually witnessed an accident. Generally, I take the *pulmonía* when I want to feel the wind in my face. We take the taxi when my wife does not want to feel the wind in her hair.

Tour van drivers: When I have had a large number of friends visit-ing, and would like to take them on a tour of the city or country I always hire a van driver. They are excellent drivers, know the tour business, and are willing to deviate from the regular tour upon request. The company I prefer is Mazatlán's Tour Guide Association, on *calle* Laguna in the Golden Zone. They have air-conditioned vans that accommodate up to 10 passengers. Rates for half-day tours (three–four hours) are $150 and $180 for a full day. They also have a special for two people: $36 for a three- to four-hour city tour. The telephone number is 916-5714, or email, *tourguides@mazatlan.com.mx.*

I have used three or four drivers and my personal favorite is Jesús A. Osuna. One day I asked him to take my group to a cockfighting ranch. I didn't know the name of the place, but knew it was north of Mazatlán. Jesús told me he had never been there before, but he would find out the name. The next day he and his wife took a "test drive". Two days later, he took my group on a spectacular tour of the cockfighting ranch and cheese factories in El Quelite. Contact him personally by calling 983-2196. He will take you on a regular tour, or personalize a trip at your request, and I've found his rates to be the best.

Chapter 9

Staying Healthy

Staying healthy in Mazatlán can best be accomplished by using common sense. Standards of sanitation in the city are high compared to many other places in the world. Most people coming to Mazatlán are concerned about food or water sources. Accidents while swimming, boating or falling are more likely to occur than problems with food or water.

Food and Water

Moderation is the key word. Mexican food is heavy and spicy compared to U.S. and Canadian food. If you gorge yourself with rich Mexican food, pitchers of strong Mexican beer and margaritas, you can count on problems. Although many of my colleagues who live in Mazatlán year-round ingest food from street or beach vendors without having health problems, I don't recommend it. My primary reason is the **sometimes** unsanitary food-handling conditions that are evident if I see no place near the vendor for periodic hand-washing. As in traveling anyplace else in the world, I recommend frequent hand-washing.

Only purified drinking water and ice is served in hotels and restaurants. So please don't embarrass yourself or friends by asking if the water or ice is purified. Most grocery stores sell bottled water, water purification tablets and iodine crystals to those of you that may be backpacking in the area.

"Turista" or Montezuma's revenge

When people travel to a foreign country they may undergo a period of adjustment to the new gastrointestinal flora in the area they are visiting. There is no way to prepare for this unpleasant occurrence. This may affect some people and not others. Mexican doctors call this *"turista"* because it affects tourists, but not the local population. The symptoms of turista are nausea, fever, diarrhea and sometimes stomach cramps. Remember that eating and drinking in moderation will help to prevent the worst of the symptoms, which rarely last more than a day or two. If it's any consolation, I have been told by Mexican friends that they suffered the same symptoms while traveling in the U.S.

If you come down with a case of turista, the best thing to do is drink plenty of fluids to replace those lost. Do not drink tea, coffee, milk, fruit juices or any alcoholic beverages. Eat only bland foods. I don't have to tell you to get plenty of rest, because that is all you will feel like doing between making trips to the bathroom. Pepto-Bismol or other peptic-based remedies usually help. None of this is a cure. Only time will cure traveler's diarrhea. If symptoms persist, see a doctor. Most hotels have doctors on-call, and they usually make house calls.

I use a preventative method when traveling to foreign countries. I usually take the prescribed amount of Pepto-Bismol for the first four days in country. It works for me.

Sunburn

It's my guess that sunburn affects more Mazatlán visitors than all illnesses and accidents combined. The nice warm sunshine and cool ocean breezes will lull you into a false sense of comfort. I have witnessed fair-skinned tourists get severe sunburn from just two to three hours in the sun. Rare cloudy days do not protect your skin from the sun.

Bring along a sunscreen with a sun protection factor of at least 25—and use it. Apply it to all exposed parts of your body—head to toe. I mention that because sunburned heads and feet are especially uncomfortable because your hair must be combed and or brushed, and shoes worn. My warnings to visiting friends and relatives to wear hats and apply sunscreen to bald heads have been mostly unheeded, with uncomfortable results. Even though the sunscreen bottle may say that the contents are waterproof, don't take any chances. Apply sunscreen before and after swimming.

If you go fishing or on an excursion in a boat, bring along not only plenty of sunscreen, but a pair of long pants and a long-sleeve shirt. You never know how long you will be out on the ocean. Engine failure or bad weather could cause delays.

Dehydration

Perspiration causes body water loss, so it is important to replace fluids by drinking plenty of water. Consume at least eight, 8-ounce glasses per day—more if you perspire excessively. No, all those cervezas and margaritas will not help keep you from becoming dehydrated. Neither will coffee, iced tea or cola with caffeine. In fact, they will all increase your potential for dehydration.

Symptoms of dehydration include urine that is much darker than usual and/or difficulty urinating, flushed face, profuse sweating or an unusual lack thereof. Sometimes these symptoms also occur: headache, dizziness and feeling of malaise.

If dehydration occurs, get the victim out of the sun right away and cover him/her in a wet sheet or towel. Get fluids into them slowly and continuously. Depending on the size of the patient, up to six liters may be necessary to regain normalcy. There are several home remedies, but water or the new electrolytic drinks such as Pedialyte (commonly available in every *farmacia* in Mazatlán), are the best.

Motion sickness

If you have little or no boating experience and you go on a fishing trip or boat excursion in the ocean, you may suffer from motion sickness. The repeated rolling and rocking of the boat affects an individual's equilibrium. The smell of diesel or gasoline fumes can add to the motion or seasickness. Further, the sight or smell of the vomit from a victim may cause a chain reaction among other guests.

Don't let seasickness spoil your trip. Take preventative measures to avoid motion sickness. Don't eat a heavy meal prior to boarding the boat. Take the prescribed amount of Dramamine or Phenergan (Promethazine). I caution about the use of those drugs, however, as they may cause drowsiness. My wife, another couple and I took Dramamine before embarking on a jet boat trip from Seattle to Victoria. All of us slept through some of the most breath-taking scenery in the world. Motion sickness prevention patches, worn behind the ear, or wrist bracelets are effective for some people.

If you are out on the ocean and you feel seasickness coming on, resist the urge to lie down—even though drowsiness is one of the symptoms. Stay out on deck, away from engine fumes, and breathe in fresh air while focusing your eyes on the horizon. The disturbed inner ear is usually the cause of motion sickness and watching the horizon will help stabilize the inner ear.

Safety

It is always wise to travel with a companion. This includes swimming, horseback riding, shopping and even just strolling the beach and streets. If something unforeseen happens, you will always have someone to help you.

In Mazatlán the individual home or business owner is responsible for the sidewalk in front of the property they own. But, many people do not maintain their sidewalks. When walking the streets, keep your eyes down to avoid tripping over a broken sidewalk or hole. I make it a habit of stopping when I want to look around. Remember that Mexico has not become like the U.S.A. where almost everyone has a lawyer. Forget about trying to sue someone for tripping over a bad sidewalk.

Although pedestrians have the right-of-way in Mazatlán (yes, even jaywalkers), be very cautious crossing streets, as some Mexican drivers seem to ignore all traffic laws.

The vast majority of the beaches in the tourist area of Mazatlán are kept clean of broken glass. There may be times when a drunken lout may break a bottle on the beach. Accidentally stepping on the glass could ruin your vacation. Dead bees are still dangerous, as the stingers remain active and so are jellyfish washed up on the beach. I suggest that you wear sandals when walking on the beach.

Most beaches do not have lifeguards so you must beware of undertows or riptides. There is a system of colored flags to indicate ocean and swimming conditions for swimmers:

Blue or green flag indicates it is safe to swim.

Yellow flag means that conditions are uncertain so use caution.

A red flag means dangerous conditions – do not swim in that area at that time.

White flags mean there are jellyfish in the area. If a jellyfish has never stung you, you do not want to experience it.

Much has been said in the Canadian and U.S. press about the safety problems in Mexico. Mazatlán is no different than any other like-sized city in Canada or the U.S. Contrary to media reports, Mazatlán has been specifically excluded, by name, in U.S. and Canadian government travel advisories.

Alcoholic beverages

I put this section in the "Staying Healthy" chapter because too much booze causes many of the health problems encountered in Mazatlán. I'll say it again: Drinking too much booze causes many of the health problems in Mazatlán for tourists. Alcohol is relatively cheap in Mazatlán, and since you are on vacation and don't have to get up and go to work, one has a tendency to "let it all hang out". Mexico has some fine domestic alcoholic drinks if they are consumed in moderation. Be sure you understand that like anywhere else, you pay big-time for imported liquor. Since I am allergic to alcohol, I cannot provide first-hand knowledge, but I can tell you what my friends and relatives think of the local spirits.

Beer: Most Mexican breweries are run under regimented German guidelines, and are often compared on a level with European beers. There are some snowbirds, and even a few tourists that have difficulty readjusting to American brew after being hooked on the tasty Mexican beer. There are companies in Mazatlán that will deliver beer to your hotel. I have friends that have a regular weekly beer delivery service, just like the Avon lady in the U.S.

The beer of choice by most tourists is Pacifico, which has been produced in Mazatlán since the turn of the 20th century. German brewers developed this light pilsner beer. Other common brands in Mazatlán are Modelo, Negra Modelo, Tecate, Dos Equis, Carta Blanca, Indio, Bohemia and Dos Equis XX Lager Especial. With all those choices, I'm sure there is something for even the most discerning beer drinker.

Alcohol content of Mexican beers is about the same as beers in the U.S., 4.5%, except for the "Light" beers. But be careful with Negra Modelo, Noche Buena, and possibly some others, as they have a high alcohol content of nearly 6% (Mexico's legal maximum for beer—no malt liquor is brewed in Mexico). Fortunately, and differently than the U.S., all beers in Mexico are required to show the alcohol content on the label or can, so it's easy to know just what you're drinking.

Wine: Not many Mexicans drink wine, even though the country produces both red and white wine, and **some** are truly outstanding, comparable to the best American or French wines. I don't see many of my friends drinking Mexican wines. There are many imported wines available in supermarkets and liquor stores throughout the city. Chilean and Spanish wines are probably the most available of the imported wines.

Tequila and Mezcal: For tourists, tequila is as common a drink as beer. Mezcal, on the other hand, is usually purchased by the bottle and taken home as a gift. The worm at the bottom of the bottle of mezcal seems to be the main attraction. It is customary for the person who gets the last drink of the bottle of mezcal to also eat the worm. I'm told that the worm is just as tasty fried.

Tequila and mezcal are almost the same—tequila is a type of mezcal, just like scotch is a type of whisky. True, tequila is made from *agave tequiliana*, the blue agave plant, and only that grown in specific regions of Mexico, mostly in the state of Jalisco. Mezcal can be made from many different types of agave, even blue agave not grown in the approved tequila regions (very common, although hardly ever called mezcal, but just shown as being distilled from 100% blue agave). The sword-like agave (also call maguey) plants are not cacti, but big brothers of the yucca plants common in the southwest U.S. and are also related to the decorative century plants grown in the U.S. There is a mezcal distillery about 45 minutes northeast of Mazatlán near La Noria, although everyone calls it a tequila factory, even though it is not labeled as such, nor is it labeled mezcal.

Some purists without deep pockets (the best tequilas can be quite expensive) actually prefer mezcal, as it is less expensive and hardly ever diluted with grain alcohol, as the cheaper tequilas are (something allowed by the tequila law).

Oddly enough, considering all the tales of tequila inebriation, tequila and mezcal are actually milder drinks than the whiskies, brandies, gins and vodka consumed elsewhere. Those run (in the U.S.) either 40% or 50% alcohol, and tequila and mezcal here in Mexico are only 34% alcohol.

To summarize, beware of being caught up in the tequila shooters or jello shooters contests at the local watering holes. Finally, the margaritas in Mazatlán taste terrific, but the bartenders don't skimp on the booze. One minute you can be having a wonderful time with your friends and the next minute wake up in your room with the sunlight hitting your aching head like a bolt of lightning. If you use common sense, do things in moderation, and plan ahead, your vacation in Mazatlán will be much more pleasant.

Chapter 10

Medical or dental problems

Medical Care

This is of interest to everyone, either visiting or considering relocating. I have first-hand knowledge of medical care facilities in Mazatlán and I have talked with many people from north of the border about medical care here.

There is a popular misconception about the qualifications of doctors in Mexico. Many Mexican doctors are trained in U.S. facilities. Conversely, many U.S. doctors are trained in Mexico. I believe that you can get medical care in Mazatlán as good as most places north of the border. The medical facilities in Mazatlán are among the best in Mexico.

Doctor training in Mexico: I have heard many comments by people concerned about the training of Mexican doctors. Dr. Marco A. Alvarez Arrazola of Mazatlán was willing to provide the following information:

"As a local Mazatleco physician trained in both Mexico and the U.S., I find that there is a lack of knowledge in the way medical training is achieved here in Mexico. Almost everywhere in the world, getting accepted in a prestigious medical school is difficult. Candidates often need to go through several examinations and in some cases even through an extensive interview process. This is particularly true at Tec de Monterrey's School of Medicine where I trained.

"In Mexico we start medical training right after high school. I believe this to be too early, especially compared to my colleagues in the U.S. that have four years of pre-med. Medical school in Mexico takes five to six years, depending on the school. The last phase of undergraduate medical training is called internship and lasts from one to two years, depending on the school. In the U.S., the internship is done after the four year medical school is finished and lasts one year.

"In Mexico, all newly graduated M.D.s must work a year for the Mexican Health Care Agency (*Secretaría de Salud*). This is called *servicio social*, or community service. Most of us work in rural villages and small community hospitals.

"All this means that following six or seven years you are officially an M.D. and that you can legally work as a General Practitioner. If you want to pursue further formal medical training, or residency, you must take the *Examen Nacional para Residencias Medicas*. This is an examination administered yearly by the federal government in which you compete for a spot against all the physicians taking the exam in the country. There are usually five times more applicants than residency vacancies. For example, in 2004, 21,643 physicians took the exam for only 3,908 positions available in all of Mexico. If selected, you have three to five years of residency.

"Fellowships follow residency and last from one to three years. In the past 10 years, the trend is that all new graduates from Residency and Fellowship take the Board examination for their own medical specialty after completion of the program. While some specialties vary, most "boards" must be renewed every five years by proving a record of Continuous Medical Education (CME) or by retaking an oral or written exam.

"In Mazatlán there is a new generation of physicians who work as a team, are well-trained, board-certified and regularly attend and lecture in national and international medical conferences.

"In my particular case I went through six years of undergraduate medical training at Tec de Monterrey. The last two years were in a hospital setting at the San José-Tec de Monterrey Hospital and at the Baylor College of Medicine in Houston, TX, at the Methodist Hospital, Houston Veterans Administration Hospital and the Harris County Ben Taub Hospital.

"My social service was in a rural community and a small rural hospital in Nuevo León state. After that I pursued four years of Diagnostic Imaging Residency (Radiology) and a year of Fellowship in Musculoskeletal Radiology at Louisiana State University in New Orleans, for a total of 12 years of formal medical education. I am a board-certified member of the Radiological Society of North America, European College of Radiology and have lectured in major medical congresses in Mexico, the U.S. and Canada.

"I realize that there are some physicians, both in Mexico and the U.S., that are money-driven. Some even lack the basic moral values and even worse, sometimes they lack proper training. This is a crisis that medicine is facing around the world as technology evolves. In Mazatlán the local medical association is working to fulfill the special medical needs of our foreign community."

Dr. Alvarez's office is located at *Unidad de Radiologia Clinica*, Insurgentes #1390, *colonia* López Mateos. Tel: 983-9080, or via internet at *marcoalvarez@gmail.com*.

The cost for medical services will usually be much less in Mazatlán than in the U.S., but if you don't have insurance (or usually even if you do) you will have to pay the bill yourself. Reimbursement from your insurance company is possible, but copies of itemized billing are usually required. Some Mexican medical facilities accept U.S. and Canadian insurance, but check with the hospital prior to check in.

Are house calls ancient history in your hometown? Most doctors in Mazatlán still visit ailing patients in their homes. There are many bilingual doctors in Mazatlán.

Sharp Hospital: A first-class medical facility, with a staff that is well-trained, and seems to always have English-speaking staff available. Many doctors are specialists and the hospital offers everything including cardiac care and plastic surgery, and they also have dialysis equipment. Most of the doctors are bilingual. I would have no qualms about taking a friend or relative there for any kind of medical treatment.

Sharp offers a special "S.H.A.R.P. Card" service to foreigners that includes discounts for certain medical services. For just over $25 for a 2-year period you can be placed in the Sharp Hospital computer system. You give the hospital your medical, insurance and contact information, and you receive a laminated photo-ID card with an emergency number to call as well as a message in Spanish on the back of the card to transport you to Sharp Hospital in case of an emergency or accident. Discounts include 30% discount for hospital stay; and 15% discount for the following: Use of emergency room and emergency consulting, laboratory tests, MRI, X-rays, and medical examination. Call 986-5678 and ask for foreign assistance for further information.

In the spring of 2005 my wife, Katherine suffered a mild stroke while dining at a restaurant. Within a few minutes the Red Cross ambulance arrived to pick her up. I insisted that they take her to Sharp Hospital. The driver called the hospital and by the time we arrived a specialist met us. She received immediate attention and I attribute the lack of serious effects from the stroke to the speed and effectiveness of the hospital staff. She had a private room and numerous tests and medication. Our bill, after three days, was less than $2,000. I sincerely believe that had she had the stroke in the U.S. she would have had some paralysis.

Naturally, prices as of this printing will be higher, but still quite a bargain.

In February 2007, I had extreme pain in my left leg, and when it was found I had a herniated disk, I had no qualms about having back surgery. After the operation the pain was gone, and six days later I was at home. Within two weeks I could walk with no assistance. The services I received were first-rate.

If you are not happy with your bill, treatment or need questions answered, check with the manager who understands English and is very accommodating. If he is not available call 986-5678, press "O" for English and ask for a foreign representative.

Central Medica Quirúrgica: This is a hospital solely for surgeries. My friend Dick Hubbard had his gall bladder removed there. He claims that the facilities are as good as Sharp Hospital, but with a more relaxed "atmosphere" than is expected by many people from north of the border. He had a private air-conditioned room with TV and a sleeper/couch. It was very clean and modern. The address is Ejército Mexicano #2207, *colonia* Palos Prietos. Tel: 985-0997 and 985-0730.

Red Cross (**Clinica Cruz Roja**): This emergency clinic is located in El Centro. It handles all kinds of emergencies, but I recommend it particularly for quick stitching of minor wounds. A couple of years ago I had a large cut on my hand from broken glass and I asked my friend Paco to take me to Sharp Hospital emergency room. He replied, "No, it might take too long to get treatment. I'll take you to a faster place."

When we arrived at the *Cruz Roja* clinic no one spoke English so Paco explained the situation. They took me into a room where my hand was examined by a doctor. The nurse cleaned the wound and under supervision of the doctor, stitched the cut and wrapped the hand. They asked me for a donation of about $5 and told me to return every day for five days to get the wound cleaned and bandage changed and then the stitches removed. For each office call they asked for a $2 donation. The treatment was superb and it goes without saying that I made a large contribution to Mazatlán *Cruz Roja*.

Rezomaz Diagnostic center: I include this "one stop" medical center because it has virtually everything in the way of medical testing. The prices will surprise you as they are a quarter to a third of the cost in the U.S. For example the cost of an MRI is about $300, instead of CAT scan they have multi-slice CT of the entire body for $150–$250, and ultra sound $60.

In 2007 I had an MRI, x-rays, and blood tests there in preparation for a back operation. I was very pleased with the treatment. The place is clean, modern, and the staff is very professional. They also have the only digital x-ray machine in Mazatlán, which provides a faster and clearer picture. And yes, ladies, they provide mammograms, but not any more comfortable than in the states, I'm told. They have a diagnostic cardio-pulmonary department, which includes an echo-cardiogram and stress test machine. In addition they have a Holter ambulatory electro-cardiography heart monitoring device and ambulatory blood pressure monitoring equipment. The well-equipped laboratory is on-site. So when your doctor sends you to get tests I suggest you contact Rezomaz, across the street from Sams Club. Dr. Mock is the resident radiologist. Tel: 986-6122 or 121-1122. or their website at *www.resomaz.com*.

IN MED: This shop, located at *calle* Zaragoza #701 on the northeast corner of *calles* 5 de Mayo and Zaragoza across from the Zaragoza park in El Centro, sells and rents medical supplies, including wheelchairs and medical beds. They also sell all types of braces and other orthopedic equipment. Tel: 981-7333.

Medical complaints: If you have a significant problem with a medical professional, either billing or treatment, you may file the complaint with CONAMED – *Comision de Arbitraje Medico*. Write them at: *andador* José Gonzales, *calle* Hermosillo #1297 P.B. (*Piso Bajo* – ground floor)

Lázaro Cárdenas/Calzada Insurgentes, Culiacán, Sinaloa, Mexico. Their telephone numbers are 01-667-761-5089 and 01-667-714-1013 from Mazatlán (drop the 01- and use the 011-52- prefix for calls from the U.S. and Canada) and the office hours are Monday through Friday, 8 A.M. to 3 P.M. You should have all pertinent dates, charges, receipts, names, addresses, phone numbers, plus details of the problem.

Local doctors

My wife and I have been very fortunate to have had all our health needs met. All of my friends here tell me of the great luck they have had with their doctors.

Dr. Jorge Sánchez: He is a General Practitioner and pediatrician who speaks good English and does not charge "gringo prices". Both my wife and I have used him for minor problems, with excellent results. His office is at Rotarismo #215 (east of the stoplight one block north of Fisherman's Monument) downtown and is easy to get to by bus from the tourist zones. His office is on the left side of the street in the same building as a pharmacy. He also owns the pharmacy, so will give you a discount on any prescriptions needed. Tel: 985-0848.

Dr. Miguel A. Guzmán: He is a board-certified surgeon from Creighton Medical School in Omaha, Nebraska, and also practices as a General Practitioner in Mazatlán. His office is in The Inn at Mazatlán, Tel: 981-2587. And get this; you can reach him at home at 981-5117, or cell phone, 044-669-918-1070 and he makes house calls. How many doctors do you know who give out their home or cell phone number?

Dr. Saul Santana: A world-class neurosurgeon who surgically corrected my herniated disk and sciatic nerve. He has an entire team of medical personnel that assists him in surgery. He visited me twice a day while I was in the hospital and daily in my home after I was released. Dr. Santana has offices on the fifth floor in the Polimedica building in front of Sharp Hospital. While he speaks good English, his receptionist may not. Tel: 984-2923 or 986-2337.

Dr. Jorge Córdova Carreon: A highly recommended ear, nose and throat specialist located in the Polimedica building in front of Sharp Hospital in suite #311. The doctor speaks English and has reasonable rates.

Dr. Levid Tórres: Is a General Practitioner and board-certified trauma surgeon with offices in El Centro at Carnaval #1611 Suite #1. He makes house calls for about $30 a visit. Raised in the U.S. and Mexico, the doctor speaks excellent English and is fully bicultural. Tel: 981-0855, or email: *levidtorres@mzt.megared.net.mx.*

Dr. Jorge Eduardo Montoya: Is an OB/GYN with an office in the Polimedica building on Rafael Buelna in front of Sharp Hospital. He can be reached by telephone at 990-1920, and by email at *drjmontoya@ hotmail.com.*

Dr. Elias Avelino Javer Fernández: Is well-known as the best gas-troenterologist in Mazatlán. Even as a specialist, Dr. Javer's office visits are about $40, and he makes house calls at about $50. He speaks good English and his office is in the Polimedica building, #606, in front of Sharp Hospital. Tel: 984-2484 or cell: 044-669-918-0460.

Dr. Sergio Acoltzi: He is also a gastroenterologist. Dick Hubbard had a gall bladder removed laproscopically with a minimum of dis-comfort and an overnight stay in the hospital. In the States you are in the hospital about five hours and then sent home. His office is also in the Polimedica building, suite #402. Tel: 112-0100, and his cell: 044-669-116-1906. His English is quite good.

Optometrist

By far the best optometrist, with reasonable prices, is at Galería Óptica in the Golden Zone. Dr. José Machado is a real professional, speaks good English and the eye exam is only $20. They have excellent English-speaking staff in their optical shop. Galería Óptica is located on Av. Camarón Sábalo # 1664-A, across from the Balboa Club, near Constantino's leather store. The phone number is 913-8419. Several of my family members and friends have been there and been completely satisfied.

Dentists

Like doctors, there are many well-qualified dentists in Mazatlán. Some are more expensive than others. Some are less painful than others, but all that I know of are conscientious to a fault.

Dr. Estrada: About 10 years ago, I was having a problem with a crown. I asked my friend, Teresa Iglis-McFarland from The Inn at Mazatlán, for the name of a good dentist, and she recommended Dr. Estrada. It turned out that I had an abscess in one of my front teeth. He said he could either do another root canal or a bridge. Since I had already undergone two painful root canals on the tooth, I chose the bridge. He made a four-tooth permanent bridge and the entire job was completed in a month, and it looks better than the crowns it replaced. Anyone who knows me will tell you that there is only one thing I hate more than criticism and that is pain. That means this is high praise for Dr. Estrada. A very expensive specialist in the U.S. had put in the two crowns.

When I spent a year in the States, I went to a different dentist and he mentioned that I had had a lot of dental work. I agreed and asked him if he could tell me what the U.S. specialist did or the one from Mexico had done. He said he could not tell the difference and all the work was outstanding. By the way, the cost of the bridge was less than the deductible I paid with my insurance plan for the two crowns. Dr. Estrada speaks good English and has offices in the small mall building with the Subway Sandwich Shop and Dr. Backman, the chiropractor, on Camarón Sábalo about a block north of the HSBC bank in the Golden Zone. Tel: 914-1622.

Dr. Eduardo Ibarra: His office is located at Canizales #502, in El Centro, one block south of the Central Mercado and then about one and a half blocks west of Av. Benito Juárez. Tel: 981-8724 or his cell: 044-669-994-4771 or email him at *dr_ibarraz@yahoo.com*. His hours are 9 A.M. to 1 P.M. and 4–7 P.M. He speaks excellent English. Be sure to tell him I referred you, as this will get you the best price.

Dra. Susanna Pedrero de la Cruz: Is a dentist and orthodontist and speaks English well. Tel: 981-8221 or cell: 044-669-120-0132. Her office is across the street from Dr. Ibarra's, at Canizales #509 suite 5, behind a small *farmacia*.

Her family owns an excellent dental lab in El Centro. The name is *Laboratorio Central Remo-Dent*. Since you would need to speak fairly technical Spanish there, I suggest you contact Dra. Susanna first if you need dental lab work, so she can have them properly handle your problem.

Dr. Ernesto Bertrand: His office is located at 5 de Mayo #1725 Bis (*bis* means the building next door to #1725) suite D-2 in El Centro. He is a root canal specialist – endodontist – and is an associate of Dr. Ibarra; their offices are only about two blocks apart. I have had three root canals and my wife two and we are both satisfied customers. Tel: 981-1260 or 985-6150 and cell: 044-669-129-7147.

One thing that is quite different than the States or Canada is that many of the less expensive, i.e., not in the tourist area, dentists do not have their own X-ray equipment, but write a prescription for you to go to an X-ray imaging lab like ResoMaz, and there are many in Mazatlán. Fortunately, the cost for dental X-rays at these labs is very, very low, usually much less than a dentist in the States would charge for the same X-rays.

Veterinarian

Why post veterinarians in the same chapter with doctors and dentists? There are some of us that love our pets dearly and treat them as members of the family. Los Amigos de Los Animales, or humane society in Mazatlán. Tel: 986-4235.

*Dr. **Marco** Antonio **Cárdenas** Avila:* This is an awesome veterinary clinic, with reasonable prices. They have a doggy wash and groomer on the premises, and can also board your critter if you have to be away. The vet speaks English…and pet-talk even better! The clinic is at *calle* Río Baluarte #1034. Tel: 982-6727 or 984-4115. You can also email them at *vetpac@hotmail.com.*

Dr. Marco will give your animal an examination and an International Health Certificate that can be used for returning home with your pet.

Mobile dog groomer: There seems to be an interest in this service so I had to place it somewhere in the book. Her name is Martita. Tel: 193-4103, cell: 044-669-431-3962. She is a busy woman so call early for an appointment.

Legal Drugs

Prescription drugs in Mazatlán often cost less than half what they cost in the U.S. Most are even the very same drugs as those sold in the U.S., made by the very same laboratory. If you take a lot of prescription drugs you can save a ton of money purchasing them in Mazatlán. Many of the pharmacists in the tourist zone speak English.

There are Farmacia Similares drugstores throughout the city that sell government approved generic drugs at reasonable, i.e., very low, prices. They also have doctors' offices right on-site with licensed doctors who can make a diagnosis and write prescriptions. In the Golden Zone there is one at the traffic light on Camarón Sábalo, across the street from the Dolce Mami Café, and just north of Domino's Pizza.

No matter where you are in the world, you may have medical or dental emergencies. It is my belief that quality emergency care from doctors, dentists, other medical personnel and veterinarians is far more available in Mexico than in the U.S.

Chapter 11

Where do you stay in Mazatlán?

Where you stay is a matter of personal taste and financial consideration. The original tourist area in Mazatlán was downtown and in Olas Altas. Many of the hotels there are older and lower-priced. As hotels were built north along the Malecón, then in the Golden Zone, tourism moved farther north. Mazatlán is one of the few Mexican resort areas that offers modern deluxe resorts alongside budget beachfront hotels. Check out this website for special deals: *http://www.tripadvisor. com/ShowForum-g150792-i257-Mazatlán_Pacific_Coast.*

And for a complete map of Mazatlán, showing all (or very nearly all) of the hotel and resort properties in Mazatlán (and many other things also), go to this fabulous website (it comes up centered on Valentino's at the south end of the Golden Zone, but is interactive, so you can move it around anywhere you like): *http://www.wikimapia.org/#lat=23.2385217&lon= -106.4460692&z=18&l=3&m=b*

This is an invaluable and interesting site. Use it.

Many of Mazatlán's attractions, particularly the beaches, are in the Golden Zone, but so are most of the tourists and noise. There are also hotels further north, in the new Marina and Cerritos and even beyond, where the beaches are not as crowded and there is less noise. El Centro

Histórico and Olas Altas have many excellent tourist activities but there can be lots of noise at Carnaval time.

The Hotels (Estimated rack rates)
Most expensive

Casa Lucila Boutique Hotel: This up-scale hotel opened in 2007 in Olas Altas near the motorcycle monument. It is a completely remodeled 19th century home with eight elegant suites. The rooms are spacious, with gorgeous furniture and décor and the original high ceilings. In-room amenities include flat-screen plasma TVs, coffee maker, iron and ironing board, bathrobes, safes and gorgeous bathrooms.

There is an infinity pool on the third floor that overlooks the Pacific Ocean right out front. On premises is a restaurant and a lobby that resembles a living room/dining room. Room service is also available. Price for these suites range from $100–$200 per night plus a 19% tax. Check out their website at *www.casalucila.com.* Tel: 982-1100, if calling from the U.S. or Canada, don't forget the 011-52-669- prefix.

Pueblo Bonito Emerald Bay: This resort sits on an isolated beach (a small area at the south end of Playa Delfín) on 20 acres overlooking the Pacific Ocean at the very north end of Mazatlán. It is billed as "away from it all – but not too far away". The property is 20 minutes north of the original Pueblo Bonito Mazatlán resort, past the end of all the bus routes, so they run a shuttle service between the two for the convenience of their guests.

It is designated as an all-suites resort. There are about 250 suites, divided into 10 independent ocean-front buildings. All suites have kitchenettes, terraces or balconies and an ocean view. Two large pools with swim-up bars, a large spa, tennis courts, three outdoor Jacuzzis, and a gourmet restaurant add to the charm.

The shuttle service is available every half-hour to Pueblo Bonito Mazatlán in the Golden Zone. Double occupancy rates are from $140 to $350 per night depending on the time of year, room size and location.

The property has a security gate and you must call 24 hours in advance to be admitted if you are not a guest. Tel: 989-0525. If you like isolation and exclusivity, this is the place for you.

Wyndham Las Villas Hotel and Spa: It is located within the gated community of Estrella Del Mar on Stone Island. Their shuttle service can bring you to their property in only 10 minutes from the Mazatlán International Airport. Unfortunately it is a 40-minute taxi ride to downtown or to the Golden Zone for other activities.

The hotel and rooms are of traditional colonial Mexican design and located right on a 3.5 mile long secluded beach and is right next to the resort's gorgeous Robert Trent Jr. designed 18-hole golf course. Price for a room with a king-size bed is $105 and other rooms are available, including a two-bedroom Presidential Suite for $265. Tel: from the U.S. 1-888-587-0609, from Canada 1-866-703-7161, from Mexico 01-800-727-4653. Their website is *www.mazatlanhotellasvillas.com.*

Expensive

The Inn at Mazatlán: This is my personal favorite; I have been a time-share owner since 1985 and have never regretted it. This property is also a hotel and has a beachfront restaurant that is open to the public. Located in the Golden Zone, just south of the El Cid Mega resort, The Inn added a tower in 2000 (about) and a second, larger swimming pool. Its main selling point is that most employees have been there for years, and the service is simply the best. The beautiful Teresa Inglis-McFarland handles time share re-sales, and she is most helpful whenever a guest has a problem. The popular Papagayo Restaurant is located on the grounds and has an excellent breakfast buffet.

The Inn has a qualified Activities Director and also a lifeguard on duty on the beach. They have a complimentary nurse on duty from 10 A.M. to 6 P.M. and a doctor on-call as well. Other amenities include safe deposit boxes, concierge service, business and fitness center, laundry, computer room and babysitting service. There is also a fantastic gift shop in the lobby. Double occupancy rates run from $120–$180. Tel: 913-5354.

Pueblo Bonito Mazatlán: This complex is among the most beautiful in Mazatlán. The suites have colorful Mexican décor and gorgeous tile kitchens. Set right on the beach with a large swimming pool surrounded by *palapas* and umbrellas, as well, it can easily accommodate the most discerning sun-worshiper. Breakfast in their open-air café and dinner at Angelo's, one of the best Italian restaurants in Mazatlán, make the trip more appealing.

Double occupancy rates are approximately $158 for junior suites and $193 for a one-bedroom suite in November, and $182 for junior suites and $215 for a one-bedroom suite in April. Tel: 989-8900 or at their website, *www.pueblobonito.com.*

The Riu Emerald Bay resort: This is a very large, high-rise, all-inclusive luxury hotel with 716 rooms/suites, located right on Bruja beach, about six miles north of the Golden Zone. There are four restaurants on-site, an exercise room with sauna, WiFi, a giant heated swimming pool, ocean water sports and live music and dancing every night in an actual open-air theater on-site.

For more information, Tel: 986 1816 or visit their website at *www.riu.com.* Email is: *hotel.emeraldbay@riu.com.*

Hotel Ramada: (formerly Hotel Los Sábalos Mazatlán): Located at *calle* Playa Gaviotas #100, at the south end of the Golden Zone, this is a large resort on the beach, surrounded by bars and restaurants. The Las Gaviotas oceanside bar is perfect for sun-worshippers, and Mazatlán's famous Joe's Oyster Bar, a popular seafood restaurant by day and hip club for the younger set by night, is right next door. The on-site, beachfront restaurant is the Ocean Terrace and across the street is Vittore Italian restaurant. The staff is well-trained and extremely helpful. It has 200 rooms and the rack rates are $130–$150 during high season but there are always "specials". Tel: 983-5333.

Tórres Mazatlán: A seven-story resort with 80 one-bedroom, 40 two-bedroom and six penthouse suites—all with unique Mexican-Caribbean décor, a private lanai or deck and amazing ocean views. Each has a kitchen, with coffeemaker, dishwasher, refrigerator and toaster. Located on a long beach just north of the new Marina area, amenities include a beach volleyball court, shuffle board, a huge heated swimming pool and hot tub. The beautifully manicured grounds have a reputation for being the perfect site for weddings or souvenir photos.

This four-star resort also has a fine restaurant, activities director and two lifeguards, one at the pool and one on the beach. On the grounds one can get a pedicure, manicure and massage. While most suites are timeshare, there is always opportunity for rental or exchange through Resort Condominiums International. It is located about five miles north of El Cid Marina on Av. Sábalo Cerritos. Go to *www.tripadvisor.com/ShowForum-g150792-i257-Mazatlán_Pacific_Coast* for specials and more information about this beautiful resort. Tel: 989-8611.

El Cid Mega Resort: The complex includes the Granada, which is the oldest, across the street from the Castillo and El Moro high-rise towers.

The newest addition to the El Cid resorts is the Marina El Cid Hotel and Yacht Club, at the north end of the Golden Zone. It is a low-rise Mediterranean-style building with 200+ units that include junior suites, one- and two-bedroom suites and presidential suites. Rooms feature marble floors with marina views and balconies. Junior suites feature two queen-size beds, living area and kitchenette. The one-bedroom suites have a private bedroom with king-size bed, living/dining room and kitchen. There are two swimming pools, both with swim-up bar, waterfalls, slides and whirlpool. There is a Jacuzzi, wading pool and children's pool.

On-site is an outdoor game area and children's playground, two restaurants and a snack bar. To get to the beach you take a short water taxi ride, provided free-of-charge by the hotel, across the marina channel.

The El Cid Mega Resort Complex has 27 holes of golf, 14 tennis courts, a marina, eight swimming pools, a spa, disco, exercise room, shopping arcade, an aqua sports center and 15 restaurants and lounges. Double occupancy rates are from $140 at El Castilla to $250 at El Cid Marina Hotel. Tel: 913-3333 and the website is *www.elcidresorts.com.mx.*

Hotel Costa de Oro: Located next to The Inn at Mazatlán in the Golden Zone, this large, quaint complex is divided into three separate areas. The original beachfront building has 120 standard rooms, some with ocean-view. The all-suite tower features spacious suites with a separate bedroom area, kitchenette, ocean view and balcony. There are about 60 standard rooms in their Margarita's building, just as comfortable, but more economical because of their location across the street next to the three tennis courts. They have a large pool overlooking the ocean, a beachfront restaurant, as well as super-friendly staff that makes the Costa de Oro consistently one of the most popular hotels in Mazatlán. Besides all of this, facing the street they have several shops, a mini-market and pharmacy and the Social Café Lounge, which has live, soft music several evenings each week, making it an ideal "meet and greet" place. Double occupancy rate ranges from about $80 to $165 depending on time of year, size, and location of room. Tel: 913-5344.

Royal Villas Resort: A 12-story high-rise on the beach in the Golden Zone, with 130 deluxe suites and studios, all with ocean view and balcony. Suites are available with one or two bedrooms as well as spacious studios. There is a large open-air lobby complete with fishponds and waterfalls. The swimming pool overlooks the ocean. There is a health club and game room available. There are two restaurants and a poolside bar. Rooms include a fully equipped kitchenette and satellite TV.

Rates range from $145 to $225, depending on time of year and number of bedrooms. Tel: 916-6161 or visit their website at *www.royalvillas.com.mx*.

Quijote Inn: This is a five-story complex located on the beach in the Golden Zone, just north of The Palms Resort and the Mar Rosa RV park. There are 67 studios and suites beautifully decorated in traditional Mexican style.. Each suite has a fully equipped kitchen. There is a swimming pool and restaurant on-site. Rack rates for double occupancy run from $95–$180, depending on time of year. Tel: 914-1134.

Less Expensive

Hotel Playa Mazatlán: The Hotel Playa Mazatlán is Mazatlán. The quaintness of the brick archways, columns, and tiles make this resort look like a Spanish villa. It is located in the center of Golden Zone activity. There are excellent shops on-site as well as a super restaurant and romantic beach. Four swimming pools have daily activities including water aerobics classes and other poolside activities. Rates are approximately $90 for a double (garden view) and $110 for ocean-view. Two children 11 or under can stay with their parents free. Tel: 989-0555.

The Palms Resort (previously the Holiday Inn Sunspree Resort): Just up the street north from the El Cid complex, The Palms is a comfortable beachfront hotel with good value and "no surprises". There is a restaurant on-site. Most rooms have wonderful ocean views. Rates are about $87–$145 for a double. Tel: 913-2222.

Hotel Posada Freeman Express: This was opened in 1944 and beautifully renovated in 2002. The hotel is on the Malecón in Olas Altas, overlooking the water, steps from museums, art galleries, restaurants and the Plaza Machado. From the rooftop pool deck or the 11th floor lounge (open to the public) you have a breathtaking 360-degree view of Mazatlán. Rates are about $100 for a double. The price includes a buffet breakfast. The breakfast buffet is open to the public daily from 7–11 A.M. and costs about $8 for adults and $4.50 for children. Tel: 981-2114 or check out their web page, *www.posadadelrio.com.*

A newer Posada Freeman hotel in the Golden Zone opened between El Cid and The Inn at Mazatlán. The price is a little higher since it is right on the water. Tel: 989-4400.

Fiesta Inn: A nine-story hotel with more than 115 rooms in the Golden Zone, each room has a balcony and most have an ocean view. The pool faces the beach and has a wading pool attached. There is a restaurant, bar, travel agency, business center and snack bar on-site. Single and triple rates are available. Double occupancy rates are from $70 to $120 depending on size, time of year and location. Children under 12 can stay free, and the hotel has many rate "specials". Tel: 989-0100.

Quality Inn: This hotel opened in 2011 across the street from the Hotel Playa Mazatlán in the Golden Zone. All the suites have internet connections at no extra charge and there are hair dryers, safe deposit boxes and coffee makers in every room. There is a restaurant on-site, as well as two heated pools, a snack bar and ballroom. Rack rate for double occupancy is $85–$125 except during Easter week and between Christmas and New Year's. Ask for their specials. Tel: 989-2317.

Hotel Aquamarina: Is a very nice, older hotel on the Malecón across the street from the beach, just a few blocks north of the Fisherman's Monument. A double suite costs $88 and $110 and all rooms have air-conditioning, phone and cable TV. There is a pool, an excellent restaurant and bar and travel agency on-site. Tel: 981-7080.

La Casa Contenta: Some of the apartments are rented long-term, but the real value is in the brick, Spanish-style cottages on the beach. They are great for family getaways. Furnishings are far from spectacular, but, hey, how much time does one spend in the room while on vacation? Parasailing and sailboat rentals are close by. It is located in the heart of the Golden Zone, north of the Las Flores hotel, but before you get to the Ocean Palms tower, and is sometimes noisy, especially during Holy Week. Rates are $89 for one-bedroom units, to $217 for three bedrooms. They have special rates for monthly rentals. Tel: 913-4976.

Moderately priced Hotels

Azteca Inn: Across the street from the Hotel Playa Mazatlán in the heart of the Golden Zone, the Azteca is an inexpensive way to be close to where the action is. I stayed there two nights and found the rooms to be clean, and surprisingly, not very noisy, despite the location. All of the rooms open into a courtyard, parking and swimming pool area. There is an excellent restaurant on the grounds. Rates are about $55–$75 per double. Tel: 913-4425.

Hotel Las Flores: A 12-story hotel with twin towers located in the heart of the Golden Zone, on the beach near the Seashell Museum. There are 119 studios, suites and standard rooms. Studios have a kitchenette area, with a table and chairs and an additional table and chairs on the deck, and two double beds. The one-bedroom suites have all of the above and more, with a separate bedroom that can be closed off for privacy. In addition to the studios and suites, there are 15 standard rooms, most without an ocean view or deck. There is a large, open-air lobby with a view through to the ocean. The swimming pools overlook the ocean. Double occupancy rates range from $42 to $80 per night, depending on the size of room and time of year. Two children, ages 11 and under, can stay free with their parents. Single, triple and quad rates are also available. Tel: 913-5100.

Bungalows Mar-Sol: Is located in the Golden Zone on Camarón Sábalo, across the street from the Pueblo Bonito Mazatlán resort. They have clean, quiet, comfortable rooms with a beautiful common area and a friendly staff. They have daily, weekly and monthly rates. Daily rates for a room for two people are from $52 to a suite for three people, $60 Tel: 914-0108.

Bargain priced Hotels

Hotel La Siesta: Located next to the Shrimp Bucket restaurant in Olas Altas. The ocean views (especially the sunsets) are terrific from the rooms on the front, all of which have a balcony. A beach for swimming is right across the street, and it is close—an easy walk—to El Centro Histórico with its beautiful old buildings, plazas, museums, art galleries and restaurants. It is in the center of the Carnaval street dancing area, so if you like partying, be sure and get reservations at least six months in advance. You can get a double for about $40 most of the year. Tel: 981-2640.

Hotel De Cima: On the Malecón, across the street from the beach, just a couple of blocks north of the Fisherman's Monument, at Av. del Mar #48. Rooms are $30 double and have two beds. Some rooms surround the pool, while others face the beach. There is parking and a restaurant and bar on-site, as well as a lovely beach club and bistro, La Corriente, right on the sand. You can walk under the busy street in a gaily painted tunnel to get there. Tel: 982-7311.

Hotel Del Sol: This small hotel is across the street from the beach on Av. Del Mar. There is a pool, private parking, sun deck, video room and travel agency on premises. A double is $45 and with kitchenette, $55. Each room has A/C and cable TV. Prices are considerably lower from Easter to November. Tel: 985-1103.

Hotel Mariana: Is on the northwest corner of Camarón Sábalo and Priv. Costa Azul, half block south of and across the street from Gus & Gus. All information is on their website *http://www.marianahotel.com/*

Very low priced Budget Hotels (often referred to as "backpacker" hotels)

My friend Dee Hulen provided a few places that she found acceptable which cost less than $30 a day.

Hotel Centro: The address is *calle* Belisario Dominguez #1607, in the middle of El Centro Histórico. It is walking distance to Olas Altas beach, the central mercado, museums and plazas. In the lobby they have computers with an internet connection, free for guests.

Rooms are small and no-frills, and the location, while central, is on a noisy, busy street with little or no atmosphere. There is no pool. The people at the desk are very nice and speak English. Price around $25 for a double.

Hotel Del Río: The address is Benito Juárez #2410, El Centro, 3 blocks south of the Malecón. Rates are about $25 for a double. Tel: 981-4639.

Hotel Plaza Río: Is a newer hotel owned by the same owner as Hotel Del Rio. It costs about $25 for a double. They are located at Av. Gutiérrez Nájera #320, El Centro, about 3 blocks east of the Fisherman's Monument. Tel: 982-4430 or cell: 044-669-115-6234.

Hotel Lerma: It is known as a backpacker hotel and is located on *calle* Simon Bolivar between Aquilles Serdan and Benito Juárez in El Centro about two blocks from the beach and four blocks from the Central Mercado. It has secure parking, but no pets are allowed. It is managed by the owner and his son, Carlos Lerma, who speaks English. Rates for the basic rooms are as low as $10 double, year-round. Tel: 981-2436.

Villa Bonita Hotel: Located in the heart of the Golden Zone on Gabriel Ruíz, a block off Camarón Sábalo across the street from Rico's Café, close to the beach. Prices range from $24 to $48. Tel: 916-5319.

Bed and Breakfast

If you like to have company with your breakfast, and a "community life" during your vacation, Mazatlán has the B&Bs for you. In my travels I have never found B&B proprietors that were not personable, and there are no exceptions here.

Casa de Leyendas: This B&B is just a block from Olas Altas beach, and is simply too beautiful for words. The historic home has been carefully restored and renovated to include every comfort imaginable for guests while retaining all its 19th century charm. There are five comfortable bedrooms, each different (named after local celebrities, including the Pedro Infante and the Lola Beltrán rooms), all with modern private bath, A/C and ceiling fans. Two of the rooms have an ocean-view *terraza* and the others also have lovely views.

There are many areas in the house where guests may relax, including a media room, equipped with large screen for TV or movies, a library of books and movies, a computer with WiFi and plenty of comfortable seating. A charming courtyard has a tiled pool, plants and seating for breakfast or afternoon wine and cheese. The *mirador* – rooftop patio – has a wonderful view of the ocean and the city and is equipped with a grill for guests' use.

A full breakfast is served each morning from the gleaming kitchen and guests have the option of being served in their rooms or joining others in the dining room or any other place in the house! The kitchen and pantry also are available for use by guests. With advance notice, the hosts, Glen and Sharon Sorrie, can arrange for special occasions such as honeymoons and family reunions, or for such things as corporate retreats or fishing excursions.

The address is Venustiano Carranza #2 & 4, El Centro Histórico, across the street from the Mazatlán Art Museum and the Mazatlán Membership Library. Tel: from U.S. is 1-602-445-6192 and locally is 981-6180. Email is *info@casadeleyendas.com* and website is *www.casadeleyendas.com*.

The Loro de Oro Inn: Just 100 yards east of the Plazuela Machado at *calle* Constitución #622 in El Centro Histórico, this lovely B&B offers everything from bungalow suites to different sizes of studio suites. There is a swimming pool and the property has WiFi everywhere. Tony and his wife Lucy are some of Mazatlán's most popular hosts. Rates are from $60 to $115 with 10% discounts for a 7 seven day stay and even bigger discounts for longer stays. Tel: 982-8996 or, from the U.S. or Canada 1-714-798-7994 or email *tony@lorodeoroinn.com*.

The RV Life

There are numerous gorgeous RV parks in Mazatlán, ranging from those on the beach to others close to the center of the Golden Zone and still more in the remote beauty of Stone Island. I suggest you make  reservations well in advance, especially for the busy winter season. Prices vary according to time of year and location.

Roads are not as good as most in the U.S. and Canada, so have good tires and don't overload your rig. If you drive from Nogales to Mazatlán, take the toll road (*cuota* or *maxipista*). The cost is worth it in wear and tear on your vehicle and time saved. Don't believe the misconception that RVs have a special toll rate. Tolls for most are based on the number of wheels you have (or maybe axles).

Mexican mechanics are magicians in making parts, so don't worry about breakdowns. It may take some time, but what the hey! Just relax in your bedroom with a good book until your vehicle is fixed.

Let's take a look at some of the RV parks in Mazatlán

Tres Amigos RV Park: Is on the beach on Stone Island. It has wonderful amenities and is right on miles of beach. The only downside is the road to Stone Island from Estrella del Mar is unpaved and not too good. There are 60 lots. For current rates check out their website at *www.mazinfo. com/rvpark*, or email them at *info@kingdavid.com.net*. You can reach them by telephone at 914-1444.

Mar Rosa RV Park: Great location, right on the beach between The Palms resort (previously the Holiday Inn) and the Quijote Inn in the Golden Zone. You can go to bed with the sound of the waves crashing. Tel: 913-6187 or email: *marrosarv@gmail.com*.

Punta Cerritos RV Park: This is another RV park on the ocean, at Cerritos Point, at the northern tip of Cerritos beach. They have daily, weekly, monthly and yearly rates. Amenities include concrete pads and patios, WiFi access, heated swimming pool, tennis/volleyball courts, laundry room, restrooms and showers and convenient access to a small grocery store, coffee shop and restaurants. For further information visit their website at *www.rvcerritos.com*, email them at *puntacerritos@live. com.mx* or telephone/fax: 988-1505.

A Unique Rental Home

Casa Bonita: Located a block from the beach in Olas Altas, this is a beautiful 19th century home turned into a rental that's perfect for groups or large families. There are seven bedrooms, six baths, a lovely pool, beautiful modern kitchen, big living room and all that you could want in a house. Casa Bonita is rented by the week only, and the whole house is yours, even though the owners live on the property. Maid service is included, as is everything you will need to enjoy your stay. All but one bedroom has AC. Rate for 6 people is $800 a week, with an extra charge of $100 a person, per week, for more than six people. The place can easily accommodate 12 to 15 people. For two, they charge $700 a week. Their website is *www.choice1.com/casabonita.htm*.

Timeshares

Many of the resort hotels in Mazatlán are also timeshare hotels. From the airport to the streets and beaches of the Golden Zone, and even in some restaurants, timeshare salespeople will hound you. Whether or not a time-share is a good buy depends entirely on personal tastes and circumstances. When I purchased a timeshare in 1985, I was a "workaholic", who needed a good reason to take a vacation. Timeshare ownership forced me to get away from my job once a year. I thoroughly enjoy my suite at The Inn at Mazatlán. Although I no longer stay there (because I have a house four blocks away), I have used it as gifts for relatives and for fundraising auctions. I am also a member of Resort Condominium International, which allows me to swap my weeks for similar accommodations worldwide.

There is a downside to timeshares. They must be paid for in cash within a short amount of time. An annual maintenance fee is charged, and the amount increases periodically. Sometimes it is difficult to plan your vacation to coincide with the week(s) you own, and trading weeks is often troublesome. There are "floating" weeks and "advance use" weeks that further confuse buyers.

Salespeople will offer you free meals, free tours and even cash to entice you to go to a two-hour "presentation". If you want to trade beach time for presentations, you can get a good value. I gave my grand-daughter a week in my timeshare for her honeymoon. Crystal and her new hubby paid for numerous things they wanted to do by attending several presentations. Be forewarned that most of the salespeople at the presentations are high-pressure, and it is sometimes difficult to extricate yourself, get your gift(s) and get back to the beach.

Since I don't want any more timeshares, I simply tell the salespeople that I'm not interested because I already own a home in El Dorado. That stops most of them because homeowners don't buy timeshares.

Don't be cajoled into buying without considering all of your options. If you impetuously purchase a timeshare and wake up with buyer's remorse, Mexican law allows buyers five days grace period before the deal is legal. If you change your mind, go back to the salesperson and void the contract.

All these places to stay in paradise make you want to stay longer. In the next chapter we will talk about retirement opportunities in Mazatlán.

Chapter 12

What about retiring in Mazatlán?

I F YOU'VE BEEN DAYDREAMING about retirement, about being able to just lounge in a comfortable beach chair with a cool margarita, you're in good company! During a period of roughly two decades (1946–1966), Canada and the United States experienced an unprecedented increase in population. This generation, the so-called "Baby Boomers," has begun a transition into retirement in great numbers. They have higher expectations and look forward to a longer life than any previous generation in history. As such, the interest in international travel is increasing. Public and private organizations are coming forth to meet the needs of these traveling Boomers with a variety of resources designed specifically to assist them in making the most of their retirement years.

You've heard many stories about life in Mexico, I'm sure. I've found some to be true, some to be false and most rather amusing. There are many expatriates living year-round in Mazatlán and loving it. There are also stories of people who have purchased a home in Mazatlán, yanked up their roots in the States or Canada and headed south with all their worldly belongings…only to become disillusioned and move back to their home country.

Even though I didn't do it, my advice is to rent a home for three to six months and give Mazatlán a trial period (see Chapter 13 for rental management companies). If you plan to live here year-round, take six months and include the summer. Mazatlán weather is fantastic from November to June, but the hot, humid summers have beaten down some of the heartiest of people. Not to mention the complexities of adapting to a new culture and language far from home.

Can you live in Mazatlán on $900 per month? It is certainly possible, but you would have to pinch your pennies. The majority of my friends choose Mazatlán because of the weather, the friendly local people and the relatively low cost of living compared to other Mexican resort cities. Most of them do not attempt to live on $900 a month.

Dee Hulen, who helped me with this book, lives in a two-bedroom apartment in Mazatlán and says that she can live on $900 per month—not including traveling costs for seeing the rest of México. Her electric bills during the winter average only $10 per month! Because of the year-round warm weather, heavy winter clothing is not needed and you will have no heating bills. Here are some of the average costs of living in Mazatlán:

My average bills in a three-bedroom home are:

- Propane gas used for the stove, hot water heater and gas dryer: about $32 per month.
- Electricity is also cheap, costing about $35 during November through April, but with air conditioning it **could** run as much as $300 during the hot muggy summer months (June-October) if over-used.
- Water is cheaper, with the average cost about $5 for tap water and bottled water for drinking about $10 per month, or about 20 pesos per five gallon jug.
- A home telephone costs about $20 per month, unless you like to call the U.S. or Canada. Long-distance rates are becoming more competitive every year, though.
- Pay-as-you-go cell phones are widely available and easy to use too.
- A full-time housekeeper costs about $50 per week. Our house-keeper/maid works a four hour day once a week and it costs

us about $13 weekly. A gardener costs about $15 every two weeks. But most expats or snowbirds don't have gardens, yards or backyards to maintain.

- Cable and satellite TV and internet cost about the same as the States and in Canada. A package with basic phone service, cable TV and internet runs about $50–$70 per month.
- For some reason, all my friends say they eat out more in Mazatlán, so those costs would increase their cost of living.

Check with people who either live here year-round or are snowbirds. They can answer any questions about Mazatlán you might have. I know because I have asked them! Some of the best sources I've found for information about Mazatlán are the following groups, of which anyone can become a member:

http://groups.yahoo.com/group/mazinfo

http://whatsupmaz.org

http://www.tripadvisor.com/ShowForum-g150792-i257-Mazatlan_Pacific_Coast.html

http://www.mexconnect.com/cgi-bin/forums/gforum.cgi?

http://thepeoplesguidetomexico.com/

You will be fine in Mazatlán if:

- **You keep an open mind and are ready to try something new.** Can you move into a neighborhood and meet new people that speak a different language? Are you willing to get out of your comfort zone? Are you willing to become "the minority"? If you answer "yes" to those questions, you should be okay.

- **You can accept things as they are.** Mexico has its way of doing things, just as we do. Sometimes it may seem like their way is not as good as ours. Since I am a snowbird, I'm able to compare the U.S. and Mazatlán all the time. You know what? I've found that plumbers and electricians in Spanaway, Washington are just as slow as those in Mazatlán—but those south of the border are much less expensive.

- **You're not completely left-brained.** Everything does not have to be precise. I spent 20 years in the army and quite frankly, developed a love for regimentation. Upon retirement, I took a job as a teacher on an Indian reservation. I became quite frustrated with the lack of "precision", but it only took me seven years to adapt to a more relaxed concept of "time".

- **You have a love of people.** Yeah, I like the winter climate in Mazatlán, but I love the people in the city even more. I have found the Mexican people very easy to get to know. I live in a neighborhood where everyone on my block is Mexican. When I have had problems in my house, my neighbors have been more than willing to help. All of the craftsmen and professionals that I have contracted with have become my friends. Even people from north of the border are more approachable in Mazatlán. On the streets or in stores I find myself starting up conversations with people I would never have bothered in the States.

A few years ago, I drove our friends Keith and Jean to Concordia to buy furniture. At one of the furniture factories/stores, they found a table and rocking chair that they liked. Only the table would fit in the trunk of our car.

Another couple were there looking at furniture, a Mexican woman and a man who looked like the typical "Hell's Angel". He was a big man, with long hair, a big black unkempt beard, a huge earring and several tattoos. And he was wearing blue jeans that showed way too much of his rear end.

He overheard us talking about how to get the rocking chair home. "Where do you live?" he said.

"El Cid," Keith replied.

"I used to work for El Cid. I know exactly where it is," he said. "If you want, I'll load your rocking chair on my truck and drop it off at your home this afternoon."

The four of us exchanged glances, and Keith said, "That would be fine. We would really be grateful."

The man's wife began negotiating prices in Spanish with the storeowner for our friends' furniture. We drove away 15 minutes later, having paid less than we originally bargained for the furniture.

Keith asked me, "Do you think the guy will really deliver the rocking chair?"

I thought to myself, *why didn't he ask me that before he agreed to the deal?*, but I said, "Yes, I think he will."

By the time I dropped them at their home the man had called and an hour later dropped off the rocking chair.

Keith likes to tell that story and always ends it by saying, "I was really surprised that I not only gave a man who I would not even talk to in the States my rocking chair, and then that he actually delivered it."

- **A sense of humor is helpful.** Being able to laugh at yourself will get you through many difficulties in Mazatlán, just as anywhere else. Most Mazatlecos have a tremendous sense of humor. If you don't have a sense of humor when you arrive, I'm betting that if you stay long enough, you'll acquire one. Mexicans are wonderful "kidders" and quick with a "comeback". They also laugh at themselves just as much as they laugh at me.

191

- **Mazatlán is a nurturing community.** Regardless of the quality of life you enjoy in your home country, I believe it will be improved in Mazatlán. The year-round warm weather will make your body feel better almost immediately. Waking up to sunshine every day will improve your disposition. Your spirit of adventure will be rekindled by experiencing so many new things. You will meet new friends faster than in any community you have lived in previously. And in some cases you will be leaving old problems behind and starting a new life.

If you expect to live in Mazatlán year-round, or more than six months per year, you have three choices for documentation to be able to do so legally. One, play it safe: a little before the 180 day expiration date of your tourist permit (FMM) you can make a trip back over the border (for just a few minutes), to the States or Canada, and return with a new 180 day tourist permit.

You can also apply for *No Inmigrante – rentista* status (the most common, formerly called the FM3 and still referred to that way by most folks), which allows you to live (but NOT work) in Mexico with unlimited exits and entrances. You get this laminated card in Mazatlán at the *Instituto National de Migración* (immigration - INM) office. Requirements for a *No Inmigrante – rentista* card change occasionally, but at press time these were the requirements:

- Photos (front) 4X4 cms, color. Kodak or other shops that take these photos will know the exact size and requirements.
- Original and one copy of a recent utility bill (to establish residence). This doesn't need to be in your name if you are just renting.
- One copy of all 24 pages of your passport—even the blank pages.
- Original and one copy of valid visa, if renewing.

- Original and one copy of three months of your most recent bank statements to prove a monthly income from outside Mexico of approx. $1,200 monthly.

If spouses apply at the same time the same bank statements can be used, but the monthly income is approx. $1,800 monthly. The required minimum monthly income at publication was about $1,200 per month, but changes annually (Jan. 1), as it is calculated at 250 times the minimum daily wage for general laborers in Mexico City.

If you do not have a monthly income you must have proof of a certain amount of dollars invested or in savings. Check with the immigration office to confirm the amount and required proof. Home ownership in Mazatlán lowers the monthly income requirement, but check with the immigration office for details.

Sometime between 8 A.M. and 1 P.M., take the paperwork and hop a taxi to the immigration office downtown at Prolongation Aquiles Serdan #408 in Playa Sur. The office is staffed with friendly, helpful bilingual folks who will help you through the process. Many folks use the services of two folks just outside of the immigration office to help with the documents, photos and everything else. They say the small amount charged (about $20) is worth it.

I recommend a man named Ángel Cruz. He is bilingual and knows exactly what documentation and forms are needed. He also takes the required photos. And if you have a car permit, he will do the Aduana paperwork for you too. Upon request he will take your email address and keep your info in his computer. A week prior to the annual renewal date he will send you a reminder via email. Tel: 193-6441 or email: *angc9898@yahoo.com.*

You must renew your *No Inmigrante – rentista* card in the same place in Mexico where you are registered, usually where you first registered. If

you move, you must report the move to immigration within 30 days—
even if you just change addresses in town.

What are the benefits of having *No Inmigrante – rentista* status?

You will not be required to renew your vehicle permit every 180 days.
But, if you drive the vehicle out of Mexico, you **must** turn in your permit
and its paperwork and upon return get a new one.

You will also be able to bring your household goods to Mazatlán
without paying duty. The one-time exemption of import taxes for
household goods (*Menaje de casa*) must be used within six months of
obtaining your *No Inmigrante – rentista* status and costs about $180
at any Mexican consulate in the U.S. or Canada. The exemption from
duty for moving your household belongings is a once-in-a-lifetime
privilege.

If over 60 years of age you will be eligible for an INAPAM card
that allows you to get reduced prices at several places including a 50%
discount on inter-city bus tickets. Great for those who want to see more
of Mexico.

Working in Mexico

This question is asked over and over. The answer is always: "It is difficult but not impossible." The first thing you must know is that it is
illegal to work in Mexico unless you have a *No Inmigrante – actividades
lucrativas* or *Inmigrante – actividades lucrativas* status, but with the latter you cannot have a foreign registered car in Mexico. This requires a
letter from a prospective employer stating why and for what exact job
he wants to hire you.

Many of the timeshare companies hire foreigners and take care
of all the legal requirements for their employees. Other employers give
you the letter and expect you to get the *No Inmigrante – actividades
lucrativas* card on your own at a cost of about $200. Even if you're

married to a Mexican citizen and work together you must have the *No Inmigrante – actividades lucrativas* card with the proper permission to work for your spouse.

Forming a Mexican corporation is possible with only an FMM (the tourist permit), but unless you get the properly documented *No Inmigrante – actividades lucrativas* status, you will not be able to receive any pay except for dividends or be allowed to work at the location of the business. The corporation must hire either Mexican employees or properly documented (*No Inmigrante – actividades lucrativas* with the permission that they may work for your corporation in a specific capacity) foreigners. To form a Mexican corporation legally, requires the services of a *notario* – a special type of attorney who is specially trained and licensed to do this (and who also acts as a north-of-the-border title company for buying property in Mexico.)

You can be self-employed by getting a *No Inmigrante – actividades lucrativas* status using a letter from you to immigration (INM), requesting permission by stating the name, address and the activities of the business and your position in that business. Then you must apply at Hacienda (the Mexican federal tax department-SCP) for a tax number (R.F.C.)—lots of paperwork, but at no cost to you.

If you want to have an income by purchasing a large home and renting apartments or converting it to a Bed & Breakfast operation or just renting out your condominium when you're up north, you must have all the proper documentation to be self-employed, as you must pay the 16% Value Added Tax (IVA), the 35% income tax (very approximate), and the various withholding and other taxes for any employees. A good accountant – *contador-(L.C.P)* – is absolutely necessary as only he or she can keep you legal.

I know of some people who don't register their business venture, but they are risking both seizures of their assets and deportation. And I also know many U.S. citizens who don't report their Mexican income to the U.S. Internal Revenue Service (they're supposed to, by U.S. law), as they consider that the IRS won't know anyway.

Whether you're self-employed or forming a corporation there are a few businesses foreigners aren't allowed to be in, commercial deep-sea fishing being the biggie, the others are unlikely. It's best to hire your accountant before starting the process as he can help you get through the paperwork and keep you from making costly errors. A good, English-speaking accountant will only charge you about $80–$100 monthly (more for corporations) and will take care of everything, tax reports, payroll tax computations, enrolling of employees with the Mexican Social Security office (I.M.S.S.) as required by law and lots more.

The main, and seemingly only, concern of the government for foreigners establishing businesses in Mexico, is that all of the appropriate taxes are paid—on time.

The only concern of the Mexican businessperson is that you're not in competition with him. If you are, count on being checked closely and often for any violations of Mexican law, as he knows exactly where and to whom to complain if he thinks you are acting illegally in any respect.

Most foreigners who are successful have businesses that are not in competition with Mexican businesses and have a good Mexican accountant.

Many others work via the Internet and have the money paid to them in the U.S. (or their own country), which is somewhat of a legal gray area, but doesn't seem to have attracted any attention from the Mexican government at this time.

Very likely to attract attention, though, is to live here and rent out rooms or apartments by accepting money paid in some other country. This HAS attracted the attention of the Mexican government, and some expats have been hit pretty hard when the tax inspectors come around. And if immigration hears of it, they must get the *atividades lucrativas* permission on their immigration permit too (and probably pay a fine).

Another possibility is to work in your own country for six months and bring your money to Mazatlán for the other six months of the year—a very attractive alternative.

David Bodwell of Mazatlán Book & Coffee Company (a bookstore) and his publishing company, Editorial Wisemaz, has been in business here for many years and would be happy to answer any questions you may have about working in Mexico or going into business in Mexico. You can either stop by his bookstore or call him. He has also provided information about lawful payment of Mexican employees for this book, in Appendix 4. Tel: 984-5078 or email: *mazbook@yahoo.com*.

What about investing in Mexican Stocks and Bonds?

There are many Mexican investment companies that would love to have you invest in their stocks and bonds, and many expats have made good investments in Mexican stocks in the past. My caution to you is that if you are looking at the weak U.S. stock market returns and see a brighter future in Mexican stocks…think again, unless you are a professional investor and truly know the ropes in Mexico.

Reasons for spending more time in Mazatlán far outnumber the reasons not to. For a discussion of home rental, building, buying and selling, check out the next chapter.

Chapter 13

Real Estate

Rental Services

I have never rented an apartment or house in Mazatlán. Many people have told me "Yes, there are cheap rentals available," and, "Yes, you get what you pay for." I would never rent anything-long term (one month to over one year) without seeing it. Some rental agencies have pictures and descriptions on their web sites. It has been my experience that the pictures look better than the homes.

I have been told that there is a major difference in renting in Mexico than in the U.S. In the U.S., if you have a problem with maintenance, you call the landlord and—usually—he will see that it is fixed promptly. In Mexico, if you have a maintenance issue it is more often than not the tenant's responsibility to fix it or get it fixed.

In El Centro Histórico, a two-bedroom rental, usually an apartment goes for about $250–$600 per month year-round, depending on what level it is furnished, and the price will usually be double that if you rent only during the winter months. For the same size and type of rental in the Golden Zone are between $500–$2,000 per month during winter season. I recommend that if you are dealing with a Spanish-speaking person you have a bilingual person help negotiate (and explain) the contract.

Once you have found a rental you should have an agreement in Spanish (Mexican courts only recognize contracts in Spanish) that covers these points:

- The price and amount of any annual increase.
- When and in what form (pesos, check, deposit in landlord's account) the rent will be paid. Contracts showing the rental price in U.S. dollars are not legal in Mexico.
- What the price includes.
- The length of the contract. Leases in Mazatlán can only legally be for a maximum of 3 years duration (for the best price), but often the renter can get out of one, IF the owner can raise the rent prior to renting to someone else.
- Description of the owner's maintenance responsibilities.

Finally, there is a difference in finding a rental. Yes, there are the classifieds…if you can read Spanish. If you see a sign in a window, knock on the door. It may not be for that home, but it can provide you with a lead. You can also post requests on the *groups.yahoo.com/group/mazinfo* and *whatsupmaz.org* Internet forums at no cost, and the latter has a free classifieds section.

Word of mouth and signs in windows are used quite a bit in Mazatlán. Also, ask everyone you know, and those you meet for the first time. If you don't know anyone, go to El Canucks de Leon restaurant in Olas Altas any Friday between 4–6 P.M. Or go to Las Flores Hotel in the Golden Zone (by the pool) any Sunday between 4–6 P.M. Mexican and expat groups meet every week and can provide you with leads.

You may not have time to do that, so some enterprising people have formed rental companies to assist you. And if you would like to rent out your home, these folks might be helpful. That is how they get their listings.

Mazatlán Rentals: Two of my favorite people in Mazatlán are the proprietors, Marlene, from Canada, and her spouse, Humberto Santana, from Mazatlán. The advantage you have with them is that you get a native English speaker and another person who is bilingual and can help you deal with things specific to Mazatlán. Their motto is: "We hit the streets while you hit the beach." They have houses and apartments all over, but primarily in the central part of town. You can email them at *mazrentals@gmail.com* or check out their website at *www.mazatlan. homestead.com.* Marlene has been in business a long time and has provided the following information about renting in Mazatlán:

"Expectations vary, as do cultural differences. Each rental scenario is completely different and nothing is ever 'standard'. We hope this list helps those who have chosen to search for a private rental themselves."

- Is the rental price a set peso amount?
- Location is important. Is it on a busy street with buses and traffic or noisy night activity?
- Neighbors. What is nearby? Auto body shops, mechanics, a Banda musician's practice house could be next door, or a school nearby causing major traffic problems twice a day.
- Contract. Ask for details. For example, how much notice is required to move?

- If you change your mind or your plans, what is the cancellation penalty?
- Security deposit. When will it be returned? What does it cover?
- What does a furnished unit include? Dishes, shower curtain, cutlery, bedding, linens?
- Is there anything included if the unit is unfurnished? Kitchen cabinets? Ceiling fans? Stove? Refrigerator?
- Which utilities, if any, are included? (Don't expect internet service to be ready and waiting!)
- Is off or on street parking available or will you have to pay to park in a parking lot or garage? Is there one nearby?
- Where is the nearest bus stop and how far will you have to walk?
- How are the water pressure and water pumps? Is there a water problem?
- Is hot water available to the kitchen sink and bathroom sinks, or just the shower?
- Is the hot water tank functional?
- Is the gas cylinder empty or full? Is a deposit required for it?
- Is the gas tank on the roof? How much does it cost to fill? Is it full now?
- Who owns the apartment, where do they live, who has keys? Get phone numbers and email addresses.
- Whose responsibility are major or minor repairs?
- Check for outstanding utility bills at CFE and Telmex. In Mexico, they stay with the home, not the person who received the service.
- Phone service available? (Check outstanding bills against the property – see above.)
- Ask which electric meter is yours and check its condition.
- Hallway and outside lighting in apartments—whose electric meter are those lights on?

- Ask about electric wiring and its age. Do you need adapters for your appliances?
- Maintenance responsibility for grounds, pool, water filters, etc.
- Does the elevator work? Stairwells secure?
- Maintenance staff. What is your responsibility and what is theirs?
- It sometimes floods when it rains heavily, so ask where the drains are located and if flooding is a problem in the area or on the property.
- Does the unit have screens/protective ironwork on windows?
- Doorbell that is operational?
- Where is the mailbox? (If any.)
- What type of security is available?
- Are guests or roommates permitted? Will the rent change?
- Discuss the pet policy ahead of time.
- How will you pay the rent? Direct deposit, or will the landlord visit you once a month?

Home Ownership

Let's first get past a myth about foreign ownership of real estate in Mexico. Foreigners can legally buy land in Mexico, other than the Prohibited Zone, which is anything within 50 kilometers of the coast or 100 kilometers of the country's borders. Wait, Mazatlán lies in the Prohibited Zone.

Not to worry, the Mexican government figured out a way to keep everyone happy. The *fideicomiso*, or bank trust, which encourages and allows foreigners to purchase real estate.

Two main factors have made home ownership explode in Mazatlán: First is that more foreigners are moving south of the border, and second, lower domestic interest rates are making homes affordable to more Mexicans.

Bank Trust – **Fideicomiso:** Shop around for any bank that will handle your trust. They don't all charge the same fee, and service varies. In general terms, the one-time trust permits costs about $2,500 plus an annual fee, currently around $400. Oddly, with this type of trust, the fees are denominated in U.S. dollars, since they are intended only for foreigners. Since 1993, the permits have been issued for 50 years and are renewable, and the trust allows one to designate beneficiaries and substitute beneficiaries, so there is no will to probate when the owner dies.

In practice, the bank trust is often, like mine was, arranged through the real estate company that sold the house to me. We went to Bancomer and I paid for the permit and part of the first year after I filled out some forms. I was told when my annual fees must be paid. You may not receive notice when your payments are due, so keep track of this yourself. My bank allows me to pay from my personal U.S. checking account.

As always, the seller thinks the property is worth more than it really is, and the buyer thinks the property is worth less than it really is. Everyone I talk to wants to buy an inexpensive home in Mazatlán. Some are surprised at the prices. Like any place in the world, the three most important considerations in real estate are the same: location, location and location. The location depends on your personal likes and preferences, your tolerance of any inconveniences and, of course, your financial situation.

If you are strolling around neighborhoods and come upon a house that is run down and appears to be abandoned, don't automatically think a great deal is waiting for you as a "super sleuth". Sometimes it is next to impossible to track down the owner...even if it has a "For Sale" (*Se Vende*) sign.

Real Estate Companies

It has been my experience that real estate agents in Mazatlán are much like those in the U.S. Some are better than others. Real estate agents in

Mazatlán are not required to be licensed (at the present time), however. Properties are either listed with one agency or appear on a central listing. In my judgment, a good agent is very important. Their fees are usually a percentage of the sales price and are negotiable. I provide the following Real Estate companies for your consideration:

Realtymex: Is owned and operated by my friend, Alberto Ochoa. It is a family operation that not only sells properties but also builds homes and other buildings. It is located on Camarón Sábalo, across the street from Bancomer bank. His brother César is an architect and supervises the building program. The employees speak excellent English.

I purchased our home through them and had an outstanding experience. They helped me immensely in getting through my first home-purchasing experience in Mazatlán. Tel: 914-5323 or email: *www.realtymex.com.mx*

Bernal Real Estate: It is one of the oldest real estate companies in Mazatlán. The owner, the personable Lupita Bernal, manages rental property and sells property. Check out their listings on the website at *http://www.lupitabernal.com/eng/index.htm* or email her at *lupitabernal@prodigy.net.mx*. Tel: 914-1753. I'm told that so as not to lose a single client, she leaves her cell phone on 24/7. So if you want to discuss real estate in the middle of the night, just dial her cell: 044-669-918-7735 if you're in Mazatlán or 011-521-669-918-7735 from the U.S. or Canada.

Condominiums: I am listing condominiums in Mazatlán because during the time from 2005 to 2012 there has been an explosion of condo construction. Just like any other home there are advantages to owning a condo. You own the property, and it is a place that can be closed up and left safely for an extended period of time. There is little

personal maintenance and lots of amenities such as beach access and/
or swimming pool, a gym or spa, private parking and usually 24-hour
security. The down side is a monthly maintenance fee that will always
increase, hassles with people living above, below and beside you, and
a Condominium Owner's Association that may or may not be to your
liking.

The price of condominiums varies from $100,000 to over a mil-
lion dollars, depending on size and location. The following are some
condominiums and contact information:

> Quintas Del Mar, Paraiso Costa Bonita, Paraiso Costa Bonita II,
> Marina Costa Bonita and Costa Bonita are located in Cerritos and
> new Marina areas and sold by a reputable, reliable management
> group that is part of Costa Bonita.

> La Ventana is located on Sábalo Cerritos next to Hotel Playa María.

> Las Gavias Grand is located in the new Marina area, Las Gavias Golden
> Shores is on Playa Camarón Sábalo, and Las Gavias Residencial is
> right on the Malecón. Their website is *www.lasgavias.com*.

> Condominios Tenerife is within the El Cid complex. Tel: 913-2745.

> Club Mediterraneo is at the new Marina. Tel. 913-1050.

> Ocean Palms is the high-rise tower in the heart of the Golden Zone
> on the beach behind Dairy Queen.

> Estrella del Mar is on Stone Island, near the airport. Go to their
> website at *www.estrelladelmar.com*. Tel: 914-0363, or 1-888-587-0609
> in the U.S. or Canada.

The Deal

Generally, you will be required to make a written offer. The agent will take your offer to the seller. You may receive a rejection or a counter-offer, but not always in writing. If it is a counter-offer, you may either submit a written counter-offer, or reject their offer. Be warned that I've heard that some Mexican owners are not really interested in selling their home. I've been told of occasions where buyers have made offers at the full advertised sales price and the seller rejected them. My guess is that they are testing the market. You should always execute a purchase agreement in Spanish with the seller of the house. Some agents have a fairly standard written agreement, and I have provided an example in English in Appendix 6. Once you agree on a price, the *notario* enters the picture.

Notario: *Notarios* are not like notaries public in the U.S. The Mexican *Notario* has a law degree and is an unbiased, official representative of the government a with a fiduciary responsibility to both parties. The *notario* verifies and approves the contract from a tax and legal point of view. There are only a certain number of *notarios* in Mazatlán. Most real estate agents have one or two they usually work with. Unlike the U.S., closing is not handled through a title company, but through YOUR *notario*.

In order to obtain the trust deed, the *notario* will:

- Check the Land Registry Office to ensure the property is free and clear. Additional checks are made for outstanding utility bills or municipal taxes.
- Get a permit from the Minister of Foreign Affairs to establish the trust deed.
- Put together all the documents for both the buyer and seller. The entire process takes 30–60 days.

Closing the deal: Closing was kind of an interesting experience with our first house. A couple of days after we agreed on a purchase price, the sellers, our real estate agent and my wife and I met in the office of a *notario*. The five of us sat around a rectangular table. Neither the sellers, a nice Mexican couple, nor the real estate agent could speak English. My wife and I are not bilingual. The only one that was bilingual was the *notario* and he was only in the room for about two minutes. The initial contract had not been completed ahead of time and the office employed the world's slowest word processor. After four and a half agonizing hours in which we all sat across the table and smiled at each other, we finally paid 10% of the agreed price, signed some contracts (that were in Spanish) and were able to hit the road and look for a place to get a cold drink.

About six weeks later, I received a message from the real estate agent that the final papers were completed and I would have to return to Mazatlán. I was also told that I could use my wife's power of attorney so she didn't have to come. This time I found an interpreter to go with me to be sure what I signed was what I originally agreed to. The sellers were not present at this meeting in the *notario*'s office. I brought the balance of the agreed-upon purchase price to the office.

I paid the closing costs, which included:
- A transfer tax of two percent of the assessed value of the home.
- A registration fee of .05% of the assessed value of the home.
- Fees for the tax certificate, title search fees and property appraisal, as well as miscellaneous office expenses.
- The other cost was two percent of the assessed value of the property for *notario* fees. He wanted it paid right away, but when I found out that I would not walk out of the office with a signed deed, I paid him half, with the promise that the other half would be paid upon receipt of the deed.

- It is highly recommended that you, the buyer, get your own *notario*, rather than taking just whomever the real estate agent or seller recommends. That way you are assured that he is YOUR *notario* and looking out after YOUR interests.

Augustín Noriega Galindo: I have used him for the purchase of a home, sale of a home and purchase of a lot. He is very helpful and is usually available by telephone and does not keep you waiting when you make an appointment. His office is in El Centro at *calle* Guillermo Nelson #2503. Tel: 982-6088.

Jorge Buenrostro: Jorge has provided free legal assistance to Friends of Mexico for more than a decade. Jorge, in addition to handling real estate trusts and promissory notes, can also help you set up your own Mexican corporation, and also with many other legal matters [as can any *notario*]. Tel: 981-5083 or 981-0707.

Jesús **Ernesto Cárdenas** *Fonseca:* David Bodwell recommends Ernesto because he has used him successfully for several legal matters, including purchase of two houses and forming a corporation. Ernesto has an office at Amidas de Gaula #16200. His telephone numbers are 940-2228, 940-2229 and 940-2230.

Capital Gains Taxes: The seller pays any capital gains taxes. Capital gains taxes are 35% of the difference between assessed values at the time of purchase and sale, with adjustments made for inflation and capital improvements. The law states that as a buyer you can become eligible for a one-time exemption from capital gains tax if you establish residency for two years after purchase prior to selling. In order to establish residency you must have *Inmigrante* status from immigration (previously called FM2) and all utility and phone bills in your name for six months or more.

Property Taxes: Homeowners in Mexico pay property taxes every year just like anywhere else. Fortunately, they are very low. The property tax, known as *predial* is about .08% of the assessed value, determined at the sale. We have about the same size home in Spanaway, Washington as in Mazatlán, and the tax I pay in Mazatlán is less than 10% of what I pay in Spanaway.

During January of each year, the city posts property tax statements on this website: *www.megared.gob.mx/modules.php?name=adeudopredial2*.

You will need the parcel number for your tax statement. If you pay it prior to the date on the bill, you receive a 10% tax reduction. In some neighborhoods the tax office sets up small kiosks where you can go to pick up your tax bill if you live in that area. You can take your bill to some banks and pay the taxes in U.S., Canadian or Mexican currency. Of course, if you don't have the bill, you will need to go stand in line with a few hundred other people at City Hall. Bring a good book to read and plenty of pesos.

A further reduction of 50% is available for those that live year-round, but proof must be provided. Once you receive your tax bill, take it, copies of your passport, *No Inmigrante* or *Inmigrante* card, home contract, electric/water bill and whatever cash you will need, in pesos, to the city hall downtown and tell the guard at the door that you want to pay your taxes. Most likely there will be a long line—that is where you want to be. You only have to do this once as they will place your status into the computer system for future reference.

Appraisal: As you can tell by now, the appraisal of your property by the city appraiser has a great deal to do with the amount of your closing costs and property taxes. It does not have anything to do with the true value of the property. The appraiser uses a chart that shows land values and construction per square meter. After considering the location of property, the appraiser uses a formula to compute the appraised value.

Home Values/Neighborhoods

Make no mistake about it: There are homes you can buy for $40,000 as well as homes for one million dollars or more and everything in between.

Real estate people in Mazatlán will tell you that prices are going up for home purchases. That may be a sales come-on to get you to sign on the dotted line. On the other hand, I live in a depressed area in the U.S., in which housing prices declined. For that reason I don't blame sales people for protecting themselves by telling you that Mazatlán is not a depressed area and prices will rise...and they have risen in the time I have been here. However, at publication, home prices have stagnated in Mazatlán, the same as in so many parts of the world right now. Prices have not declined much but some decline is evident.

Home values sometimes depend on the neighborhood where they are built. Let's consider the various neighborhoods, going from the docks to the south and heading north:

Playa Sur: Nearest the dock for the La Paz ferry. This is for people who like a nice neighborhood and want to live close to downtown. The homes are of the 1970s variety, many of them large with spacious yards, and run upwards from $120,000.

Cerro del Vigía: The hill where you'll find homes with a great view looking down on the fishing fleet and lighthouse. Some of the oldest and wealthiest families in Mazatlán live in these expensive homes. Not many of these appear on the market, and sometimes smaller homes sell for about $60,000, but most exceed $250,000.

El Centro Histórico and Olas Altas: This is the area from the Cathedral to the Olas Altas beach. Many of these fine homes were vacant in the early 1990s. Fortunately, many foreigners recognized the "Old World" charm of these high-ceilinged homes, and many have been restored.

Sometimes you can't judge the value of the homes from the outside because they are close together, and most lack garages. Inside may be huge rooms with a large central patio and garden and even a swimming pool. Home prices range from $50,000 to $450,000 and up. Many need extensive renovation and modernization.

Cerro de la Nevería: Known as Icebox Hill. These are mostly great view homes. When they have that view, prices are usually way above $300,000.

Los Pinos/Paseo Claussen: Back in the 1970s, this was the fancy area of Mazatlán. Houses are generally three bedrooms on irregular lots. Prices range above $200,000.

Ferrocarrilera: This is in the area near the Hotel Hacienda on the Malecón. The homes are generally four-five bedrooms. Some of the larger homes have been remodeled into business offices and schools. Prices for these homes are well over $150,000.

Estadio: About 30 years ago, this area was developed near the baseball field. Most of the homes are three bedrooms on 200 square meter lots. Some of the homes in the low-lying area are flooded during the rainy season. The prices range from $50,000 to $125,000.

El Toreo: Behind Office Depot and near the Plaza de Toros –bull-ring – this area was developed about 30 years ago and most homes are quite small and on lots of 150–200 square meters or less. There are also some homes in a low-lying area that suffer flooding during the rainy summer months. The prices for these homes usually exceed $150,000.

Lomas de Mazatlán: It is the neighborhood east of Camarón Sábalo between Valentino's and the HSBC bank (Av. Lomas de Mazatlán). There are not many lots still available for development. There are some small homes, but mostly large homes are here. Prices range from $120,000 to $500,000.

Las Gaviotas: A nice neighborhood of homes located east of Camarón Sábalo and north of the HSBC bank to the El Dorado subdivision. These homes retain their value because of the proximity to the tourist area. Prices are about the same as Lomas de Mazatlán, but there are more small houses.

El Dorado: This area runs east of Camarón Sábalo north from Balboa Towers to El Cid. Many upper-income Mexicans live in this quiet neighborhood that has a boulevard, a couple of parks and several dead-end streets. Most home prices range from $150,000 to $500,000.

El Cid: The neighborhood of choice for many Americans and upper-class Mexicans who want to live in a gated community. It is the most expensive area in Mazatlán, not only because of the price of homes, but the annual maintenance and security fees paid by all homeowners. Homes range from condos to mansions, golf site to waterfront. Prices range from $120,000 to $500,000. While the golf course is an attraction for every owner, there is a substantial annual golf membership fee.

Sábalo Country Club: East of Camarón Sábalo and north of El Cid, this neighborhood is loaded with tract homes, many owned by foreigners. If you are looking for a fixer-upper, this is the neighborhood for you. Beware of the low-lying homes and broken roads. That is an indication of flood conditions at certain times of the year. Houses sell for above $150,000.

Marina Mazatlán: Next to El Cid and the El Cid Marina and Yacht Club. The developer ran out of cash in 1995 and there are many unfinished buildings in the area. However, new buildings are now being built in the neighborhood and there are condo developments as well.

Cerritos: Although Cerritos itself is only at the north end, the area north of the new Marina, from just past the two bridges to the end of the road at Cerritos point is commonly called Cerritos. There are numerous housing developments and condo complexes, including La Marina Tennis and Yacht Club, Playa Escondido Condominiums, Villas de Rueda, Playa Linda, Real del Mar, Villa Tranquila and Royal Country. Two-bedroom condos at La Marina and Playa Escondida start at $120,000. and houses at Villa Tranquila sell for just over $125,000. The villas in Villas de Rueda go for about $400,000 and the Playa Linda homes go for between $200,000 and $800,000.

Playa Delfín: This is the northernmost part of Mazatlán and is the current frontier. There has been little development, but beachfront lots are relatively inexpensive. The Pueblo Bonito people built a huge complex called Emerald Bay several years ago. The Playa Delfín condominiums are located here. Currently, the only road is packed dirt and gravel There is now a bypass road that skirts the Golden Zone, and makes getting to the downtown and airport easier and faster—especially during the high tourist season. But the lots further north have a bridge problem where the estuary feeds into the ocean (the bridge was poorly constructed and washed out during the rainy season a few years ago and the various temporary bridges keep doing the same. The municipal government, at this time, doesn't have the funds to construct a new, properly designed bridge.)

Estrella del Mar: A relatively new development on Stone Island, and a few minutes from the airport. This beautiful gated community, surrounded by a golf course and the ocean, offers a convenience store, restaurant, hotel, swimming pools, and when completed, 1,145 home lots and 630 condominiums. Lots, homes and condos are currently on sale and under construction. Golf course custom home sites with ocean view start at $120,000 and condos at $199,000. Tel: 1-800-967-1889 from the U.S. or 914-0363 in Mazatlán.

There are many other housing areas further inland that are much less expensive, but not many foreigners venture into those neighborhoods. I have heard of subdivisions where one can purchase an semi-finished tract home for less than $25,000, but I have not talked to anyone who has bought and finished (the interior only) one.

What about building a home?

Again, this is a matter of personal taste, location and your financial situation. There are many good architects, builders and real estate people in Mazatlán.

César Ochoa: I recommend César because I have not only seen several of the buildings he built, but he completely remodeled our house and then built a new one for us. I had heard horror stories about delays in work, etc., and how if you want things done right, you must be on-site all the time. I have not had that experience. During the remodel, my wife walked through the house with César a couple of times, noting what she wanted done. They went to various stores and ordered tiles, fixtures and paint. He gave us an estimate, we negotiated the price, and I prepared a contract that included a per-day penalty if the job was not completed on time. After paying a third down, we departed for our home in Washington State. I gave him four months to complete the job and he took three.

Every other week he emailed us pictures showing the progress. We sent another third of the payment via cashier's check two months after he started, and then made the final payment after I inspected the job and gave final approval. When we arrived on site, the job was perfect and so clean we moved in the same day.

In 2003, César built a new house for us in the El Dorado neighborhood. He started it in May and it was finished completely in November. He did the job while we were gone and emailed us photos again. He asked us to come to Mazatlán two weeks prior to the scheduled date of completion and stay in the house so that any adjustments could be made prior to his turning the house over to us. The job was completed on time and better than we expected…and we had very high expectations!

I have also recommended César to several friends to assess homes prior to possible purchase to determine costs of modernization, safety factors, etc. They have all been pleased with his service, and some ended up hiring him.

He is part of a family firm, Realtymex, on Camarón Sábalo in the Golden Zone. Tel: 914-4001 or cell: 044-669-120-0761.

Santiago León *Lorda:* Santiago "Chago" León Lorda was born in Mazatlán and educated in Mexico City, but returned home and has been building quality homes for more than 30 years. If there is one thing that makes Chago different, it is his attention to detail. It is easy to tell a "Chago" house, because in addition to a pleasing visual design, there is an absence of the little problems that drive homeowners crazy. He also stands behind his work and will fix problems that crop up months after the owner has moved into the property. Tel: 916-5552.

A Cautionary Note

I feel an obligation to provide a word of caution about your vacation home. Many real estate agents will try to convince you to buy a home by saying that you can rent it out when you are not using it and the rent will make your house payments. The problem is that generally you want to use the home to get away from those cold North Dakota winters. Well, the prospective tenants want to get away from Manitoba snowstorms. So unless you only want to live in the home a month or so in the winter, or prefer to be in Mazatlán from June through October, I don't think you will be able to make your payments by renting your home. I tried it for two years, using a property manager and I got a bad first year and only about a month of renters the next.

Another consideration is that both Uncle Sam and Mexico want their cut of your rental profits. You should check with your accountant in your home country, Hacienda and your *notario* in Mazatlán before buying a rental property or renting your home out. At the very least, you will have to have *No Inmigrante – actividades lucrativas* status and be registered with Hacienda for paying your Mexican taxes.

I have looked at hundreds of homes for sale in Mazatlán and for some reason, Mexicans and foreigners alike do not "prepare" them for sale by making minor repairs and adding a coat of paint where needed. You should examine the home closely because the cost of repairs should be considered in your offer.

Salitre: I mention *salitre* here because it is a common and sometimes expensive home maintenance problem in Mazatlán. If you notice puffy, peeling paint and the concrete seems to be drying into powder and falling from the walls, you may have a case of *salitre*. It is alkaline salts in the ground moisture or even in the mortar used for building the house (often due to unwashed beach sand being used) leaching out due to ground moisture.

I'm told that the only way to eliminate this is to chip away the concrete down to the brick, and then apply a new sealer called FinSalitre. This solution neutralizes the alkaline residue. Wait five days and apply a second coat. Wait another five days and apply a mixture of cement, washed sand and city water. Be sure to let the area dry before painting. There are many reliable professionals in Mazatlán who can do this job for you.

Home Financing

Like anywhere else in the world, most sellers want cash. There are, however, some sellers that, for their own reasons, offer to carry a contract. It is not difficult to acquire home loans, but don't expect the same percentage rates enjoyed in the U.S. I recommend that if you are retired and want a second home, you take out a second mortgage on your home in the States to purchase that vacation home in paradise.

If that is not an option, Residential Mortgages for Mexico provides a 20-year mortgage at 6.5%. Check out their website at *www.rmm-mx. com* Tel: from the U.S. 1-800-778-6272 or locally, 913-3065.

Home Insurance

Home insurance companies are like any other insurance. You don't really know if you need it until the disaster happens. I've been insurance-poor all my life and will probably continue to be so until my next-of-kin collects all my life insurance benefits. The good news is that because most of the houses in Mazatlán are made of bricks, concrete and stucco, there is little chance of a fire wiping you out. The bad news is that Mazatlán lies in the path of hurricanes, although that is a very, very low risk. You should also consider accidents and thefts that could occur on your property. Further good news is that the price of homeowner's insurance is less expensive in Mazatlán.

By now you should have gathered that I recommend insurance. Not to worry, I'll also recommend an outstanding insurance agent.

Juan *Francisco* ***Chong*** *Robles:* An agent for home insurance in Mexico. His company also sells auto insurance, medical and life insurance. I have purchased insurance from Juan since I bought our first home. In 2010, I had a house break-in and Juan saw that my claim was processed in a timely manner. Once I bought car insurance from him and prior to crossing into Mexico, my car was totaled. Since I was never able to drive to Mexico, my money was promptly refunded. Tel: 982-0260 or 982-8900 or 982-3310 or cell: 044-669-918-2504. From the U.S. or Canada: 1-619-488-3717. Email: *juanchong@telmexmail. mx*, or his website at *www.chonginsurance.com*. As a last resort, if all you have is your laptop with Skype on it, his ID is juanchongmaz.

Selling your home

What if you decide, for whatever reason, that it is time to sell your dream house? The time to think about what it will take to sell it should be before and during the time you are making the purchase. You will need your deed, either a copy or the original. The information where it has been recorded on the public registry is on the last page. The *notario* will need this information to get the certificate of "Liens Burdens or Encumbrances". An up-to-date paid copy of your tax bill is also important. Your *notario* will need this to get a certificate from city hall clearing your property of pending charges. Make sure these bills are kept in a safe place.

As mentioned earlier, you may want to have capital gains taxes excused, so have the foresight to get *Inmigrante* status from immigration at least a year before and keep all the electric and telephone bills. You'll need a copy of the most recent electric bill to prove you still live there. The *notario* will require the most recent water bill paid in full, association dues receipts showing that they are paid up and trust fees if appropriate. You will also need to give him a birth certificate and driver's license or passport. If you had the home built recently, you may need a final release from Mexican Social Security (IMSS) showing that all worker's taxes have been paid. All of these papers will someday be important so don't throw them away. Keep them in a safe place.

You have made up your mind and decided to stay in Mazatlán for an extended period of time. You have acquired a place to stay. In the next chapter, you'll learn useful tips for adjusting to your new environment.

Chapter 14

Tips for home owners and long-time renters

WHEN I FIRST MOVED TO Mazatlán I had far more questions than I had answers. I received a great deal of help from friends and neighbors, but I learned more from making my own mistakes. In this chapter, I will try to provide you with some helpful tips as well as some pitfalls to avoid. I'm sure you may have other preferences, but these are based on my own experience and information given to me by other people.

The Major Essentials

Shipping your furniture/household goods into Mexico: If you have *No Inmigrante* status less than six months old, you can bring or have your furniture/household goods shipped to Mazatlán without having to pay any import duty. You will need to provide a list of items that will be transported to your nearest Mexican Consulate to get the permit that allows this. Don't attempt to bring new items to Mazatlán, as you will be assessed import duties.

Inventory the items you are importing: your inventory needs to include the make, model number and serial number of any electronic apparatus. Remember that the date of manufacture is on the item and if it is less than one year old there is a possibility of having to pay duty.

For the rest of the items, descriptions, i.e., five boxes of clothes, three boxes of kitchen articles, etc., are sufficient.

Take two copies of your inventory list and your *No Inmigrante* card to the nearest Mexican Consulate, where they will stamp it and write in your *No Inmigrante* document that you are transporting your furniture/household goods. The cost is for this permit, known as a *Menaje de Casa*, is about $180. You give these stamped inventories along with a notarized copy (done at the consulate) of your *No Inmigrante* card to your shipper. When your furniture/household goods reach Mexico, customs inspectors will check it. A customs broker is required to transport the goods across the border. Brokers' fees normally are in the neighborhood of $300. I can suggest a highly recommended professional who can facilitate moving household goods from the United States to Mazatlán.

Robert Hudson: Tony Feuer retained the services of Robert Hudson of Mazatlán to move his furniture from San Francisco to Mazatlán. Tony paid the airfare to fly Robert to the San Francisco Bay area. It took them two days to pack the largest truck U-Haul has. Robert drove the truck and Tony drove his own Suburban. By 7 A.M., two days later Robert guided him to a customs broker just before the Mexican border in Nogales where Mr. Hudson orchestrated transferring all his goods to a Mexican-plated, 48-foot tractor trailer. They then dropped the U-Haul off at a U-Haul dealer in Nogales. The tractor trailer was locked and sealed by the custom's agent. They followed the driver to the border crossing.

The truck driver went his way and they went theirs. Two days later they arrived at a predetermined location in Mazatlán where they met up with the furniture truck. Robert retained the services of a fellow with a decent sized stake bed truck and six movers. Mr. Hudson supervised the truck-to-truck transfer and six loads later everything was in the house in the exact position requested and nothing had been damaged.

The entire move cost Tony less than a third of the lowest estimate he got from a professional moving company. Mr. Hudson has a website at *www.movingtomexicoguy.com* and can be contacted by email at *movingtomexicoguy@yahoo.com.* Tel: 176-0893 and cell: 044-669-127-9074 and his U.S. number: 1-213-928-6214.

Furniture: Personally I would not go through the trouble of shipping furniture to Mazatlán. In my opinion, it is not worth the hassle, and I have furnished two houses in Mazatlán—one on the cheap and one with more expensive furniture. In addition, termites can sometimes be a problem here in the tropics and they don't seem to like cedar, which most of the locally crafted furniture is made from. There are many furniture stores in Mazatlán and also near Mazatlán. Concordia, a small town about 30 miles from Mazatlán, is best known for colonial-style furniture, but they can make many styles and have a number of different factories. Mesillas is a little town about three miles southeast of Concordia where furniture is also made.

Custom-made furniture can be made from either pictures or drawings in a reasonable amount of time. Some places will even deliver free of charge. It's not hard finding the factories, once you enter the towns.

Good furniture is also available in and around Guadalajara. Tonalá is a suburb particularly known for its rustic – *rustico* – style furniture. Linea Castores is a reliable shipping company that will get it from Tonalá to your home in Mazatlán. They enjoy a reputation for delivery in a timely manner at a decent price.

We checked all those places, and then furnished 80% of our new house from a sale at Fábricas de Francia, a huge department store in Mazatlán, for the same price as having the furniture custom-made.

Leaving a Foreign Plated Vehicle in Mazatlán

You will need *No Inmigrante* status in order to bring a car from the U.S. or Canada and legally leave it in Mazatlán year-round, unless you plan to nationalize the vehicle, something few do, as it is both expensive and complicated.

Auto ownership in Mexico: Many people have asked questions about car ownership in Mexico, and I will answer them to the best of my ability. Bureaucrats are different throughout the world, and people in the same office interpret the laws differently. What I am about to tell you is not the gospel. It is the best information available at this time.

People wonder if it is best to purchase a car in the U.S. and bring it to Mexico or buy one in Mexico. It is possible to do either or both, but there are problems inherent in both options. By and large, it is cheaper to buy a car in the U.S. and bring it to Mexico.

One advantage of buying a new car in Mexico is that new car warranties are honored on vehicles sold in Mexico, but not those purchased in a foreign country. Another advantage is that you can legally sell the car to a Mexican citizen.

Can you sell your foreign plated vehicle to a Mexican? NO, it is, and always has been, completely illegal. What happens if your car gets totaled or is not usable? Well, you can't donate it to charity or leave it sitting around. You must somehow take it back to the States for disposal.

Most foreigners purchase cars in the U.S. or Canada and drive them to Mexico. A change in the law occurred in 2011 and a rough translation is as follows:

"Temporary importing of a vehicle is required for the vehicle's entrance into the country for its use within the country for a limited time length and for a specific purpose. When the vehicle leaves the country it should be in the same condition as it was when imported.

"According to Mexican customs regulations (section 106Va), foreigners and Mexicans residing abroad can import a vehicle as long as they can prove their immigration status in Mexico by means of official documentation (Visitor's Permit-FMM, *Inmigrante – rentista*

(FM2), *No Inmigrante* (FM3). The time limit for a vehicle to return to its country of origin would be the same as the importer's legal status in Mexico. Extensions to legal status of the importer also apply to vehicles but must be requested at the closest office of Aduana.

"Once imported, vehicles can be driven on the Mexican territory by the importer, his/her spouse, children, parents or siblings, regardless of their nationality; or by another foreigner having proper immigration status in Mexico, or by a Mexican national, but in this last case, the importer or any of the authorized persons mentioned above must ride the vehicle as well.

"To import a vehicle the owner must go to a Banjercito CIITEV unit, make a cash deposit ($200–$400 for the contingent cost of the import tax that would be generated if the vehicle was not returned to its country of origin and/or the cost of fines arising from infractions to the customs regulations). If the import permit fee and deposit is paid by using an internationally accepted credit or debit card, the cash deposit is not required.

"To avoid forfeiture of this deposit, importers whose immigration status in Mexico was extended or adjusted as described in the Mexican Customs Law section 106IV, must, within 15 days of the immigration modification, present a photocopy of that extension to any Aduana – Customs – Office in the country, as well as a photocopy of the vehicle permit and a brief letter signed by the importer and stating the changes in his/her status in Mexico." [It is recommended that you make a photocopy of that letter and have the Aduana stamp your copy so they can keep the original letter and the attached photocopies].

"If you have further questions please contact the *Administración Central de Regulación Aduanera* office."

The deposits may vary from year to year and with the age of the vehicle, but the important thing to remember is that you must keep the paperwork and receipts so that you can collect the deposit when you exit the country with the vehicle.

If you have *No Inmigrante* or *Inmigrante – rentista* status you must go to Aduana and get a letter of permission to keep in your car each year when you renew that status. In June of 2011 Mexican law changed to require renewal of the car permit as soon as your immigration card is renewed. If you DON'T do so within 15 days, you will lose the deposit you made. There is no charge at Aduana for this renewal.

To get to the Aduana office in Mazatlán, go toward the docks (east) on Aleman, then turn right (south) at the docks. About half mile south, look for a two-story yellow building on the dock (east-left) side of the street. Bring the following documents:

- The original and one copy of the car permit received at the Port of Entry.
- Your *No Inmigrante* card and one copy of the *No Inmigrante* letter you get from the immigration office.
- Your passport and one copy.

There has been some speculation about driving a car from Mexico to the United States with the Temporary Import Permit hologram sticker. Some people think that there is no need to return the sticker when leaving the country, and that they can simply drive back into Mexico and avoid that annoying line at the car registration window at the border. **Wrong!** The law specifies that when the car leaves the country you must surrender the temporary importation permit (you get a computerized receipt), then it must be re-registered upon its return. Can you ignore the law and drive back into Mexico on the old hologram sticker? You can try, but you risk being told at one of the check points that it is no longer valid and that you must return to the border and get a new one.

The vehicle permit must be gotten immediately upon the vehicle's entry into Mexico at the 21km checkpoint, and the official form you'll be given must be carried in the car at all times.

Some people wonder if it is possible to get a car licensed in Arizona temporarily. Yes, it is. Simply go online at *http://www.azdot.gov/mvd* to find office hours and locations under Customer Service. An office visit and Level I inspection are required. Most offices do not require an appointment. You will need to show proof of vehicle ownership, such as the title or expired registration, and proof of identity as the vehicle owner, such as your driver's license. There is no charge for the inspection, but there is a permit fee of $15 and the temporary license is only valid for 30 days.

My friend George Keats provided the following information concerning his experience in acquiring a Mexican driver's license:

Requirements:

- A copy of your *No Inmigrante* or *Inmigrante* card.
- Utility bill (to prove residency). This may be in the name of your landlord if you rent.
- They did not ask about my foreign license and I did not show it, so I assume it is not relevant.
- Blood type—If you don't know it, they direct you to a lab two blocks away and they do it in 10 minutes or less.
- Process: First, you fill out an information form.
- At about 10 A.M. you listen to a one-hour spiel in Spanish where you are given answers to all the questions that appear in the test.
- You take a written test of about 20 questions concerning basic driving skills.
- I had been told by a friend that the English test had only 10 questions, so I requested the English test. It actually has about 20 questions...all basic stuff.
- You take a driving test around the block.

- If you pass, you pay about $24, get your photo taken and wait a few minutes for the license…about 2½ hours in total.

Recently the Mayor of Mazatlán told the foreign community that policemen will no longer take car license plates from cars until parking tickets are paid, nor will they take drivers licenses from traffic violators until their fines are paid. We've heard no reports as to whether or not this is not happening any longer.

INAPAM card (senior citizen discount card)

If you have *No Inmigrante* or *Inmigrante* status and are 60 or older you can get one of these cards at their office at Constitución #2007, near the corner of Rosales in El Centro between 8 A.M.–2 P.M. Monday through Thursday and 8 A.M.–1 P.M. Friday. It qualifies you for many discounts including a 50% discount on inter-country buses and reduced price movie tickets, medicines and some other things.

When you go to INAPAM bring along your passport and two copies, your *No Inmigrante* or *Inmigrante* card and two copies (of both sides), a utility bill for proof of residence and two copies, and two full frontal ID photos. Also, even though it is on your card, they want the original CURP document and two copies. This is available at the CURP office in the main Post Office building. Once the card is issued, it does not have to be renewed. They will give you a list of places where you can use the card, if you ask.

Schools

There have been many queries about the quality of schools in Mazatlán. For that reason I asked my friend Lani Wooll to research the subject through friends and co-workers. She reviewed private schools, with monthly fees, uniform and book costs and bus transportation if needed. There may also be other associated costs such as field trips in the more expensive schools and in the less expensive middle-class schools there may be expenses such as providing toilet paper and soap. Books and uniforms are purchased by the parents from the school.

There is generally high security at the more expensive schools. Discipline is strict, a lot of homework is assigned, parental participation is mandatory and expectations are high. Rote learning and memorization is emphasized over critical thinking.

Except for English classes, few, if any, other classes are taught in English. Although there are few native English-speaking teachers for the English classes, there are qualified Mexican nationals. This is mainly because the transient foreign population won't/don't want to work for the wages offered and the schools don't want transient teachers. I have a listing of recommended schools at Appendix 7.

Death in Mazatlán

Yes, it can happen anywhere, even in paradise on earth. Don't despair. I have spoken with Roger Culbertson and Lani Wooll who had deaths in their families and the funeral arrangements **went as smooth as possible**.

For you citizens of the U.S., the U.S. Consular Agency will assist in making all arrangements. Their office is at Playa Gaviotas #202, across the street from Hotel Playa Mazatlán in the Golden Zone. Call the Consular Agent at 916-5889 for an appointment.

For Canadians, your Consulate is on the second level in the La Marina Business and Life Commercial Center in the new Marina. The telephone number is 913-7320.

When a death occurs, take the passport or birth certificate and death certificate to the consular agency or consulate. They will provide the names of funeral homes, places of cremation and procedures for flying your loved one back to the U.S. or Canada. I'm told that even with the cost of airfare it is less expensive than in the U.S.

Utilities

I had the secretary at the real estate company where I purchased our home call the utility companies to start my service. The cost is much less than in the U.S. except for electricity during the summertime when air conditioners are running. I'm in Mazatlán from October 15 to April 15, and although I have an air conditioner in the bedroom, I never use it. My ceiling fans are enough to cool the house on those rare hot days.

Electricity: Many wall outlets are two-pronged, and many do not have the right size, i.e., one prong larger than the other, for your electrical appliances. Many appliances have a third ground plug. The cheapest way is to purchase adapters at a hardware store. In some cases, builders will put in a three-pronged outlet, but not install the grounding wire. There are no electrical inspectors required in Mazatlán so some builders will scrimp on the ground wire.

Another common problem is in the kitchens of older homes, where there may not be enough electricity to run all your new appliances. As a result, the circuit gets overloaded and the breaker switch keeps clicking off. The only way to solve the problem is to install a new circuit and put some of the outlets on it.

My electric bills usually run $20–$30 per month. It can be paid at any bank, OXXO convenience store or at a drive-through machine at the electric company office in front of Sharp Hospital on Rafael Buelna. For those who live in El Centro, there is another CFE office near the docks where you can pay your bill. You can also pay electric bills on-line. The official web page for CFE is at *http://www.cfe.gob.mx*.

Water: The typical water system in a Mexican house is a gravity flow system. The city water is piped from the street to a cistern, usually located under the carport or garage. It has an electric pump that moves the water up to a tank – *tinaco* – on the roof. The large tank on the roof has a float and when the water drops to a certain point, it turns on the pump that runs until the tank is full. When you turn on the water faucet, the pressure of the water that flows out is caused by gravity—the higher the tank, the better the water flow. Hence the slow-moving showers and long-running washing machines in one-story houses. The advantage of this system is that when the water is turned off due to an emergency, you usually have a reserve in your roof tank. Many, if not most, one story houses don't have the cistern-pump setup, but depend on city water pressure during low usage hours to refill the rooftop tank.

If you can afford it, you can have a pressure tank and water pump installed. It is pricey, but it is worth it, especially when you have house guests.

I learned how to troubleshoot my water system the hard way. If no water runs out of the faucet, first go up on the roof, take the cover from the tank and lift the float bulb. If water runs into the tank, your mechanism was stuck, and you may just have to spray some WD-40 on the moving parts (above the water line, of course). If that doesn't work, the problem is in your pump or cistern, and you'll probably need professional help.

I know some foreigners who drink water from the tap, without benefit of a purification system and never get sick, as the Mazatlán city water is rated completely potable. But most foreigners do as we did. We had a water purification system installed in our house. I also run all our drinking water through a Brita water filter.

The monthly bill for tap water runs about $4–$15. It can also be paid at the local bank or OXXO convenience store.

Electric and water bills are usually delivered by a delivery person and are not very timely or, for that matter, reliable. My friend, Sam, said he once found his water bill on the street a half block from his house. So when you are out for your morning stroll, don't just pick up that paper and throw it in the trash. Take a good look at it, as it may be your utility bill. I solve the problem by paying the entire water and electric bills for a year in advance.

Just go to the water company offices, either downtown or in Plaza del Mar (Ley #2). Tell them you want to pay by the year and they will tell you what you paid last year. I always add a few pesos more. For the electric bill you can go to the office downtown or to the drive-through in front of Sharp Hospital. Use the auto pay machine and just deposit what you think will cover the electric cost for the year. It saves me several trips to the bank—or if I forget, to the utility companies.

Propane Gas: We have a gas stove, clothes dryer and hot water heater. Our propane gas tank is on the roof of our house. Every two or three months I call Gaspasa at 981-0505 and request a delivery. I have waited for delivery anywhere from 30 minutes to two hours. Due to expansion, they never put in more than 90%. You pay on delivery. There is usually a gauge on the tank that will indicate when the tank needs to be refilled. Don't forget to check it occasionally, as cold showers are still cold, in spite of the beautiful weather outside.

Most homes have gas delivered in cylinders. The driver brings a fresh tank, connects it and takes the empty cylinder.

Cable TV: Cable TV is available all over Mazatlán, except in El Cid, with most of the channels you enjoy in the U.S. or Canada. Basic service from Megacable, with mostly Mexican channels, costs about $38 per month. For this, you get mostly Mexican channels. Satellite TV service is also available.

The Megacable bill is usually delivered to your home around the middle of the month. But don't count on it. Sometimes I don't receive a bill. On one occasion, I didn't receive a bill, and since I did not pay it, my service was disconnected. When I called to get connected, the lady acknowledged that the man failed to deliver the bill—but I still had an obligation to pay it. She told me in the future if I do not receive a statement, to go to one of the many Megacable offices throughout the city and pay the bill. You can also pay it with a credit or debit card online at *www.megacable.com* after a rather lengthy registration process.

Many people from Canada bring their Shaw network receiver and antenna down and continue their subscription throughout the year to be able to enjoy all the channels they are accustomed to.

Maz Satellite offers digital satellite service with different packages of U.S. and Canadian English-language TV. There is a set-up fee and monthly charges of $40–$55 depending on the package you choose. Tel: 668-0798 or 910-0270 or their website at *www.mazsatellite.com* for details.

Telephone: A telephone is essential in Mazatlán, although some people find a way to avoid getting one. Telmex had a monopoly on the landline phone service in the country until just a few years ago. Now you can get landline service from Megacable if you have their cable TV service or Axtel if you have their Internet broadband service. If the previous renter or owner of your address did not pay their bill, you must pay it before Telmex (or any of the other two) will connect you.

In order to get Telmex phone service, you must go to the main office in El Centro near the Cathedral or to the office on Insurgentes a couple of blocks east of Soriana on Insurgentes. I used my friend, Santana, who is bilingual, and he had me connected and operational in two days. Any phone from the U.S. or Canada will work, but I got a new one as part of a promotion. You get 100 free local calls (to other landline phones), then a small, per call charge kicks in. Also, if you call a cell phone number it will cost you at least $0.09 [approx.] (one minute minimum) per call. Federal law in Mexico says that "caller pays" for all calls **to** cell phones. This was because so many people complained that they were having to pay for unwanted solicitation calls to their cell phones. You sure don't get any blind solicitation calls on your cell phone here. Telmex bills can be paid at the bank, OXXO convenience store, online at the Telmex website or at any Telmex office (24/7).

For you "snowbirds", if you want to keep your same number when you return you must keep it connected while you are gone and pay the monthly fee.

233

Long Distance Rates: Long distance is expensive in Mexico if you don't know what you're doing. But now that there is competition for Telmex, rates are coming down. Of course, since most expats/snowbirds have Internet service, Sykpe, Magic Jack, Vonage and other Internet phone services have completely solved that problem.

Cell phones

You can buy an inexpensive pay-as-you-go cell phone from TelCel, Movitel or other companies for about $23 which includes about $7.50 worth of minutes (although they are NOT denominated in minutes). They can be purchased at any TelCel store or kiosk or at any of the big grocery stores as well. When you run out of prepaid credit, you can buy more in increments starting at $20 pesos from numerous places all over town, including OXXO, the grocery stores or any *farmacia*.

Internet connections

There are three different Internet service providers that I know of in Mazatlán. They are Telmex, the phone company that provides the Infinitum service, Megared, from the cable TV company and Axtel, another telephone company.

Telmex has ADSL. It can cost as little as $35 per month. The nice thing about ADSL is that you use it on the same line as your telephone and when the phone rings your Internet connection merely drops down in speed. Unlike cable, ADSL is like being connected directly to the backbone. However, ADSL is only good if you are within a specific distance from a switching station. It is also dependent on the condition of the copper wire from your home to the switching station. There are a lot of variables. You may get a great connection and you may get a bad one or you may be too far from the station to qualify.

I use Telmex ADSL and have been quite happy with it. In addition, before I go home in April, I can put the ADSL line on vacation for a few dollars, and when I return in October I go back to Telmex and get reconnected.

I can't find a majority of acquaintances that vote in favor of any one of the ISPs. One thing they do agree on is: Do buy a good surge protector and don't scrimp on the cost. Mazatlán has many electrical storms and surges that can fry your hard drive and cause expensive computer damage. While we are on this subject, it is appropriate to get a surge protector for your TV and refrigerator as well.

WiFi stands for wireless fidelity and uses radio frequencies between a computer and a wireless router connected by wire or cable to the Internet. For us non-computer nerds, it means that there are cafés, shops and public places where they have WiFi and we can take our laptops and go online to send emails and check the web without having to hook up with any cables. Some of the places I know of at this time are McDonalds, Pura Vida Restaurant, the food court at La Gran Plaza, Mazatlán airport, Rico's Coffee Shop, The Shrimp Bucket and almost every hotel in Mazatlán, with the list growing every month.

Speed test of internet: To check the speed of your internet, go to:
www.speakeasy.net/speedtest

Internet telephoning or VOIP

My wife likes to call my daughter every few days in Washington State. Until I found this system, I tried (to no avail) to limit her calls to 15 minutes. I solved both our problems by using the Vonage phone. Now she talks as long as she wants and my stomach no longer churns with worry about the cost.

When I had my telephone connected at Telmex, I also asked for a Infinitum ADSL Internet connection, which together with the landline costs less than $45 per month. When I am in the States, I hook up the Vonage and make calls to friends in Mazatlán for no charge. This can also be done with dialpad.com, Skype, Magic Jack [all less expensive than Vonage] and other services. We can carry the Vonage router box anywhere and the telephone number remains the same.

In October we bring the Vonage box, laptop computer and telephone to Mazatlán and hook them up to our DSL line. We can still have unlimited calls anywhere in the U.S. and Canada for the same price. Because we have a Spanaway, Washington, Vonage number, it is a toll-free call for our daughter and neighbors. For anyone else outside our local area in Washington, the long distance charge is only from their telephone to our Spanaway, WA location—they don't have to pay any international long-distance rates to Mexico! And the reception is excellent.

Megared: If you have cable TV with Megacable, you can get their high-speed Internet service called Megared. Then you can sign up with dialpad.com, Skype or other VOIP services and call the USA for less than four cents a minute (or even free).

Axtel: You can get these same services if your Internet service is with Axtel. It is a fairly new service, but seems to work well.

News of the U.S. and world in English

There are some places that sell daily newspapers like USA Today, but they are hard to find, not consistent and outrageously expensive. In addition, the news is late. Some hotels provide U.S. newspapers for their guests.

I get the news online. I put my hometown newspaper and the Seattle Times on my favorite browser, and every morning over coffee, I get on the net and read the sports section and news. Even if you go to one of the Internet cafés for a half hour, it would be cheaper than buying a foreign newspaper in Mazatlán.

There are some costs associated with Internet service.

Ink cartridges: Ink cartridges for printers are expensive in Mexico or in the U.S., but if you know where to go, you can save some money. In Mazatlán, the cheapest and most convenient place I know is Rellenables

Movil. Just call Robert at tel: 176-6613 or cell: 044-669-431-0572 and within an hour or two, someone will be at your home to remove your cartridge(s), fill them on the spot and place them back in your printer. All for about $7.50, although that varies with the brand of the printer and the size of the cartridges.

Computer Technicians: MazPC: Charles Swarts works on Microsoft, Mac and Linus. He does computer repair as well as web design. He is very responsive and charges going Mazatlán rates. Tel: 1-817-346-6432 from the U.S., cell: 044-669-110-5034, or email: *support@mazpc.com* or his website at *www.mazpc.com.*

César González Mera at Aztech is also reliable and fast and speaks perfect English. His cell phone number is 044-669-994-3705 and his website is *www.aztechpc.com.*

Satellite TV technician: Jorge Herrán set up my satellite system three different times and adjusted it a couple more. He speaks excellent English and is very responsive. Jorge is also a magician with a computer. Tel: 985-5599 or cell: 044-669-994-1518.

Home Repair, Service and Construction Materials

Building supplies: Marlene Santana of Mazrentals offers the following: Felton lumberyard in El Centro has some fabulous building supplies. The lumberyard is very efficient, and they take all credit cards AND don't go away for a mid-day meal break. She learned that it is appropriate to tip the guy that custom cuts your lumber.

> Kuroda is located across from Plaza Ley #1. This place sells tiles, tubs and sinks and is even more efficient than any building supply place she shopped at in the U.S., including Home Depot. They double-check your tiny bits and pieces against the bill that you paid prior to bagging it for you. They also have a branch next door to the Polimedica building on Rafael Buelna.

Home Depot: Just like in the states, it is a huge one-stop hardware store/lumber yard/nursery and garden store. It is located on Rafael Buelna, across the street from Soriana.

Glass and glass cutting

Con Ramírez is on Ejército Mexicano, across the street from the Plaza Ley #1 They have always done a good job for me and are fast and reliable. They do nice beveling also. They will come out to your home and take measurements and their prices are about the same as all the others.

Humberto Ruíz, owner of Vitrales Inova is located at Insurgentes #290-A. Humberto charged quite a bit less than Ramírez above. He speaks English. Going east on Insurgentes from the Malecón, his little shop is on the right just before the first stop light. It is a small shop so you might easily miss it. Just a note, glass seems to be expensive here in Mexico so don't be surprised at the price no matter who gives you a bid.

Purchase/repair of windows, screens, mirrors, and glass work: Contact José Luis Castorena—cell: 044-669-929-6282 or 044-669-137-1883. He does excellent work, is very responsive and speaks fair English.

Wrought iron work: For excellent and reasonably priced custom wrought iron work go to Las Quince Letras in El Centro. The owner is Jorge Medina, who speaks excellent English. Tel: 982-8896.

Craftsmen: Call Lani Wooll and leave a message at 989-8624 and she will return your call. Her cell: 044-669-918-1678 or email, *laniwooll@ gmail.com.* She has a whole list of reliable, honest plumbers, handymen, electricians, architects, carpenters, masons and painters. They all work or contract with the Tórres Mazatlán resort where she is the head chef. She can supply excellent references from Americans, Canadians and various hotels where they have also done work. Most can speak some English.

Régalo (emphasis on the first syllable) has done some small plumbing projects around our house, such as water heaters, leaky pipes, faucets, etc. Cell: 044-669-120-7948.

Lorenzo Enrique López is more of a plumbing and electrical contractor. He is better for larger jobs like a new cistern, serious plumbing inside walls or out to the street mains, etc. His English is slow, but he can communicate in English. I used Lorenzo to repair a toilet and he was efficient, reliable and inexpensive. Tel: 984-8696.

Electrician/Plumber: Marco Hernandez comes highly recommended both as a plumber and electrician. Marco installed a water purification system and pump in my house. He is very responsive, but speaks no English. Cell: 044-669-932-0832.

Small appliances and parts: I have had good luck on most any small appliance parts and repairs at Camacho on *calle* Zaragosa. It is on the north side of the street, just east of the 5-way stoplight at Aquiles Serdan.

My friends Herman Heynen and Dee Hulen highly recommend a small repair shop at Benito Juárez # 916 in Playa Sur, about two houses south of Av. Miguel Alemán The shop has a Samsung banner hanging outside. They had their microwave ovens repaired there. The owner's name is Jesús Osuna. Tel: 982-2978.

A good technician repaired Sophia's microwave oven on two occasions and also repairs TVs. He does not speak English. Call him before 10 A.M. at 983-3525. TV repair: Lani Wooll recommends Ivy's on Benito Juárez, between Zaragoza and the Malecón in El Centro. They also repair other small appliances. They give you a free estimate prior to doing the job.

For a gas stove repairman call Tecnico del Hogar. Yes, they do make house calls. Tel: 982-2253.

My friend Willie Bodrack recommends Semayre de Mazatlán for appliance repair. They are at Montes de Oca #807 in *colonia* Juárez. They also make house calls for large appliances. Juan Sánchez, the owner speaks excellent English. Tel: 986-5416.

Taller Especializado makes house calls for washer, dryer, A/C, dishwasher and refrigerator service. The father/son team is very responsive. The father, Agustín Figueroa, cell: 044-669-127-3074, is the boss but does not speak English. His son, Javier, cell: 044-669-122-1070, speaks excellent English.

Locksmith: If you lock yourself out of your home or simply need more copies of keys, go see Moises. The little hole-in-the-wall (literally!) shop is located on Camarón Sábalo, across from the Balboa Club in the Golden Zone. He is an excellent lock picker. I know quite well as he has opened doors in my home twice! He speaks some English and rates are excellent. Cell: 044-669-931-8971.

Sewing machine repair can be done by La Máquina Contenta Singer, Aquiles Serdan #2402, about 3 blocks north of Av. Zaragoza (at the five-way intersection). Tel: 985-4517, but if you don't speak Spanish you'll need a interpreter.

Handyman: Luis Miguel Gil does construction, tile, dry wall, home maintenance, roofing, light plumbing, electric and painting. He is reliable and speaks excellent English. He charges a little more but is worth it. Tel: 988-3518 or cell: 044-669-173-7268.

Mail

Mexican mail service is not only slow, but has a reputation of being unreliable. For every good experience story I've heard about mail delivery, I've heard 100 bad ones. I would not recommend using the Mexican mail system. Especially do not use them to pay your utility bills. But in recent years this has been changing. Now many expats use the Mexican Post Office, both to send and receive mail and report very good results.

Their MexPost service is only a bit slower than DHL courier service, but much less expensive.

Post offices: If you have no other choice than to use a Mexican post office, the main post office is located near the Cathedral downtown. There is at least one smaller post office in the *Central Camionera* (main bus depot) and there may be one in *colonia* Juárez as well. There is also a small telegraph office at *Central Camionera*.

Post @ Ship (formerly Mailboxes, Etc.): is located at Camarón Sábalo #202-4, across from (and a little bit north) Domino's Pizza, in the Golden Zone next door to Dolce Mami restaurant. They sell U.S. postage stamps and packing materials. I have found their shipping service to be reliable but pricey. Tel: 916-4010.

Quick Delivery **to** Mazatlán: Fedex or UPS. With either one you need the exact Mazatlán address written the Mexican way. Like mine here:

Charles A. Hall
calle Balboa #108-B
Fracc. El Dorado
C.P. 82100 Mazatlán, Sinaloa
Mexico

Even if you decide to use the Mexican mail system, your letter has a better chance of getting to you if you have it addressed the same way. The *Colonia* or *Fraccionmiento* is important. It's definitely part of your correct address. I live in, Fracc.(ionmiento) El Dorado, David Bodwell lives in Col.(onia) Sánchez Celis, most people in El Centro live in Col. Centro which includes El Centro Histórico and Olas Altas. Basically, everything between Av. Gutiérrez Najera on the north and Av. Miguel Alemán on the south, Paseo Clausen on the west and Av. Emilio Barragán (alongside the docks) on the east is Col. Centro. There are three small colonias around and on Cerro de la Nevería that aren't part of Col. Centro, although usually included when casually speaking of El Centro.

I send mail back to the States whenever possible with a friend or acquaintance that is heading back to the States and is willing to drop the envelope in the nearest mailbox in the U.S. Every Sunday at the Vineyard Church on Camarón Sábalo, about 150 yards north of Panama Restaurant and Bakery, the last thing the minister asks is, "Are there any people heading back to the U.S. or Canada who would be willing to post letters?" There are always people who answer in the affirmative. I use this method all the time and have never had a problem with slowness or loss. [This works pretty well during the tourist season – mid-October thru mid-May, not so well the rest of the year.]

Quick delivery out of Mazatlán: The only real choice is DHL, which has an office in the Golden Zone almost next door (a bit north) to Domino's Pizza and cattycorner to the HSBC bank.

For routine utility bill payments for my home back in the States, I use my checking account and credit card for automatic monthly payment.

The intercity bus service in Mexico is very reliable, though pricey, for sending and receiving packages. I have known people who have made purchases in Guadalajara and had them shipped to themselves in Mazatlán via the bus service.

Grocery stores/Supermarkets: I have shopped at all the supermarkets, Mega, Soriana, Ley (#1 in Plaza Ley near El Centro and #2 in Plaza del Mar near Wal-Mart) and Wal-Mart and found them to be about the same price. They don't charge the same prices for everything and they don't all carry the same products. We have found that we often have to go to two or three supermarkets to fill our needs. Prices for foods produced in Mexico are usually significantly cheaper than the same thing produced and purchased in the U.S. Food imported from the U.S., however, costs more than in the U.S.

Sam's Club requires about a $35 per year membership fee. You can cut the cost of membership in half by going into partnership with someone else. They allow two cards for the annual dues.

Special foods

It is difficult to identify "special foods", because some of the foods we take for granted in the States are not available in Mazatlán or are hard to find. The following are items that I have found or have been told about:

Tofu: Can be found in most major grocery stores, Sam's Club and at a little store just off Zaragoza, around the corner east of *calle* Guillermo Nelson.

Soy milk: Is now available at most supermarkets.

Coffee: Being from the Pacific Northwest, I've grown accustomed to good coffee. No! I'm not a Starbucks' snob. I've not been able to bring myself to pay $4 for a latte or espresso—but my wife drinks enough for both of us.

We especially like the El Marino export gourmet coffees of Oaxaca, beans or ground, espresso, beans and all of the flavored coffees sold at the El Marino shop/booth in the Central Mercado and the wonderful Café Aroma Real from the state of Nayarit sold at Mazatlán Book & Coffee Company, located in the mini-shopping plaza on Camarón Sábalo, across the street from the Hotel Costa de Oro, behind the Banco Santander in the Golden Zone. David Bodwell has the best coffee for the price in Mazatlán.

There is a fairly good health food store on calle Zaragoza, around the corner east of calle Guillermo Nelson (cattycorner across from Zaragoza park).

Vehicle repair

Mazatlán has as many good mechanics as there are cars. They can do wonders—especially with older models. Many of my friends have favorite mechanics in Mazatlán. I have first-hand knowledge of only one garage. I have heard they can service any car, old or new, foreign or domestic.

GL Auto Servicios: (GL stands for Gonzalo Llausas, the owner.) I was impressed by the sense of professionalism and the many late-model vehicles being worked on in the shop. They have seven full-time mechanics and all the computer equipment to handle newer cars and trucks. Gonzalo is very knowledgeable and has two degrees from U.S. schools and colleges in automotive repair. His English is close to flawless. The result was always a reasonable bill, an excellent repair and an altogether pleasant experience. GL Auto Servicios is on Camarón Sábalo #316 in the Golden Zone, right next to the Hertz car rental.

Auto body shop: The Convertiauto Mazatlán, located on Rafael Buelna, next to the Nissan dealer, does outstanding body work. They have a big operation with modern tools and computer-aided paint matching. I took my 2003 auto there to get a small panel painted. It cost almost $90, tax included. I had the same thing done to a car in the U.S. about five years ago and it cost close to $400. They have a service department as well, so I had scheduled maintenance performed too. And the car was finished on time! Of course they also do insurance work—free estimates on request. Tel: 986-7696.

I also recommend Felton's, on *calle* Sierra Rumarosa, visible from and just off Rafael Buelna, about a half-block east of the PoliMedico building. Tel: 984-2291. Their email address is *alexfeza@hotmail. com*. Just like in the U.S. and Canada, I recommend more than one estimate.

Electric window repair: Fernando Plasencia does an excellent job of repairing power windows and door locks. His address is Rio Piaxtla #178, *colonia* Estero. Going north on Ejército Mexicano turn right onto Rio Piaxtla, which is the street at the stoplight (and overhead pedestrian walkway) in front of Ley #1. Go six blocks east and it's located on the left—a small yellow house with a one-car garage.

Spanish Language Classes

While it is not necessary to speak or understand Spanish, if you plan to set up housekeeping in Mazatlán, I recommend you take Spanish classes. I practice my Spanish by watching and listening to Mexican TV programs. Mexican friends are always willing to correct my Spanish diction and verb usage. There are numerous people and schools who give classes to fit the needs of just about everybody.

One that I have used is English and Spanish for All, owned by Martha Armenta of CONREHABIT, a certified and licensed simultaneous translator, located at Ángela Peralta #230, *fracc.* Flamingos. Just off the Malecón and one block south of Insurgentes or two blocks south of the La Gran Plaza shopping mall, then turn right onto *calle* Ángela Peralta. Tel: 984-8010 or cell: 044-669-106-0305.

A couple of books that will help most anyone, whether they are taking classes or not:

Enjoy México in Spanish, by David Bodwell, gives you simple, basic Spanish for a large number of cases, the correct pronunciation (very important in Spanish), proper speaking etiquette and a number of cultural tips with wit and experience, an easy way to construct sentences that make sense and much, much more.

Speaking Spanish like a Native, by Brad Kim collaborating with his Mexican wife, is a "must read", for anyone seriously interested in learning idiomatic Spanish. While I would say it is written for the intermediate Spanish speaker, as a novice speaker, I found it extremely useful in teaching me how to put phrases together. The author makes good use of humor and sports metaphors to make the reading easier and more entertaining.

Both books are available from your favorite bookstore or the Internet. In Mazatlán they can be purchased at the Mazatlán Book & Coffee Company.

Translation assistance: Ángel Cruz is not only an outstanding interpreter and translator, but is the man that has his office next to the immigration office and is a big help in filling out the necessary forms. He can also complete the form for your auto to be registered with the Aduana. Tel: 193-6441 or cell: 044-669-108-8632. Email: *angc9898@ yahoo.com.*

Legal advice: Spencer McMullen is a lawyer in Guadalajara. He provided this information to share with foreigners. If you need to hire an attorney, this could be a big help!

"I see all sorts of mistakes that attorneys make and I doubt even 1% of their clients know they make these mistakes, and some are huge.

"Here in Mexico there are no oral proceedings for the most part [as of 2012, Mexican court procedures are being reformed and oral proceedings are being introduced, although, as of this 2012 edition, the vast majority still follow the written request method] and most everything is done by turning in a written request and then the court issues a ruling. If you are involved in litigation ask your attorney to provide you a copy of each request turned in to the court within 24 hours of doing so. It doesn't matter that you speak or understand Spanish as it will help you build a file, something which few people have, and if their attorney turns out to be a real dud, they'll need a full copy of their file to have the next guy clean up the mess. Only an attorney with something to hide will not provide this to his client or one that is lazy or cannot afford an $800 peso scanner or one peso for a copy.

"More importantly than a copy of the request to the court is what the court answers back. Sometimes the court orders can be from one page to three or more. The heading is really what matters as reading it you'll know if your attorney screwed up.

"On the top it says "AUTO" (meaning court ruling) Then the following are danger signs that your attorney screwed up (these are the most common):

"NO SE ADMITE This is where your attorney did the lawsuit wrong and the court won't accept it. Sometimes the attorney can correct and resubmit, other times they chose the wrong court, manner or relief, didn't wait or do it in time, etc.

"SE PREVIENE This is where the attorney forgot to include something, perhaps as simple as a copy of the suit to be served on the other party, a copy of the plaintiff's *No Immigrante* card or other document to show they are legally in the country and sometimes they really aren't attorneys and pretending to be and have a three-day period within which to show their attorney ID, among other things. There is a time period here to act, usually three days and do things properly or else your case gets kicked out and you start from scratch.

"NO HA LUGAR This is where the attorney asks the court for something and it is denied. Commonly this is where the attorney asks the court to start or conclude an evidentiary period but perhaps they calculated the time wrong or some other improper request.

"Knowledge is power. These are general terms but will allow you to see, if your attorney seems to be always getting rulings with these headings, then maybe they don't know what they are doing or the court just hates them. Either way it is not good news for you. The court also makes mistakes (they are human but this isn't too common) so everything needs to be taken into consideration, but some attorneys just don't know what they are doing and have no business practicing and preying on the naïveté of the foreigners by showing off their sparse English skills.

"Just because another gringo recommends an attorney doesn't mean they know what they are doing. Litigation is what separates the men from the boys. Some cases a monkey can win, others will challenge even the most experienced jurist."

Legal Assistance: If you are robbed go to the legal office located in the building adjacent to Playa Mazatlán resort on calle Playa Gaviotas that was once the Canadian Consulate office, right across the street from the U.S. Consulate Agency. Now the sign on the front of the building has the Sinaloa state seal and SINALOA in big letters followed by an unbelievably long name in Spanish that **very** roughly translates as State attorney for crimes against tourists. There the people will get you started as to which legal office to go to to report whatever happened to you. It is the "District Attorney" for foreigners and they can describe what they do in perfect English.

Miscellaneous

Internet sites: This is a list of the most popular and reliable websites with news and information about what's going on in Mazatlán:

http://www.maz-amor.com/
http://pacificpearl.com
http://mazatlanlife.com/
http://www.mazatlanmycity.com/
http://mazmessenger.com/
http://groups.yahoo.com/group/mazinfo/
http://www.whatsupmaz.org/
http://www.countdowntomexico.com/
http://www.friendsofmexicoac.org/

Google map of Mazatlán: If you cut and paste this link to your web browser you will find a general map of Mazatlán. Just click on the little orange man above the zoom in/out icon and bring him to any area in Mazatlán and you'll get a picture of that place. Ain't technology wonderful?

http://maps.google.com/maps?f=q&source=s_q&hl=en&g=Ej%C3%A 9rcito+Mexicano%2C+82000+Mazatl%C3%A1n%2C+SI%2C+M exico&q=Mazatlán+sinaloa

but if you REALLY want to see where places are, go to the wikimapia map:

http://www.wikimapia.org/#lat=23.2385217&lon=-106.4460692 &z=18&l=3&m=b.

And if you prefer a "real" map to carry around, go to Mazatlán Book & Coffee Company.

Everybody complains about the weather, but no one does anything about it. If you want to check the weather for specific dates use this website, *www.wunderground.com.* Get the Mazatlán weather page displayed and scroll to almanac and history. Personally I am just interested in the weather today (I can look outside and see the sunshine), and the next few days (which are usually more sunshine).

Fibah Beauty Salon: Laura Delia Habif has the reputation for using make-up to make pretty women beautiful and beautiful women gorgeous. She also does haircuts, color and styling, facials, manicures and pedicures, permanents and more. Look for her shop in the Lomas de Mazatlán residential area, at Sierra de Venados #415, the street running east next to Dolce Mami restaurant. Just two blocks east of Camarón Sábalo in the Golden Zone. Tel: 914-0150.

Gaby's Beauty Shop has fast become a favorite with the women of Mazatlán. Aside from the usual cut, shampoo and color, she does permanents, and highlighting. They have estheticians that specialize in massage, reflexology, pedicure, manicure, acrylic nails, waxing, fake eyelashes and laser hair removal. Her shop is located on Camarón Sábalo # 3001, in Sábalo Country, across the street from Chile's Pepper and Tony's on the Beach restaurants. Tel: 044-669-120-5379 for an appointment.

Naomi Paredes and her father Luis have a unique business in Mazatlán. Naomi does all of the things any beauty shop can do (and speaks really good English) and her father, Luis (not much English), is a men's barber. AND they do it by all appointment, right in your home. Cell: 044-669-123-2372.

Framing of photos and pictures: For a beautiful job at excellent prices, try Marcos y Molduras, El Pinito at *calle* 5 de Mayo #1517 in El Centro. It is easy to find, right behind the City Hall (*Palacio Municipal*). They have many samples and can do a job overnight. I had them frame six paintings, four pictures and a mirror and the job was completed in three days. Tel: 982-5643.

Vivero Diana: A *vivero* is a nursery or greenhouse business. They have flowers in pots, plants, fountains, trees and shrubs as well as yard ornaments. They are located on the corner of Rio Fuerte and Cruz Lizárraga one block off the Malecón behind the Hotel Aquamarina near downtown. Operating hours are from 10 A.M. to 7:30 P.M. Monday through Saturday and 10 A.M. to 2 P.M. on Sunday. Tel: 985-6050.

If you like driving there is a good selection of plants at a *vivero* a couple miles past the turn-off to the airport on highway 15. It is on the left and has no signage.

Mazatlán Home Rentals: In addition to finding you a place to stay, they provide personal assistance in solving your problems as well as working with Spanish-speaking community members. Santana is bilingual as well as having a great sense of humor. He knows where everything is and you don't waste a lot of time asking for directions. I'm told he set a new record by having my Telmex phone connected in just two days! Check their web page at *http://www.mazatlán.homestead.com*.

Bazar – **Bazaar** – this is a second-hand store for you bargain-hunters. It is located on Belisario Dominguez, four blocks south of the Fisherman's

Monument. From the Malecón, turn left onto Belisario Dominguez and go about two blocks and look for it on the left.

Garage door repair

My friend Lou Raskin recommends Jorge Medina Osuna, Las Quince Letras, at Franciso Villa #2309 in El Centro. They repair both doors and garage door openers. The owner speaks "Spanglish" and can be communicated with. Tel: 982-8896 or email: *las15ltras@yahoo.com*.

I receive excellent service from Rodolfo Medina Osuna, who specializes in automatic garage doors. His shop is at Canonero Tampico #421 in El Centro. He speaks some English. Tel: 981-3981 or cell: 044-669-994-1609.

Are the insects bugging you?

Many people have told me that ants and cockroaches have gotten into their homes. We have not been bothered much by insects. The reason is that we have an exterminator come and spray our house every couple months. The non-toxic chemicals cause a slight clean-up problem 24 hours after application, but it is well worth it. We use Eco Fumigaciones, who charges us approximately $15, but they charge by the size of the house (and ours is pretty large). They do a good job and actually show up when they say they will. Tel: 986-7921.

Several residents have complained about the tiny ants on the kitchen counters. I use "Hot Shot" by Maxattrax, and it works great.

Sewer problems: Since most of Mazatlán is at sea level (or slightly below or above) and sewers are gravity-operated, drainage problems can occur, especially in heavy rains. Sometimes during heavy rains, water from the street may back up into your sewer. If so, you have an old sewer line from your house to the street. To prevent this from happening in the future, have a flap installed on your line at the street. Water will exit your pipe, but the flap prevents water from entering your sewer.

If you need your sewer cleared, call the Plomero Company. Roberto Carlos did an excellent job for me. No one there speaks English, but I did fine demonstrating with hand gestures. The cost was very reasonable. Tel: 981-1447

Foam for mattress top: Some people complain about the hardness of beds in Mazatlán—especially in the hotels. Well, the expensive route is to get the expensive kind of memory foam from Wal-Mart, or go downtown and get the less expensive foam type.

The less expensive foam is available at Telas y Tapices, an upholstery shop that also sells upholstery supplies. They are at *calle* Teniente Azueta #2510, right across the street from east side of the main city flower market (which takes up an entire square city block!). The owner's name is Jorge Ramos, and he speaks English. He has what you want in several different sizes, thicknesses and "firmnesses". Tel: 982-1633.

Getting cash from U.S. and Canada

For those of you who live here from five or six months to all year, there is an excellent way to get your money to Mazatlán at a better exchange rate. The Casa de Cambio is called Intercam, which is located on Camarón Sábalo in the Plaza Balboa (at small strip mall at the front of the Balboa Club). They specialize in converting personalized U.S. and Canadian checks to pesos and give a better exchange rate than the banks.

If you need money wire-transferred you can have it transferred to yourself c/o Intercam at their U.S. bank in California and you'll not only get a lower wire-transfer fee from your bank and a better exchange rate than the local banks give, but you'll avoid the fees many of the local banks charge for receiving a wire transfer.

They will also cash personalized dollar checks you have been given by someone else as long as you guarantee them. For legal reasons they will NOT cash any U.S. government check or U.S. Post Office money orders.

You will need to provide copies of your *No Inmigrante* or *Inmigrante* card, passport and utility bills in your name or your landlord's name if renting, to get registered with them. The manager is Miguel Ochoa, L.A.E., and he speaks good English. Telephone him or his assistant Rafael (who speaks really good English) at 916-7517. They are also an agent for investments, stock market and insurance policies.

I hope this book has been helpful in making your stay in Mazatlán an enjoyable one. I wish you many happy returns to paradise on earth!

Spanish Words and Phrases

W ITH ASSISTANCE FROM Sra. María del Rosario Romero de Rodríguez of the "English and Spanish for All" school and David Bodwell.

To learn conversational Spanish, it is important to learn the correct pronunciation of the Spanish words. If you cannot pronounce a word, you will not be able to recognize it when it is spoken to you.

Mexican Spanish Pronunciation Guide©
from
Editorial Mazatlán

A guide to Mexican Spanish pronunciation, based on common western and midwestern U.S. and western Canadian English pronunciation:

The vowels

a as in father
e like the ay in bay *or* like the Canadian "eh"*
i as in machine
o as in cold

---

* see notes for perfectionists

u like the oo in food

y, when used as a vowel, like the i in machine

The diphthongs

The following are the common Spanish diphthongs (ai – uo), really pseudo-diphthongs, as both letters are pronounced, one slightly weaker than the other (the i or the u). This guide will always indicate these 13 diphthongs with a dot (·). Any vowel pair represented **without** the dot is pronounced as two separate, distinct letters. Note that the "y" is sometimes interchangeable with the "i".

ai(y) like ah·ee

au like ah·oo

ei(y) like ay·ee

eu like ay·oo

ia like ee·ah

ie like ee·ay

iu like ee·oo

oi(y) like oh·ee **except** for English loan words such as boiler where it is pronounced like the oy in boy, e.g., BOY layr (a hot water heater).

ou like oh·oo

ua like oo·ah, but commonly slurred as wah

ue **or** üe like oo·ay, but when …

ue is after g **or** q the u is silent, **not** a pseudo-diphthong.

ui(y) **or** üi like oo·ee, but when …

ui is after g **or** q the u is silent, **not** a pseudo-diphthong.

uo like oo·oh

ae, ao, ea, eo, oa, oe are **not** pseudo-dipthongs, but in ordinary speech are pronounced almost like one. Try to pronounce the two vowels separately but quickly. In the phonetic versions they will be shown with a dot just as the regular diphthongs are unless the two vowels are in separate syllables.

oa like oh ah, **not** a pseudo-diphthong, but sometimes slurred as wah, e.g., the Mexican city of Oaxaca is **correctly** pronounced as wah HAH kah.

Notes on diphthongs:

Spanish has **no true diphthongs** (as we know diphthongs in English), as you can see from the above phonetic renderings. However, the two letters are pronounced (only **rarely** slurred into one sound – a phoneme – like we do in English) so close together that it is very hard for an English speaker to HEAR them as separate. Normally, if a Spanish diphthong has an "i", the "i" is only slightly pronounced. The same applies to the "u".

When first learning Spanish words, you should make the effort to pronounce both letters, even though that is not truly correct, otherwise some bad **mispronunciations** could cause you to be misunderstood. **If** the vowel combination has an accent mark over one of the vowels, this "splits" the combination and they are pronounced totally separately. Unfortunately, **in México**, the common suffix, -ria that should **almost** always have the accent mark, **ría**, rarely has it, so be careful. It's pronounced RREE-ah, **most** of the time.

Some pseudo-diphthong examples:

six – **seis** – say·ees **not** says as in "he says..."

comb – **peine** – PAY·EE nay **not** PAY nay

dance – **baile** – BAH·EE lay **not** BUY lay

The consonants

b as in boy

c before e **or** i, the same as s, but before any other vowel, like the
   c in care.

ch tch as in watch, with the "t" pronounced.

d as in dog when an initial or final letter of a word or a ***stressed***
   syllable or after **n** or **l**, otherwise, like a soft **th** as in the word
   think, but the normal English **d** sound will be understood if
   you find this difficult.*

f as in fair

g before **e** or **i** like the h in hair, but before any other letter, like
   the "g" in game.

Note: In some dialects of Mexican Spanish, particularly those in
southern México, "gua" is pronounced "wah" instead of the correct
"goo-ah" or "gwah". Wah sounds like baby talk to folks in the rest of
México so please don't get in this habit.

   *gue like the word gay

   *gui like the word ghee, the clarified butter used in India.

   *güe like goo-ay

   *güi like the word gooey (goo-ee)

h always silent

j like the h in hair

k like the c in care

l like the l in like

ll like the heavily stressed **y** in **YES!,** as when your team scores.
   Often, in México, you will hear it pronounced like the **j** in
   jelly or the **g** in **beige**. All three pronunciations are acceptable.

m as in man

n as in name

---

* see notes for perfectionists

ñ like the ny in canyon, but more terse and not split between two
   syllables

p as in pan

q always followed by ue **or** ui, but the u is silent

   *qui like the word **key**

   *que as "kay" in the word **okay**

r as in rowdy, **rolled,** i.e., **lightly trilled**, except between two vowels, where it is pronounced like the soft **d** in medicine in casual
   central/western U.S. speech.*

rr r as in rowdy, **strongly trilled**, no real English equivalent.

s as in sun

t as in top

v the same as b, **but** if you find this difficult, the normal English **v**
   sound will always be understood.

w as in wander

x as in exit, **except** in words borrowed from the various Mexican
   native languages, e.g., Xalapa hah LAH pah and México, MAY
   hee koh, where it is the same as the **h** in **hair** or **often** like the
   sh in she and **sometimes** the **s** in sun.

y before a vowel, see **ll**, otherwise the same as **i**

z like the s in sun

Stress/emphasis (for pronunciation):

The stressed syllable in **most** words depends on the last letter of the
word: If it's a vowel (**a e i o u**) or **n** or **s**, the stress is on the **next-to-last**
syllable, e.g., táco, señóra (*accent marks only for these examples*), otherwise
it's on the **last** syllable, e.g., señór, nacionál, comér (*accent marks only
for these examples*). Only words that **don't** follow these two simple rules
are written **with** an accent mark to let you know which is the stressed
syllable. There are **a very few** nouns in Spanish that don't follow these

---

*   see notes for perfectionists

three rules, but are always stressed on the last syllable unless the word has an accent mark elsewhere.

In México, when a word is written in all capital letters, the accent marks are frequently **not** used, so it's easy to make pronunciation errors. Be aware.

Some written words have an accent mark that has nothing to do with pronunciation, but is only there to differentiate the word from one with the identical spelling and pronunciation, but a different meaning, e.g., c**ó**mo – how between question marks ¿~? or exclamation points ¡~! or como – like or as (a comparison), s**í** – yes, si – if or **é**l – he, el – "the" before a masculine noun.

Sometimes the accent mark is used to "split" a vowel combination (so it's **no longer** a pseudo-diphthong) such as **í**a or **ú**o, which puts the stress on the syllable with the accented letter.

Notes for perfectionists:

Some consonants, particularly "p" and "t" (sometimes "b"), are pronounced in English with a *plosive*, i.e., a sort of puff of air that lays a little extra stress on the letter. Spanish pronunciation, while nearly identical with the English for these letters, NEVER does this.

One of the reasons English speakers hear Spanish as "very fast" is that spoken Spanish is **NOT ENUNCIATED AS SEPARATE WORDS**, but until you are fluent, continue to enunciate the separate words, as you would in English. This merely sounds somewhat theatrical to those listening; it won't be misunderstood **if** you pronounce the words properly.

Another reason English speakers hear Spanish as "very fast" is that spoken Spanish gives only approximately ½ the **time** to a vowel that spoken English does. Spanish speakers will hear the person learning Spanish pronounce words as if they are heavily "drawled". English speakers will hear a native Spanish speaker sound as if he is "clipping" his vowels.

Good examples are the words yes and no – **sí** and **no**. You and I, English speakers, will usually say these as the English words see (sseee) and no (nnoo), but a Spanish speaker will say them as see (**see**) and no (**no**), exactly the same sound, but so "clipped" and abrupt that these two words may sound rude to an English speaker.

These are the main reasons that it may be difficult for you to **understand** a native Spanish speaker, even though your Spanish is **understood** by native Spanish speakers.

When using the phonetic versions of the Spanish words, you should practice saying them until you can say them all run-together, otherwise your pronunciation will be considered a little "odd", but not wrong.

*The Spanish "e" is pronounced most of the time in normal—as opposed to beginner—speech exactly like the Canadian interjection "eh" or the "a" in late…but very "clipped" and not always. Until you become more proficient in Spanish, it is best to always pronounce it like the "ay" in bay.

The soft Spanish "d". This is tough. It's really not pronounced like the soft English "d" in medicine, as that will be **misunderstood by Spanish speakers as a soft "r". It's more like a soft English "th". Probably the **best** example is the **th** in **think**. A common word for pig/pork, **cerdo**, is pronounced SAYR thoh with this sort of **th** sound.

***The "ue" and "ui" after "g" and "q" are **not** pseudo-diphthongs, as the "u" is totally silent. In the case of the "g", the "u" is inserted after the letter to indicate that the "g" before "e" or "i" is pronounced as a hard "g" instead of the normal "h".

The "üe" and the "üi" after "g" **are** normal pseudo-diphthongs. They just have the dieresis (those two little dots) so you will know that the "u" is **not** silent and the g is still a hard g.

The "u" after "q" is there merely because Spanish borrowed the "qu" from Latin in order to represent the "k" sound before "e" or "i", and the "u" has never been dropped, it's just silent.

****The soft Spanish "r". This is real tough. The word for newspaper, **periódico**, will be **heard** by most English speakers as "pediódico". But the English word medicine, when spoken **casually** (the tip of the tongue lazily resting against **lower** teeth) by a central/western U.S. English speaker, will be heard by most Spanish speakers as "mericine", so the best way to describe the pronunciation of the soft "r" is that it is like the soft, casual "d" in medicine.

Here are a few words to get you started understanding Spanish. The capital letters are emphasized. For example, hello is spelled hola, but pronounced OH-lah.

Good morning	buenos dias	bway-nos DEE·ahs
Good afternoon	buenas tardes	bway-nas TAR-des
Good evening	buenas noches	bway-nas NO-ches
Hello	hola	OH-lah
Goodbye	adiós	ah-de-OHS
Friend	amigo	ah-MEE-goh
Thank you	muchas gracias	MOO-tchahs grahs-ee·ahs
You're welcome	de nada	day-NAHD-ah
Sir (mister)	señor	say-NYOHR
Miss	señorita	say-nyohr-EE-tah
Madam (Mrs.)	señora	say-NYOHR-ah
Yes	sí	see
No	no	noh
Excuse me	con permiso	cohn payr-MEE·soh
Please	por favor	pohr fah-BOHR
I'm sorry *or* Excuse me	discúlpame	dees-KOOL-pah-may
Pardon	perdón	payr-DOHN
Go ahead (pass)	adelante	ahd-ay-LAHN-tay
What's your name?	¿Cómo se llama?	COH-moh say ÝAH-mah
My name is…	me llamo…	may ÝA-moh…
Nice to meet you	mucho gusto	MOO-tchoh GOOS-toh

How are you?	¿Cómo está?	COH-moh es-TAH?
Fine, thank you	bien, gracias	bee·ayn, GRAH-see·ahs
And you?	¿Y usted?	ee oos-TAYD?
What's happening?	¿Qué pasa?	KAY PAH-sah?
Not much	nada	NAH-dah
Until later	hasta luego	AH-stah LOO·AY-goh
Until tomorrow	hasta mañana	AHS-tah mah-NYAHN-ah
I don't speak Spanish	no hablo Español	no AHB-loh es-PAH-nyohl
Do you speak English?	¿habla inglés?	AHB-lah een-GLAYS?
Who?	¿Quién?	key·ayn?
What?	¿Qué?	kay?
Where is/are?	¿Dónde está/estan?	DOHN-day ays-TAH/ ays-TAHN?
When? or At what time?	¿Cuándo? or ¿A qué hora?	KWAHN-doh? or ah kay OH-rah?
Which?`	¿Cuál?	kwahl?
Why?	¿Por qué?	pohr-KAY?
How much?	Cuánto?	KWAN-toh?
What is price?	¿Cuánto vale?	KWAHN-toh BAH-lay?
Too expensive!	¡Muy caro!	moo·ee KAH-roh!
A lot of money	mucho dinero	MOO-tchoh dee-NAYR-oh
Inexpensive	barato	bahr-AH-toh
How many?	¿Cuántos?	KWAHN-tohs?
Small	chico or pequeño	TCHEE-koh or pay-KAY-nyoh
Medium	mediano	may-DEE·AH-noh
Large	grande	GRAHN-day
It's good	está bueno	ays-TAH BWAY-noh
It's bad	está malo	ays-TAH MAH-loh
Cold	frío	FREE-oh
Hot	caliente	kahl-EE·AYN-tay

263

NOTE: caliente is for things ONLY. If you want to say "I am hot/cold." you say,

	tengo calor/frío	TAYN-goh KAH-lohr/FREE-oh
The menu, please	el menú, por favor	ayl may-NOO pohr-fah-BOHR
The check, please	la cuenta, por favor	lah KOO·EEN-tah pohr fah-BOHR
The bathroom, please	el baño, por favor	ayl BAH-nyoh pohr fah-BOHR

Days of the week

Monday	lunes	LOON-ays
Tuesday	martes	MAHR-tays
Wednesday	miercoles	mee·ayr-KOH-lays
Thursday	jueves	HOO·AY-bays
Friday	viernes	BEE·AYR-nays
Saturday	sábado	SAH-bah-doh
Sunday	domingo	doh-MEEN-goh

Numbers

1	uno	OON-oh
2	dos	dohs
3	tres	trehs (NOT "trays")
4	cuatro	KOO·AHT-roh
5	cinco	SEEN-koh
6	seis	say·ees
7	siete	SEE·AY-tay

8	ocho	OH-tchoh
9	nueve	NOO·AY-bay
10	diez	dee·ays
11	once	OHN-say
12	doce	DOH-say
13	trece	TRAY-say
14	catorce	kah-TOHR-say
15	quince	KEEN-say
16	diez y seis	dee·ays-e-say·ees
17	diez y siete	dee·ays-e-SEE·AY-tay
18	diez y ocho	dee·ays-e-OH-tchoh
19	diez y nueve	dee·ays-e-NOO·AY-bay
20	veinte	BAY·EEN-tay
21	veinte y uno	BAY·EEN-tay-e-OO-noh
22	veinte y dos	BAY·EEN-tay-e-dohs
23	veinte y tres	BAY·EEN-tay-e-trehs
30	trienta	TREE·AYN-tah
40	cuarenta	kwahr-AYN-tah
50	cincuenta	seen-KOO·AYN-tah
60	sesenta	say-CEN-tah
70	setenta	say-TAYN-tah
80	ochenta	oh-TCHAYN-tah
90	noventa	no-BAYN-tah
100	cien	see·ayn
101	ciento uno	SEE·AYN-toh-OO-noh
200	doscientos	dohs-SEE·AYN-tohs
300	trescientos	trays-SEE·AYN-tohs
400	cuatrocientos	kwaht-roh-SEE·AYN-tohs
500	quiñientos	key-NYEE·AYN-tohs

600	seiscientos	say·ees-SEE·AYN-tohs
700	setecientos	seh-tay-SEE·AYN-tohs
800	ochocientos	oh-tchoh-SEE·AYN-tohs
900	novecientos	noh-bay-SEE·AYN-tohs
1000	mil	meel
5000	cinco mil	SEEN-koh-meel

Appendix 2

Conversion Tables

Temperature

Fahrenheit	Celsius/Centigrade
100	37.8
95	35
90	32
85	29.4
80	26.6
75	23.8
70	21.1
65	18.3
60	15.5
55	12.7
50	10
45	7.2
40	4.2
35	1.6
32	0

Volume

Milliliter= .34 ounce   Ounce= 29.57 milliliters
Liter= 2.11 pints   Pint= .47 liter
Liter= 1.06 quarts   Quart= .95 liter
Liter= .26 gallon   Gallon= 3.79 liters

Weight

Gram= .15 ounces   Ounce= 28.35 grams
Kilo= 2.2 pounds   Pound= .45 kilo

Length

Centimeter= .4 inch   Inch= 2.54 centimeters
Meter= 3.28 feet   Foot= .3 meter
Meter= 1.09 yard   Yard= .91 meter
Kilometer= .62 mile   Mile= 1.62 kilometers

On the Road

Kilometer	Miles	Liters	Gallons
1	.62	1	.26
5	3.1	4	1.06
10	6.3	10	2.64
20	12.5	15	3.97
30	18.8	20	5.2
40	25.8	30	7.92
50	31.3	40	10.6
60	37.6	50	13.2
70	43.9	60	15.8
80	50	70	18.5
90	56.3	80	21.1
100	62.5	90	23.8
120	75	100	26.4

Types of Mexican Restaurant Food

Agua Fresca: Could be anything from fruit-flavored water drinks to mashed sweetened rice mixed with ice water. They are made with purified water and ice.

Asada a la Plaza: Grilled beef, cut into pieces, served with potatoes or vegetable with lettuce, onions and tortillas.

Birria de Borrego/Chivo/Res: Stew of lamb/kid/beef in a sauce spiced with chiles, cinnamon, cloves, cumin and oregano.

Burrito: A flour tortilla rolled around seafood, beans or meat.

Carne Asada: Grilled beef that is served with cut up pieces of vegetables or potatoes, or, if chopped up is served on a taco.

Chalupa: A crisp, whole tortilla topped with beans, meat or seafood. (This is also known as a tostada.)

Chiles rellenos: A mild chile stuffed with cheese, dipped in egg batter, deep-fried and served with a *ranchero* sauce.

Enchilada: A corn tortilla dipped in chile sauce, then rolled around a filling of meat, chicken, cheese or seafood and covered with a chile sauce and served warm (sometimes baked in the oven).

Enfrijolada: Like the enchilada except it is dipped in a sauce of refried beans instead of chile sauce.

Flauta: A small corn tortilla roll generally stuffed with chicken or beef and fried.

Gordita: A small, thick, corn tortilla stuffed with a spicy meat mixture.

Huarache: A large, flat, thick, oval-shaped tortilla topped with fried meat and chiles.

Menudo: A thick soup made with pigs' feet and tripe. It is seasoned with chiles de arbol, oregano and fresh chopped onions.

Posole: Stew of nixtamalzed corn (the world's first "hominy"—much more flavorful than U.S. hominy), with pork or chicken and garnished with lettuce or cabbage, radishes, oregano, onions, chile, salt and lime.

Picadillo: A dish spiced with chopped or ground meat with chiles, raisins and onions.

Quesadilla: A flour tortilla folded over sliced cheese and grilled or fried without oil or shortening.

Sope: A small, thick, round corn cake with dimpled edges, topped with a spicy meat mixture and crumbled cheese.

Taco: A corn tortilla folded around anything and eaten with the hands.

Tamales: Nixtamalized corn dough – *masa* – wrapped in a cornhusk and steamed. They are usually stuffed with sweet corn – *elote* – pork, chicken, shrimp or turkey (before wrapping up and steaming) and sometimes quite spicy.

Appendix 4

Responsibility toward hired help

Printed with permission of David Bodwell

Here is the final word on any discussion about how house-keepers/maids are paid legally. I talked to my accountant and he gave me the exact lowdown. Here goes:

The emphasized words are those of the accountant.

First, the law itself (paraphrased, and not all of it by any means) says that certain workers may decide voluntarily to be included in the obligatory IMSS program (my take on this is that they have to voluntarily opt to not be registered. Read on and you'll see why.). These workers include: artisans, craftsmen, casual day workers or non-salaried workers and domestics, i.e., maids, cleaning ladies, cooks, nannies, housekeepers, etc., who work only in a person's home.

My accountant reminded me of something I already knew, and that was that, in Mexico, a dispute between worker and employer is almost always decided in favor of the worker.

In my case, the accountant said, since my FM3 was never "rentista" but was "visitante-activadades lucrativas", my first accountant probably registered my maid just for my safety from possible enquiries from "hands out" IMSS inspectors (and at that point it cost me very little). Of course now she also works at the bookstore so she has to be registered, as she is no longer just a "doméstica".

It's my feeling that any foreign resident would be wise to have a contract to protect themselves from any possible trouble if there happened to be an unfriendly "parting of the ways" with a domestic worker that did not want to register with IMSS by not offering the option, i.e., registering them with IMSS, paying the taxes (small), getting the worker's comp insurance (automatic and cheap for domestic workers). The IMSS program not only gives the worker free medical, but gives it to their dependents also, AND IMSS pays for any "sick leave" when they are unable to work more than three days. It's somewhat of a pain to do so, but any licensed accountant can handle if for you for a nominal charge, and, at least for me, the idea that I'm not responsible for all those things IMSS provides takes a load off my mind.

If you have construction workers doing some repairs or remodels on your house, my accountant said they always have to be registered, BUT in reality, unless the job was very long (weeks, not days) or needed a "city hall" permit, they normally would not be registered since they would be called casual day workers or non-salaried workers (the voluntary bit still applies, if they ask to be registered, you MUST do it—this applies to domestic help too). If the job was a long one or needed a permit you HAVE to register them. The IMSS inspectors usually check the workers at all the permit jobs, and if a job lasted any length of time (and, I assume would be noticeable from outside), it could draw their attention, which would result in a check.

Note: If you have a contractor he does this for you, but almost always registers them in your name, not his. This should be negotiated in advance as that last IMSS billing can be a real killer when you finally get it—one or two months after the job is completed

Since Mexico doesn't have a category of hourly workers (they all are salaried by the day, week, bi-monthly, or monthly) non-salaried means that you are paying a fixed amount for the job no matter how long it takes. If you pay by the number of days they work, they suddenly become salaried workers. This means that if you don't register them, you should get a fixed price for the job, in writing, ahead of time, from each one of them. Mexicans do it with a handshake, but a foreigner better have it in writing (at least in my opinion).

The law requires that the following items must be paid by every employer whether or not the worker is registered with IMSS:

1. The *aguinaldo* (Christmas bonus) must be paid before 20 December – although many employers pay it on the payday which precedes that date.
    *   The aguinaldo must correspond to 15 days of salary.
    *   Roughly, divide the number of days worked during the year past by 365. Multiply that figure by 15 times the daily salary to determine the amount of the *aguinaldo*.
        Examples:
    *   If you have an employee who works one day a week for $100 pesos:
        52/365 x 15 x 100 = $213.70 pesos = *aguinaldo*
    *   If the worker is paid $500 pesos per week:
        $500 x 2.14= $1070 pesos = *aguinaldo*
    *   The *aguinaldo* must be paid in cash. Gifts, Christmas baskets and other presents do not fulfill the statutory requirement.

2. It's *Vacación* Time Again (if you haven't given your worker paid vacation at the 125% of daily pay rate).
    *   I'm not certain there is any specific date in the law, but it needs to be paid by the end of the year so I pay it with the *aguinaldo*.
    *   The *vacación* pay must equal 6 days (the first year) of salary PLUS 25%.

- Roughly, divide the number of days worked during the year past by 365. Multiply that figure by 7.5 to determine the amount of the *vacación* pay due. As you can see this is exactly ½ of the *aguinaldo*.

  Note: This is ONLY the first year worked. It increases every year by 2 days until 12 days are reached. The next year it jumps to 15 days a year and never goes any higher. At the 10 day level you would use a multiplier of 12.5 instead of 7.5.

  Examples:

- If you have an employee who works one day a week for $100 pesos:

  52/365 x 7.5 x 100 = $106.84 pesos = *vacación*.

- If the worker is paid $500 pesos per week:

  $500 x 1.07 = $535 pesos = *vacación*

3. A reminder. If your worker worked on any of the Mexican legal holidays and you did not pay double time plus the holiday pay, i.e., triple time, you owe the balance to the worker. If the worker was paid for the holiday, but didn't work, you don't owe anything, but you cannot deduct it from the "days worked" in the preceding computations. If the worker is part-time and doesn't work the day the holiday falls on, no holiday pay is required.

A minor addition to the above. If your worker worked on any Sunday, you owe them an additional 25% for working on Sunday.

Mexico's Legal Holidays

Jan 1 New Year's Day

First Monday of February* Constitution Day Memorial

Third Monday of March* Benito Juárez' Birthday
    Memorial

May 1 Labor Day
Sep 16 Independence Day
Third Monday of November* Revolution Day Memorial
Dec 1 Presidential Inauguration Day every 6 years
(2012)
Dec 25 Christmas Day
*Note: *These three observed holiday days subject to change
in any given year depending on the mood of the Federal
Legislature.*

David Bodwell has two FREE things at the bookstore, one is a spreadsheet that is simple and really works for figuring the *aguinaldo* and vacation pay. Expats and snowbirds all over Mexico are using it. The second is a MUCH more complete overview of the entire legal situation regarding domestic help than this short "primer". All you have to do is drop by the bookstore, or email him at *mazbook@yahoo.com* with NEWBIE in the subject line and he will email them to you.

Sample Purchase Agreement

Printed with permission of Henry Laxen

PUBLISHER'S NOTE and WARNING: This sample purchase agreement is for information only. To be LEGAL in México or in Mexican courts, it MUST be in Spanish and SHOULD be denominated in Mexican pesos. Otherwise it has no LEGAL standing whatsoever. Have YOUR *NOTARIO* prepare ALL documents such as this BEFORE ANY MONEY changes hands, something which should ONLY happen in his, the *notario's*, office. THIS INCLUDES EARNEST MONEY. If the real estate agent has a pre-printed purchase agreement, IN SPANISH, YOUR *NOTARIO* MUST SEE IT and approve it BEFORE you sign it.

Purchase Agreement

Purchase agreement entered between Mr. Hernan Cortes henceforth called the seller and Mr. Christopher Columbus and Felipa Perestrello Columbus henceforth called the buyers. The object of this transaction is the house located at 1 Pennsylvania Avenue at the El Cid development in Mazatlán, Sinaloa, Mexico. Both parties agree to celebrate this agreement according to the following:

Declarations

Seller Declares: To be a Mexican citizen, of legal age, married, with address 1 Pennsylvania Avenue, El Cid, Mazatlán, Sinaloa, Mexico.

To be the legal owner of the property above described according to deed number 65,536 Volume LXIV, dated June 15, 1994, in the notorial records of lawyer Perry Mason and registered in the property registry number 128, Book 256, Part II, dated June 16, 1994. Said property has the following description: three bedrooms, two and one-half bathrooms, living room, dining room, kitchen, terrace, common area, swimming pool, two parking spaces.

He wishes to sell the property to the buyers.

Buyers Declare: To be United States citizens of legal age, married, with address 77 Sunset Strip, Los Angeles, California, and local address Hotel Playa Mazatlán, Room 1002, Mazatlán, Sinaloa, Mexico.

They wish to acquire the property object of this agreement.

Both parties agree to celebrate this agreement according to the following:

Clauses

First: Both parties agree that the total price for this transaction is the amount of $41,000 (forty one thousand dollars and 00/100 U.S.C.Y.) and will be paid as follows:

1. The amount of $1,000 DLLS, (One thousand dollars and 00/100 U.S.C.Y.) will be paid once both parties have signed this contract.
2. The amount of $4,000 DLLS. (Four thousand dollars and 00/100 U.S.C.Y.) will be paid 15 working days from this date.
3. The balance of $36,000 DLLS (Thirty six thousand dollars and 00/100 U.S.C.Y.) will be paid on the closing date of August 16, 1999.

Second: Both parties agree that the property will be transferred free of all liens, burdens, and encumbrances, and current in all municipal, federal, state taxes, as well as in maintenance fees. Any dues or fees, which are paid on a yearly basis, will be prorated on the day of closing.

Third: The seller will be responsible to pay the capital gains tax, if any, and real estate commissions.

Fourth: The buyers will be responsible to pay all closing costs.

Fifth: Property will be deeded to Mr. Christopher Columbus and Felipa Perestrello or to whomever they designate.

Sixth: This transaction is to include five fans, three air conditioners, stove, curtains, light fixtures, hot water heater, water tank, pump, telephone line, and gas tank. All other furnishings, decorations, and personal items are not included.

Seventh: Both parties agree that the earnest money paid is non-refundable unless the seller is unable to transfer the property to the buyers.

Appendix 6

Aduana Law to show traffic officer

**Articulo 106 Ley Aduanera en Vigor
Que Se Entiende Por Régimen De Importación Temporal**

ARTICULO 106. Se entiende por régimen de importación temporal, la entrada al país de mercancías para permanecer en el por tiempo limitado y con una finalidad especifica, siempre que retornen al extranjero en el mismo estado, por los siguientes plazos.

FRACCION IV. Por el plazo que dure su calidad migratoria, incluyendo sus prorrogas, en los casos.

 a) Las de vehículos que sean propiedad de turistas, visitantes, visitantes locales y distinguidos, estudiantes e inmigrantes rentistas, siempre que los mismos sean de su propiedad a excepción de turistas y visitantes locales. Cuando no sean de su propiedad deberán cumplirse los requisitos que establezca el Reglamento. Los vehículos podrán ser conducidos en territorio nacional por un extranjero que tenga algunas de las calidades migratorias a que se refiere este inciso, por el cónyuge, los ascendientes o descendientes del importador, aun cuando estos ultimo no sean extranjeros, o por un nacional, siempre que en este ultimo caso, viaje a bordo del mismo cualquiera de las personas autorizadas para conducir el vehiculo.

Los vehículos a que se refiere este inciso, deberán cumplir con los requisitos que señale el reglamento.

Article 106 Customs Law
Temporary Vehicle Importation Regulations

ARTICLE 106. Temporary importation is understood as the entry of merchandise into the country, which will remain in it for a limited period of time and for a specific purpose, so long as it is returned abroad in the same condition. The former applies for the following term:

PART IV. For the term of his or her migratory status, including extensions, in the following cases:

a) Vehicles owned by tourists, visitors, local visitors and distinguished visitors, students, and immigrants who are tenants, whenever said vehicles are their own, excepting tourists and local visitors. When the vehicles are not their own, requirements established within the regulations must be met. Such vehicles may be driven within the national territory by a foreigner—the importer—holding one of the migratory status referred to in this paragraph, by his or her spouse, parents or descendants, even when the latter are not foreigners: and by a Mexican as long as one of the persons authorized to drive the vehicle travels with him or her in the car.

Vehicles referred to in this section must meet the requirements pointed out in the regulations.

Schools in Mazatlán

Printed with permission of Lani Wooll

Pre-kinder – nursery school – and *Kinder* – kindergarten – are preschool, for kids from 3–5 years of age. *Primaria* – Elementary – is grade 1 through 6 and *secundaria* – junior high – is grade 7 through 9. *Preparatorio* – high school – is grade 10 through 12, and although not mandatory at this time, the Federal government is moving to make it so quite soon. The curriculum and school year doesn't vary much from school to school as it is mandated by the *Secretaría de Educación Publico* (SEP) – Department of Education, both Federal and State. All schools must meet specified criteria and guidelines.

These are some of the most popular schools although there are many more to consider. It seems every neighborhood has its own private school.

1. Instituto Británico, located at Blvd. del Marlin #34, Fracc. Sábalo Country, this school promotes small class size as well as 100% bilingual education with a great physical education program, which is very rare in Mazatlán. It is one of the newer, more popular schools amongst the upper middle class and foreign population and is non-denominational. Tel: 913-5919. *http://www.britanicoac.edu.mx/*

2. Instituto Anglo Moderno (Anglo), is currently the biggest and most popular and one of the more expensive private schools. The pre-kinder, kinder and grade school are located in Lomas de Mazatlán at Avenida Lomas de Mazatlán #242 and #222. They have also built a brand new junior high & high school (*secundaria* and *preparatorio*) in the new Marina area, Av. del Delfín #6203, Fracc. Marina Mazatlán.

   They are non-denominational with some sports and a soccer program that is linked to a top Mexican soccer team, plus a computer lab and well-equipped kitchen for culinary arts. This seems to be the upper middle class' choice. The downside to this school is very large class sizes. Telephone numbers for contact are: Kinder and Pre-kinder: 916-6029, Elementary: 913-5376, Junior High: 182-2100 and High School: 182-2100. Their website is: *http://www.anglomoderno.edu.mx/*

3. Instituto Cultural de Occidente (ICO), is a Catholic school located on east side of Ejército Mexicano at the junction with Rafael Buelna. This used to be THE school for the wealthy and powerful families of Mazatlán and outlying areas. It is very difficult for a foreigner to get into and it helps if you have connections. Class sizes are fairly large, with a decent phys. ed. program. Tel: 986-1466. *http://www.ico.edu.mx/*

4. Colegio Andes is located behind Home Depot, at Av. de la Universidad #205, Fracc. Alameda. Tel: 986-2488. This is, in my opinion, the best school in Mazatlán. It has small class size, excellent bilingual education and some of the richest, most influential people send their children there. The downside is that it is a strict Catholic, very conservative, Opus Dei education. *http://www.andes.edu.mx/*

5. Colegio Begsu is on Av. Insurgentes with two locations between the Malecón and Av. de la Marina, and is solidly middle class,

non-denominational and the popular choice of many small business owners, hotel workers, etc. Telephone them for more information at 984-5621.

6. Colegio Remington is behind Ley #1 at *calle* Rio San Lorenzo #223, Col. Palos Prietos, and is a elementary (*primaria*) school run by Catholic nuns. This school generally has more girls than boys since it used to be an all girl school and is known to be a springboard to acceptance in ICO. Their number is 981-3347.

7. Colegio Vallodolid, has two locations; one downtown on Belisario Dominguez,

> *http://www.sistemavalladolid.com/portal/index.php/directorio/*
> *72-colegio-valladolid-mazatlan-centro-*

and the other out near El Conchi,

> *http://sistemavalladolid.com/portal/index.php/directorio/*
> *59-colegio-valladolid-mazatlan-villa-verde.*

These schools are relatively inexpensive and popular with the working class families. They are non-denominational, with discipline and security not being the same as in the more expensive schools. Connections are not needed to be accepted here. Tel: 985-6333.

8. Colegio el Pacífico is at *calle* Cruz #2 in Cerro del Vigía and is a great choice for those in El Centro. This is a solidly middle class school. My bilingual co-workers who are themselves alumni are now sending their children there and believe that the English program is excellent. Contact them at 981-2215. Their website is *http://www.colegioelpacifico.edu.mx/*

9. Instituto Pedagógica Hispanoamericano, Av. de las Tórres #10100, Fracc. Los Olivos. This is also a middle–class school with good academic standards. They frequently score amongst the best in the state on standardized testing. They are nursery

(*pre-kinder*) through high school and offer many after-school activities. Telephone: 990-2101.

There are 2 new large schools. One is Colegio Rex, Av. del Delfín #6221, Fracc. Marina Mazatlán, Tel: 922-0700. They say their teachers have been trained by graduates of the University of Arizona. They offer nursery through junior high. *http://www.colegiorex.mx/*

The other is Colegio Montfort, *calle* Eduardo Fountanet #203, Fracc. Plaza Reforma, east of the Soriana on Rafael Buelna and behind the bullring just east of Av. de la Marina. Tel: 913-0267 *http://www .colegiomontfort.com/*, which opened February of 2012.

Most of what I wrote in the K-9 section applies to high schools. Preparatorio is equivalent to a U.S. prep school and is a fast track to university. There is a prep school affiliated with the Universidad Autónoma de Sinaloa, 985-5917. The Tec de Monterrey, Mexico's most prestigious university system, has its own prep school. Attendance at Tec de Monterrey prep school will virtually guarantee you a spot in the Tec University system, providing the qualifying grades are attained. A tough admissions exam is required to get into the Tec de Monterrey and it is very expensive. They have also moved to a brand new, state-of-the-art campus in the new Marina area. Telephone: 989-2000

Index